Quality Reclaimed

The Umbrella Playbook Q-Intelligence™ and the Future of Enterprise Quality

A Systems Approach to Enterprise Quality Engineering

Paul G. Kanaris

QACE Institute

Published by QACE Institute

Disclaimer:
This publication is designed to provide accurate and authoritative information regarding the subject matter covered. It is provided with the understanding that the author and publisher are not engaged in rendering legal, financial, or professional services. If professional advice is required, the services of a competent professional should be sought.

ISBN: 979-8-9966707-0-3

First Edition

Printed in the United States of America

Dedication

To the colleagues, team members, and leaders I have worked with throughout my career.

Through the challenges, failures, and successes we experienced together, you shaped the understanding captured in these pages—and encouraged me to share it.

This work reflects what we built, what we learned, and what we proved in practice.

And what remains to be built.

Foreword

Adam Sandman
Founder & CEO, Inflectra

In 2006, while working on large-scale technology programs supporting the U.S. Navy, I encountered a problem that would ultimately change the direction of my career.

The project was not lacking talent, process, or technology. We had experienced teams, established methodologies, sophisticated project management practices, and complex systems being developed for mission-critical operations. Yet despite all of that, one area remained surprisingly disconnected from the rest of the delivery lifecycle.

Quality.

When it came to testing and quality assurance, much of the work was being managed through spreadsheets, whiteboards, status meetings, and manual coordination. Teams worked hard, but visibility remained limited. We could estimate project schedules and development progress, yet when stakeholders asked seemingly simple questions—

"*How much testing remains?*"
"*What risks still exist?*"
"*How confident are we in this release?*"

—the answers were often based more on judgment than evidence.

The problem was not effort.

The problem was understanding.

That experience eventually led me to found Inflectra and create what became our first product, SpiraTest. What started as a desire to improve visibility into testing and quality quickly evolved into a much broader realization.

Organizations rarely struggle because they lack tools. In fact, they often have too many disconnected tools giving conflicting or misleading indicators.

Organizations rarely struggle because they lack talented people.
Organizations struggle because quality is often treated as a separate activity instead of an integrated organizational capability.

Over the past two decades, I have had the opportunity to work with organizations across government, healthcare, banking, insurance, defense, logistics, transportation, and technology. During that time, I have watched the industry move through wave after wave of transformation.

Waterfall became Agile.
Agile evolved into DevOps.
Automation became essential.
Cloud transformed how software was delivered.
Today, Artificial Intelligence is transforming how software is imagined, created, tested, and maintained.

Yet despite all of these changes, one challenge remains remarkably consistent.

Organizations continue to struggle with understanding whether they are building the right thing, validating the right thing, and making decisions based on the right information.

That is why *The Umbrella Playbook* resonated with me.

What Paul Kanaris presents in this book is not another methodology, testing strategy, or process framework.

Instead, he challenges readers to view quality through a broader lens.

The visibility problems that initially inspired me to build Inflectra were ultimately symptoms of a larger issue. Organizations often approach quality as a collection of activities, metrics, tools, and checkpoints. Yet quality itself emerges from something much larger.

It emerges from decisions.
It emerges from priorities.
It emerges from leadership.
It emerges from governance.
It emerges from how information moves through a system and how organizations choose to act upon what they learn.

In short, quality is a system.

That perspective aligns strongly with what I have observed throughout my own journey.

The organizations that achieve sustainable quality outcomes rarely do so because they purchased a new tool, adopted a new framework, or introduced additional checkpoints. They succeed because quality becomes part of how decisions are made throughout the organization.

Without that commitment, other forces inevitably take precedence.

Schedules.
Costs.
Velocity.
Short-term objectives.

The result is often predictable: organizations optimize activity while quietly accumulating risk.

Today, as Artificial Intelligence and agentic software development accelerate the creation of requirements, code, tests, documentation, and countless other artifacts, the need for this broader perspective becomes even more important.

AI allows organizations to create more.
It does not automatically help them understand more.

The question is no longer whether we can generate software faster.

The question is whether we can make better decisions about what we create, why we create it, and how we know it delivers value.

If anything, AI increases the importance of visibility, traceability, governance, and quality intelligence.

That is one of the reasons this conversation feels particularly timely.

Whether you are a quality leader, engineer, architect, executive, transformation leader, or practitioner, *The Umbrella Playbook* will challenge you to think differently about the role quality plays within modern organizations.

You may not agree with every conclusion.
You may challenge some of the assumptions.
But you will almost certainly find yourself thinking differently about how quality is created, measured, governed, and sustained.

And in a world where complexity continues to increase faster than ever before, that is a conversation worth having.

Adam Sandman
Founder & CEO
Inflectra Corporation

From the Author

There is a question I have carried with me through every technology leadership role I have held, across every enterprise I have served, and through every transformation initiative I have sponsored:

When did we decide that quality was negotiable?

There was no single moment. No formal decision. No executive directive. And yet, when we examine the state of software quality across large organizations today, we see the outcome clearly. Speed became the priority, and quality became the trade-off.

This shift was gradual. Delivery accelerated. Metrics improved. Dashboards turned green. For a time, it appeared successful.

But the underlying system evolved in a different direction.

Defect escape increased. Operational instability became normalized. Engineering teams shifted from building systems to managing their consequences. Organizations began to accept outcomes they would have rejected outright only a few years earlier.

This is not a failure of engineering capability. It is a failure of the operating model.

The cost is no longer abstract. It appears in customer impact, regulatory exposure, operational disruption, and accumulated technical debt. It manifests in the credibility of engineering organizations and the confidence stakeholders place in the systems they depend on.

For leaders, this is not a quality problem alone. It is a leadership problem.

The assumptions that shaped modern software development—about ownership, automation, measurement, and accountability—have created conditions where quality is no longer governed as a system. Responsibility has expanded while accountability has weakened. Activity has increased while insight has diminished.

The result is predictable.

Without structure, control, and alignment, quality does not scale.

This is where this work becomes critical.

Quality Reclaimed does not simply describe what went wrong. It identifies the patterns that led to systemic failure and frames them as consequences of design, not isolated decisions. More importantly, it introduces a structured response.

The QACE operating model—Quality, Automation, Compliance, and Engineering—provides a framework for restoring quality as a governed, enterprise capability. It integrates design, validation, measurement, and governance into a coordinated system that can operate at scale.

This is not theory. It reflects the realities of enterprise environments where quality must function under constraint, across distributed teams, and in direct alignment with business outcomes.

Across the chapters that follow, the book builds this model deliberately. It moves from identifying the conditions that caused quality to degrade, to defining the structures required to rebuild it.

This work is not about adding activity. It is about restoring system integrity.

For technology leaders, this represents a fundamental shift. Quality must be treated not as a phase, not as a role, and not as a function of tools. It must be treated as a system that is designed, governed, and continuously improved.

This book provides a blueprint for doing exactly that.

The challenges facing modern organizations—complex architectures, accelerated delivery expectations, and increasing regulatory pressure—cannot be addressed through incremental improvements alone. They require a rethinking of how quality is structured and sustained.

Quality Reclaimed offers that perspective.

It should be read not just as a narrative, but as a lens through which to evaluate your own organization. The patterns described here are not theoretical. They are present, today, in the systems most organizations operate.

The opportunity is to recognize them—and to redesign accordingly.

Paul Kanaris

Founder

QACE Institute

July 2026

Preface

Quality Reclaimed: Why This Book Exists – And What Comes Next

We Didn't Lose Quality. We Gave It Away.

Software quality did not fail in a single moment. It deteriorated gradually—through assumptions that were accepted, repeated, and eventually institutionalized.

Speed became equated with progress. Automation was treated as a substitute for design. "Shift left" became shorthand for distributing responsibility without defining accountability.

For a time, these shifts appeared successful. Delivery accelerated. Metrics improved. Reporting systems reflected control.

But the underlying system changed in a different direction.

Defects escaped with increasing frequency. Operational instability became normalized. Engineering effort shifted from building systems to managing their consequences.

The gap between reported quality and experienced quality widened—quietly, but consistently.

This book begins at that gap.

The Problem Worth Naming

The decline in software quality is not primarily a failure of engineering capability. It is a failure of system design.

Organizations did not abandon quality explicitly. They deprioritized it structurally—through planning models, organizational design, and operating assumptions that were not aligned with how quality actually functions.

Across enterprises, consistent patterns emerge:

- Quality functions were redistributed without governance structures to replace them
- Responsibility expanded while accountability weakened
- Automation scaled faster than architecture
- New technologies were introduced without corresponding validation and control models

These patterns did not occur in isolation. They compounded.

The result is not a single failure mode, but a system that produces instability as an expected outcome.

It is not a tooling issue.
It is not the result of any single methodology.

It is an operating model failure.

Quality as a System

The central premise of this book is simple:

Quality is not a phase.
It is not a role.
It is not an outcome of testing activity.

Quality is a system.

Like any system, it must be intentionally designed. It must have structure, controls, feedback mechanisms, and governance.

When those elements are absent or fragmented, quality becomes unpredictable—regardless of the tools or practices applied within individual teams.

Rebuilding quality is not about increasing activity. It is about restoring system integrity.

The QACE Operating Model

This work is structured around the QACE (Quality, Automation, Compliance, Engineering) operating model.

QACE provides a framework for organizing quality as a coordinated, enterprise-level capability—one that integrates engineering practices, governance structures, and measurement systems.

It defines quality across multiple, interdependent domains and establishes the relationships required for those domains to function as a single system.

The model is not presented as theory. It is derived from practical application in enterprise environments where quality must operate at scale, under constraint, and with direct impact on business outcomes.

In the chapters that follow, QACE is used not as a concept to be described, but as a structure to be applied.

The Purpose of This Book

The Umbrella Playbook is not a collection of techniques or isolated best practices.

Its purpose is to:

- Define the conditions under which quality systems degrade
- Establish a shared language for evaluating quality at the system level

- Identify the structural gaps that prevent quality from scaling
- Provide a coherent model for restoring quality as a governed capability

Each chapter builds on this foundation—progressing from problem definition to structural analysis, and ultimately to system design.

The goal is not incremental improvement.

The goal is alignment.

The Transition

The starting point is clarity.

Before systems can be redesigned, assumptions must be examined. Before models can be applied, definitions must be stabilized.

The next chapter establishes the foundation for that work.

It defines the core premises this book challenges—and the conditions under which quality systems either stabilize or fail.

Quality is not lost.

It is unstructured.

And what is unstructured can be rebuilt.

How to Use This Book

This book is not intended to be read as a sequence of chapters alone. It is intended to be used as a framework for understanding and transforming how quality operates within an organization.

Throughout the book, certain concepts are marked with cross-reference notation to help readers locate supporting material without interrupting the flow of reading. References in the form [[GL:Term]] point to definitions in the Glossary, while other references may point to appendices, acronyms, models, or related concepts. These references are intended as navigation aids and may be consulted immediately or explored later as needed.

The Umbrella Playbook establishes a system-level view of quality—one that moves beyond individual practices, tools, or roles and instead examines how quality is produced, governed, and sustained across the enterprise. It is written for leaders and practitioners responsible for improving outcomes in environments where complexity, scale, and delivery pressure expose the limitations of fragmented quality approaches.

This includes:

- CTOs, CIOs, and engineering leaders responsible for enterprise delivery outcomes
- Quality engineering leaders tasked with transforming QA organizations into system capabilities
- Architects, developers, and practitioners seeking to move beyond activity-driven validation toward engineered quality systems

The book can be used in two ways.

First, it can be read as a continuous narrative. In this form, each chapter builds on the previous, moving from the identification of systemic problems to the definition of a structured operating model and, ultimately, to the design of a governed quality system.

Second, it can be used as a diagnostic reference. Individual chapters can be applied to specific conditions within an organization—allowing leaders to isolate failure patterns, evaluate their current state, and determine where intervention is required.

Transformation does not begin with selecting the next improvement initiative. It begins with understanding the organization.

Effective change requires a clear view of:

- Where breakdowns occur across the lifecycle
- Where quality is reactive rather than engineered
- Where ownership exists without accountability
- Where measurement exists without meaningful insight

Only after this assessment can meaningful transformation occur.

In many organizations, improvement begins at the source—product definition and requirements—where unclear intent and inconsistent inputs propagate failure downstream. At the same time, development practices and validation approaches must be aligned so that quality is integrated into the system rather than applied after the fact.

From this foundation, additional domains can be addressed based on need, including automation architecture, non-functional quality, governance structures, and system observability. These domains are interdependent and must be engaged as part of a coordinated system rather than as isolated initiatives.

This approach defines how the broader Q-Intelligence™ Body of Knowledge is intended to be applied. The series is not a prescribed sequence of books. It is a structured set of domain expansions that can be engaged as required—based on organizational maturity, constraints, and transformation priorities.

The Umbrella Playbook provides the foundation for this work.

The chapters that follow begin by dismantling the assumptions that have shaped modern quality practices. From there, they establish the structure required to rebuild quality as a governed, enterprise capability.

Table of Contents

Chapter 1: The Case for Q-Intelligence™

Chapter Introduction

This chapter establishes why traditional QA and quality models fail at enterprise scale and why quality must be reconceived as an intelligence discipline before any framework or solution is introduced.

1.1 The Modern Quality Paradox

Enterprise technology organizations are investing more in quality than at any point in history—yet quality outcomes continue to deteriorate. (Krasner & Consortium for Information & Software Quality [CISQ], 2022) This contradiction is not anecdotal; it is systemic.

Budgets expand, headcounts grow, tooling proliferates, and process maturity models advance, while production incidents increase, release confidence declines, and failures surface later and more publicly than ever before.

Figure 1.1 – The Modern Quality Paradox

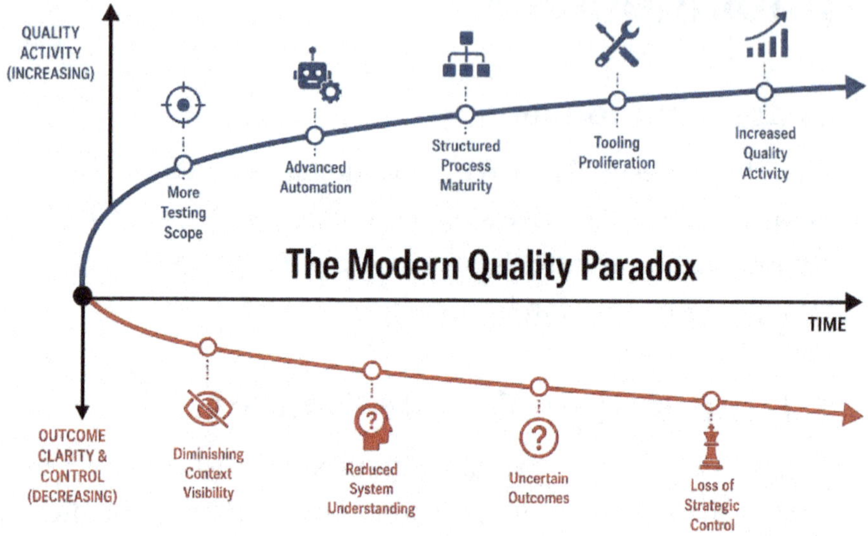

Despite rising investment in quality tooling, automation, and process, outcome predictability and control decline at enterprise scale.

This tension defines the modern quality paradox [[GL:Modern Quality Paradox]]: the simultaneous rise of quality investment and degradation of quality outcomes. What makes this paradox particularly corrosive is that, on paper, quality appears healthier than ever.

Test coverage charts trend upward. Automation pipelines execute thousands of checks per deployment. Dashboards shine with pass rates and green indicators. Governance [[GL:Governance]] artifacts multiply.

And yet—despite unprecedented levels of activity—organizations find themselves discovering critical defects in production, responding reactively to customer-impacting incidents, and absorbing mounting systemic risk.

The problem is not effort. It is not intent. It is not even tooling in isolation. The paradox exists because modern quality systems increasingly optimize activity while failing to produce insight.

Recognizable Situation:

A deployment proceeds with confidence. Test execution completed successfully. Coverage targets were achieved. Quality dashboards reported healthy status across the release pipeline. Within days, customers begin reporting issues that none of the metrics suggested were possible.

The organization did not lack activity. It lacked the insight needed to understand what the activity actually meant.

Investment Without Control

Over the past decade, quality functions have been scaled aggressively. Enterprises have expanded test automation programs, formalized quality engineering roles, embedded testing into continuous delivery pipelines, and layered governance on top of increasingly complex architectures. These moves were rational responses to accelerating delivery demands and rising technical complexity. But scale has introduced its own failure modes. As organizations grow, quality work fragments across tools, teams, and checkpoints. Ownership diffuses. Signals scatter. The very mechanisms designed to increase control instead generate noise. Quality becomes something that is performed rather than understood.

In this environment, additional investment does not yield proportional improvements. Instead, it amplifies inefficiency. More tests are written, but fewer are trusted.

More metrics are tracked, but fewer inform decisions. More reviews are conducted, but systemic risk remains invisible until it manifests as failure. The paradox is not that organizations failed to invest in quality. It is that much of that investment was directed toward scaling activity, automation, tooling, and process while the underlying understanding of how quality emerges at enterprise scale advanced far more slowly. It is that funding has outpaced understanding.

Activity Mistaken for Assurance

Modern quality organizations are extraordinarily productive. They generate artifacts at scale: test cases, automated suites, reports, dashboards, audit evidence, and compliance mappings. Success is often measured by volume—runs executed, defects logged, coverage achieved, gates passed. Yet volume is not assurance. Activity provides comfort because it is observable. It can be counted, charted, and reported. Insight, by contrast, is harder. It requires synthesis across signals, interpretation of patterns, and an integrated view of how risk propagates through systems over time.

This is why organizations often experience confidence collapses immediately after "successful" releases. The metrics said everything was fine. The checks all passed. The governance gates were cleared. And still, something fundamental was missed. The paradox deepens when leadership responds to failure by demanding more controls—more tests, more reviews, more reports—without addressing whether those controls are producing actionable insight. Activity expands. Blindness remains.

Late Discovery as the Core Symptom

If the modern quality paradox has a defining symptom, it is late discovery [[GL:Late Discovery]]. Critical issues are rarely unknown in absolute terms. Signals often exist early—subtle, fragmented, or dismissed—but they are not recognized as risk until impact is unavoidable. By the time defects are confirmed, options are constrained. Responses become costly, reactive, and externally visible.

Late discovery is not a timing issue; it is a failure of judgment driven by insufficient intelligence. In healthy systems, risk is surfaced while choices still exist. Trade-offs [[GL:Trade-Off]] are made consciously. Uncertainty is bounded. In paradoxical quality systems, risk accumulates silently. It is obscured by dashboards optimized for pass/fail status rather than systemic understanding. Late discovery persists even in highly automated environments because automation alone cannot interpret significance. It executes instructions. It does not reason about context, convergence, or trajectory.

When Scale Breaks Intuition

At small scale, quality can be managed through intuition and proximity. Engineers understand how changes ripple. Test failures have discernible meaning. Risk feels tangible.

Enterprise scale destroys this intuition. Dependencies multiply. Release boundaries blur. Teams operate asynchronously and geographically. Systems evolve continuously rather than episodically.

In this environment, localized success says little about global health. Traditional quality controls were never designed for this level of complexity. They were built to validate artifacts, not systems.

They assume stability where there is constant change, and linear causality where effects emerge from interaction. When these assumptions break, activity fills the gap left by lost intuition. Organizations do more because they see less.

The Illusion of Control

From the outside, modern quality programs often appear mature. They are well-documented, heavily tooled, and procedurally rigorous. Internally, however, teams frequently express a shared unease: despite all the checks, no one feels fully in control.

Executives sense the risk but lack visibility into where it originates. Quality leaders manage ever-growing backlogs of effort without a clear line of sight to impact. Engineering teams navigate conflicting signals about readiness and risk. Everyone is busy. No one is certain.

The paradox persists because it is self-reinforcing. When outcomes degrade, organizations respond by intensifying the very patterns that obscure understanding. More activity replaces insight. More structure substitutes for clarity. More investment deepens the illusion of control [[GL:Illusion of Control]].

Framing the Problem, Not Solving It—Yet

This section does not argue that quality practices are unnecessary, nor that automation, testing, or governance are failures. It makes a narrower, more consequential claim: the modern quality problem is not lack of effort, but lack of intelligence.

Increased investment without improved outcomes is not a temporary anomaly. It is a structural signal that the industry's prevailing assumptions about quality no longer hold at enterprise scale. Understanding why this happened—and how quality engineering arrived at this point—requires tracing the historical path that produced today's systems. That examination begins next.

1.2 How Quality Engineering Got Here

To understand the present condition of enterprise quality, it is necessary to trace this progression—beginning with traditional quality assurance (QA) [[AC:QA]], moving through the rise of automation, and culminating in the systemic challenges introduced by scale—into what is now understood as quality engineering [[GL:Quality Engineering]].

From Verification to Assurance

In its earliest modern form, software quality was primarily a verification function. Quality assurance teams operated as downstream validators, responsible for confirming that delivered systems matched predefined requirements.

Development tended to follow linear or phase-gated models, where design, implementation, testing, and release occurred in distinct stages. Within this structure, quality activity was naturally positioned late in the lifecycle.

This arrangement reflected both technological and organizational realities. Systems were smaller, release cycles were longer, and change frequency was limited by tooling and infrastructure. Manual testing, document review, and checklist-based validation were sufficient for the scope of what was being built. Feedback delays existed, but their impact was constrained by modest system interdependencies and relatively stable requirements. Quality assurance, in this context, was not expected to guide system design or influence upstream decisions. Its role was to verify conformance and surface defects before release. Within the bounds of those expectations, the model functioned predictably.

The Emergence of Automation as a Response

As development velocity increased, particularly with the adoption of iterative and agile methods, the limitations of manual verification became apparent. Release cycles accelerated, codebases grew, and the cost of late defect discovery rose. Automation emerged as a practical response to these pressures.

Initial automation efforts were targeted and tactical. Test scripts replicated manual checks, enabling teams to rerun validations more frequently without proportional increases in headcount. Regression testing, in particular, benefited from this shift. Automation promised consistency, speed, and repeatability—attributes well aligned with fast-moving delivery pipelines. Over time, automation became synonymous with quality advancement. Tooling ecosystems expanded, frameworks matured, and organizations invested heavily in building and maintaining automated test suites. In many environments, the presence of automation itself became an indicator of quality maturity. This phase represented progress, but it also marked a subtle shift in emphasis: quality activity increasingly focused on executing tests efficiently rather than understanding what those tests revealed about system behavior.

Scaling Changes the Nature of the Problem

Enterprise scale does not simply increase the amount of work being performed. It changes the nature of the quality problem itself. Assumptions and practices that function adequately in smaller, more predictable environments begin to break down as systems, teams, dependencies, and decision pathways multiply.

At enterprise scale [[GL:Enterprise Scale]], the number of potential interactions between components expands dramatically. Change frequency increases, while blast radius becomes harder to predict. Failures no longer originate solely from isolated defects but from emergent behaviors across systems, environments, and organizational boundaries.

Small, locally rational changes interact in ways that are neither linear nor predictable from any single vantage point. Timing effects, configuration drift, data dependencies, and cross-team decisions combine to produce outcomes that no test suite or checklist can fully anticipate. Cause and effect separate in time and space: the decision that introduces risk is often far removed from the moment—and location—where that risk finally manifests.

Assumptions That No Longer Hold

At scale, foundational assumptions do not merely weaken—they invert, producing the very risks they were designed to prevent. Several assumptions that were reasonable in earlier phases begin to show limitations. These assumptions were not errors when they were adopted; they reflected the realities of the systems and delivery models for which they were created. The strain emerges when organizations continue to apply them unchanged, even as scale fundamentally alters operating conditions.

The Collapse of Deterministic Testing

Enterprise complexity alone would challenge traditional quality models. Artificial Intelligence introduces an additional shift by changing the nature of software behavior itself.

For decades, software testing has operated on a simple but foundational assumption:

Given the same input, under the same conditions, a system should produce the same output.

This assumption enabled repeatable testing, predictable regression outcomes, and the widespread use of pass/fail validation models.

That assumption is now beginning to break.

With the introduction of AI-enabled systems, software behavior is no longer strictly deterministic. The same input may produce different outputs—not because of a defect, but because the system itself is designed to operate probabilistically rather than procedurally.

This shift introduces a fundamental challenge:

- There is no longer a single “correct” result in many scenarios
- Test outcomes may vary without any underlying system change
- Traditional regression assumptions no longer reliably indicate stability

As a result, validation can no longer depend solely on exact comparison or binary success criteria.

Instead of asking:

"Did the system return the correct output?"

The more relevant question becomes:

"Did the system behave within acceptable boundaries?"

This represents a subtle but critical transition—from validating correctness to evaluating bounded behavior.

Figure 1.2 – Deterministic Testing [[GL:Deterministic Testing]] vs. Non-Deterministic Testing

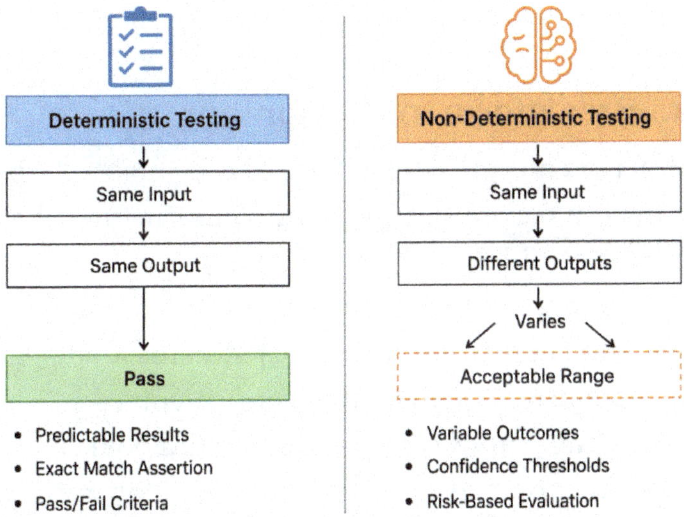

Deterministic testing assumes consistent outcomes (same input → same output → pass/fail), while non-deterministic systems [[GL:Non-Deterministic System]] introduce variability, requiring evaluation based on acceptable ranges and bounded risk.

At the same time, development velocity continues to accelerate, increasing the volume and complexity of systems entering the lifecycle. However, the models used to validate those systems have not evolved at the same rate.

The result is not simply a tooling gap.

It is a growing misalignment between how systems are built and how they are validated.

This shift marks an early signal of a deeper structural change—one that will require rethinking how quality is defined, measured, and embedded across the software lifecycle.

This concept will be expanded further as we introduce the Quality Engineering operating model and the emerging frameworks for validating AI-enabled systems.

From Breakdown to Recognition

What many enterprises experienced as a quality "crisis" was, in practice, a recognition moment. The structures that once supported confidence began producing noise instead of clarity. Metrics increased while certainty declined. Remediation efforts multiplied, yet systemic understanding remained elusive. Quality engineering evolved incrementally, but its core positioning did not keep pace with the environments it was expected to govern. The transition from QA to automation addressed speed. Scaling exposed a deeper issue: the absence of mechanisms to interpret quality signals across complex, adaptive systems.

This trajectory does not suggest missteps or mismanagement. It reflects an industry advancing through successive problem spaces, each solved with the tools and thinking available at the time. The current inflection point is the result of accumulated progress intersecting with new forms of complexity. Understanding how quality engineering arrived here is a prerequisite for understanding why incremental optimization is no longer sufficient—a theme that continues in the sections that follow.

1.3 Structural Limits of Traditional QA Models

We are no longer explaining how this happened—we are showing why it cannot work anymore. The historical logic that once justified these models now defines their limits. What follows is not a continuation of how quality evolved, but an explanation of why its prevailing structures can no longer function at enterprise scale—regardless of intent or effort.

Traditional quality assurance models emerged in an era when software systems were comparatively bounded, release cycles were longer, and organizational accountability was easier to localize. These models reflected the prevailing assumptions of industrial production: work could be decomposed into functions, progress could be staged into phases, and quality could be verified by inspecting outputs after the fact. For decades, these assumptions shaped how quality was organized, staffed, and measured.

As systems have become larger, more interconnected, and more continuously evolving, the structural limits of these models have become increasingly difficult to ignore. The limitations are not primarily a matter of tooling, staffing levels, or execution discipline. They are structural: rooted in how traditional QA defines responsibility, timing, and evidence of quality.

Three patterns are particularly persistent—function-based QA, phase-based testing, and coverage-centric measurement—and each introduces systemic blind spots that modern systems can no longer absorb.

Function-Based QA and the Illusion of Containment

Function-based QA organizes quality responsibility around a designated role, team, or department. Quality becomes something that "belongs" to QA, as distinct from design, development, product management, or operations. This structure appears efficient on paper: it creates a clear owner, a defined process boundary, and an apparent safeguard against defects entering production.

In practice, function-based QA fragments accountability. When quality is structurally assigned to a separate function, upstream decisions are implicitly decoupled from downstream consequences. Requirements can remain ambiguous, architectural constraints can be deferred, and risk can be normalized under the assumption that QA will "catch it later." The organization may still value quality rhetorically, but structurally it has positioned quality as a checkpoint rather than a governing concern.

This separation reshapes behavior across the system. Development teams optimize for throughput, feature delivery, or velocity metrics that are orthogonal to quality outcomes. QA teams inherit artifacts they did not shape and are expected to validate them within fixed time windows. When defects surface under these conditions, the failure mode is framed as "missed testing" rather than as an accumulation of earlier decisions that narrowed the space for quality to emerge.

Function-based QA further assumes that quality attributes are inspectable in isolation. It treats quality less as an emergent property of the system and more as a set of discrete conditions that can be verified against predefined criteria. This assumption weakens as systems grow more dynamic. Integration effects, cross-team dependencies, data flows, and operational variability rarely map cleanly to a single function's scope. The result is organizational blindness: issues arising from interactions between components or teams fall between functional boundaries, noticed only after they escape formal QA ownership.

Over time, the QA function is left managing the consequences of structural decisions it did not control. Its authority expands procedurally—more gates, more documentation, more sign-offs—while its influence over system behavior diminishes. Quality becomes both everyone's stated priority and no one's structural responsibility.

Phase-Based Testing and the Myth of Sequential Assurance

Phase-based testing extends the same logic into time. Work progresses through defined stages—requirements, design, implementation, testing, release—each treated as sufficiently complete before the next begins. Testing, by definition, occurs after development, reinforcing the belief that quality can be assessed once construction is largely finished.

This model assumes relative stability between phases. Requirements are expected to be settled, designs largely fixed, and scope changes treated as exceptions. Under these conditions, testing appears as a rational verification step: confirm that what was built matches what was specified.

Modern systems do not behave this way. Requirements evolve as understanding increases, integrations shift as dependencies change, and operational realities surface continuously rather than at the end of a cycle. When change is persistent, phase boundaries become artificial. The issue is no longer whether late discovery is costly—by this point, it has become structurally inevitable.

Testing performed "at the end" is necessarily constrained by earlier commitments that may no longer be valid. Phase-based testing compresses learning into the latest possible moment. Signals that could have informed design or architectural choices are deferred until after those choices are costly to revisit. When defects or risks are discovered late, organizations face false tradeoffs between schedule and quality—tradeoffs created not by necessity, but by the sequencing of work.

The emphasis on phases encourages local optimization within each stage. Teams focus on completing their phase rather than ensuring system coherence across phases. Handoffs replace continuous engagement, and information degrades as it passes through documentation rather than shared understanding. Testing becomes an act of reconciliation between intent and reality instead of a mechanism for shaping intent itself. As systems scale, the latency introduced by phase-based testing becomes untenable. Feedback arrives too late to influence the conditions that produced the problem. In many cases, those conditions originated during planning, requirements, architectural, or prioritization decisions made much earlier in the lifecycle. The organization responds by adding more phases, checkpoints, or parallel testing efforts—compounding complexity without addressing the underlying temporal misalignment.

Coverage as a Lagging Indicator of Quality

If automation exposes the limits of executing checks at scale, coverage exposes a deeper failure: mistaking measurement for understanding. Traditional QA models rely heavily on coverage metrics—test case coverage, requirement coverage, code coverage—as proxies for confidence. These measures are attractive because they are countable, comparable, and auditable. They create a sense of progress and control, especially when integrated into dashboards and governance reports.

However, coverage is inherently retrospective. It describes what has been exercised or inspected, not what the system can sustain over time. (Jois, 2024) High coverage can coexist with brittle behavior, unexamined assumptions, and latent failure modes. Low coverage may signal risk, but high coverage does not guarantee resilience.

Coverage metrics also reinforce the functional and phase-based structures that generate them. Tests are written to satisfy coverage targets, not necessarily to explore meaningful system behaviors. Work gravitates toward what can be measured, often at the expense of what matters under real operating conditions. More subtly, coverage as a primary indicator shifts attention away from leading signals of degradation. Drift in decision quality, erosion of architectural clarity, and accumulation of implicit dependencies often precede observable failures but do not register in coverage reports.

When coverage is treated as evidence of quality, it becomes a defensive artifact. Teams point to numbers to justify releases, close audits, or resolve disputes about readiness. Quality discussions become quantitative negotiations rather than systemic inquiries. The metric remains stable even as the system's true risk profile changes beneath it.

Structural Consequences

Taken together, function-based responsibility, phase-based timing, and coverage-centric measurement form a closed loop. Each reinforces the others, creating an assurance model that is internally coherent yet increasingly disconnected from system reality. Quality is inspected rather than cultivated, delayed rather than anticipated, and measured after the fact rather than governed in motion.

These structures persist not because they are effective, but because they are familiar. Yet familiarity does not equal fitness. As systems continue to integrate, adapt, and operate under continuous change, the gap between traditional QA assumptions and operational reality widens. The problem confronting modern organizations is therefore not a shortage of tests, tools, or talent. It is the mismatch between how quality is structurally framed and how systems actually behave. Until that mismatch is addressed, additional effort within traditional QA models yields diminishing returns—more activity, more artifacts, and more confidence signals that arrive too late to matter. These structural limits expose a deeper issue: even when execution and measurement are functioning, the organization still lacks the ability to interpret what those signals mean.

1.4 The Intelligence Gap

Most quality organizations operate across two layers: execution and measurement. Execution focuses on doing—running tests, validating requirements, enforcing gates. Measurement focuses on counting—defects, pass rates, coverage, and cycle time. Together, they produce activity and data, but not insight. What is missing is a disciplined ability to synthesize signals, interpret context, and inform decisions early enough to change outcomes [[GL:Intelligence Layer]].

Raw data does not become insight through aggregation alone; it requires interpretation within context. Metrics do not become insight by being visualized; visualization organizes data but does not explain it. Without an intelligence layer (Q Intelligence™ context), quality data remains fragmented—useful in hindsight but ineffective in steering complex systems in real time. This is why organizations can be data-rich, insight-poor at the same time. Modern organizations are not failing because they cannot execute. They are failing because execution has outpaced understanding.

Without interpretation, signals remain disconnected from decisions. The organization can observe increasing activity without understanding whether that activity is improving outcomes.

Conceptual Interpretation: Data aggregation is similar to collecting signals from multiple instruments without a control panel that explains what they mean together. Each measurement exists, but without interpretation, no actionable understanding emerges.

Figure 1.3 – Execution, Measurement, and the Missing Intelligence

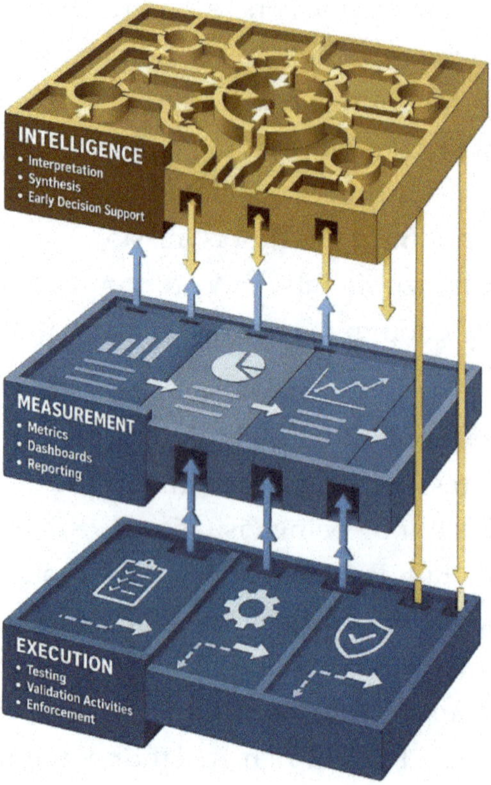

Execution and measurement generate activity and data, but without an intelligence layer to synthesize signal and context, organizations remain reactive.

Across industries, leadership teams celebrate velocity: faster delivery cycles, expanded operating footprints, and unprecedented volumes of activity. Dashboards glow green. Metrics update in real time. Reports circulate with clock-like regularity.

And yet—decisions feel increasingly reactive. Strategic pivots arrive late. Risks surface only after damage is done. Postmortems grow longer while confidence shrinks.

This disconnect signals a widening intelligence gap [[GL:Intelligence Gap]]: the structural separation between what organizations do, what they measure, and what they truly understand. This separation is not incidental. It is produced by how responsibilities for execution, measurement, and interpretation are distributed across the organization.

Execution Without Awareness

Execution [[GL:Execution]] is action—the visible motion of the organization: projects launched, processes run, transactions completed. Over the past two decades, enterprises have become exceptionally good at execution. Process optimization, automation, and scale economics have turned once-manual operations into finely tuned machines. But execution alone does not imply clarity. Activity can increase even as comprehension erodes. Teams can meet deadlines while missing the point. Entire organizations can move faster in the wrong direction.

The danger lies in mistaking movement for mastery. When execution becomes the primary signal of success, organizations reward completion over comprehension. Questions such as "Why are we doing this?", "What conditions are changing?", or "What patterns are forming beneath these results?" are deferred or dismissed as distractions from delivery. Execution answers what happened. It does not explain what it means or why it matters.

Measurement as a False Proxy for Intelligence

To compensate for blind execution, organizations turned to measurement [[GL:Measurement]]. Metrics promised objectivity. Data promised truth. If activity could be tracked precisely enough, insight was expected to follow. In practice, this assumption does not hold. Instead, many organizations fell into measurement saturation. Key performance indicators multiplied. Dashboards expanded. Reports grew more granular, more frequent, and more automated. The belief was simple: if leadership could see everything, it could understand anything.

Measurement does not produce intelligence by default. It captures signals but does not interpret them. Metrics describe states but do not explain dynamics. An organization can quantify precisely what is happening and remain uncertain about why. The result is a substitution error: measurement begins to stand in for intelligence. Leaders talk about being data-driven while relying on surface-level trends. Discussions fixate on variance and thresholds rather than meaning and implication. When metrics become the endpoint instead of the input, data becomes decorative rather than decisive.

Data-Rich, Insight-Poor

This condition has become so common that it is now normalized. Organizations possess more data than at any point in history—and less shared understanding of what it implies. In data-rich, insight-poor environments, information flows constantly but coherence does not.

Reports contradict each other. Metrics improve while outcomes deteriorate. Root-cause analyses recycle familiar explanations without resolution. Strategic decisions rely on intuition disguised as analytics. The problem is not a lack of intelligence potential; it is the absence of structures that convert data into understanding. Data arrives raw, fragmented, and decontextualized. Teams are tasked with consumption, not synthesis. Analysts produce outputs, but no one owns interpretation. As a result, organizations accumulate knowledge artifacts without building organizational knowledge.

Intelligence Is Not More Data

Intelligence begins where measurement ends. It emerges when signals are connected across domains and interpreted against context, intent, and consequence. Intelligence is meaning under conditions of uncertainty—not certainty through accumulation. Crucially, intelligence is not a function of volume. More data can just as easily obscure insight as reveal it. Without disciplined interpretation, additional inputs increase noise, not clarity.

Without structured interpretation, additional data increases cognitive load rather than clarity, making decision-making more reactive rather than more informed.

This distinction is often lost because intelligence is quieter than execution and harder to visualize than metrics. It does not fit neatly into dashboards. It provokes discomfort by challenging assumptions. It forces decisions before proof is complete. For this reason, intelligence is frequently underweighted in organizational design. It is treated as an individual trait rather than an institutional capability.

When Intelligence Arrives Too Late

The cost of the intelligence gap is timing. Most organizations can explain failures perfectly—after they occur. Compliance breakdowns, quality escapes, market misreads, and strategic reversals are dissected in exhaustive detail once consequences are unavoidable. These analyses are often accurate but irrelevant. They describe what intelligence should have been rather than what intelligence was at the moment of decision. The true failure is not incorrect action but delayed understanding. Intelligence that arrives after execution is historical accounting, not decision support. An organization that learns only from outcomes is condemned to learn slowly.

The Structural Nature of the Gap

The intelligence gap persists because it is structural, not personal. Executives do not lack intelligence. Analysts are not incompetent. Frontline teams are not blind. The issue is that most organizations are designed to optimize delivery and reporting, not explanation and insight. Responsibilities for action are clear. Responsibilities for measurement are explicit. Responsibilities for synthesis—integrating signals into understanding—are often undefined or dispersed. Where no one is accountable for intelligence, everyone assumes it exists somewhere else.

Intelligence as Organizational Sensemaking

At its core, organizational intelligence is collective sensemaking—the capacity to distinguish signal from noise, anticipate second-order effects, recognize emerging risk before metrics breach thresholds, and understand not just whether performance is changing, but why it matters. This capacity cannot be retrofitted through tools alone. Nor can it be outsourced entirely to specialists. Intelligence must be designed into how organizations think, not just how they operate. Without this design, execution accelerates, measurement intensifies, and intelligence lags ever further behind.

The Consequence of Ignoring the Gap

The most dangerous aspect of the intelligence gap is that it appears productive. Activity is high. Reports are plentiful. Decisions are constant. Yet beneath this surface, organizations grow increasingly fragile. They rely on lagging indicators. They confuse correlation for causation. They repeat avoidable mistakes with refined efficiency. Eventually, complexity overwhelms control. When unexpected events occur—and they always do—leaders discover that what they knew was insufficient for what they needed to decide. This is not a failure of data, effort, or capability. It is a failure of intelligence. When this intelligence gap persists, its most visible consequence is late discovery—and the enterprise costs that follow. The rest of this book argues that closing this gap is neither optional nor cosmetic. In environments defined by complexity, uncertainty, and consequence, intelligence is no longer a supporting function. It is the operating condition for survival.

1.5 The Enterprise Cost of Late Quality Discovery

The absence of Q Intelligence™ carries a compound cost that extends well beyond defects or test failures. Strategic decisions are made without visibility into long-term quality impact. Tradeoffs favor speed over resilience without understanding downstream consequences.

Remediation work displaces innovation. Trust between engineering, quality, and leadership degrades as surprises accumulate. Over time, quality becomes viewed as a tax rather than an asset—a necessary burden instead of a source of organizational advantage.

These outcomes are not caused by insufficient testing. They are caused by insufficient intelligence.

Late quality discovery is often treated as an execution problem—a defect escaped, a test was missed, or a release cycle moved too quickly. At enterprise scale, this framing is incomplete and dangerously misleading. The impact of discovering quality issues late does not remain confined to development or testing functions. It propagates outward, compounding financial loss, eroding trust, increasing customer attrition, and introducing persistent organizational friction.

Figure 1.4 – Cost Curve of Late Quality Discovery

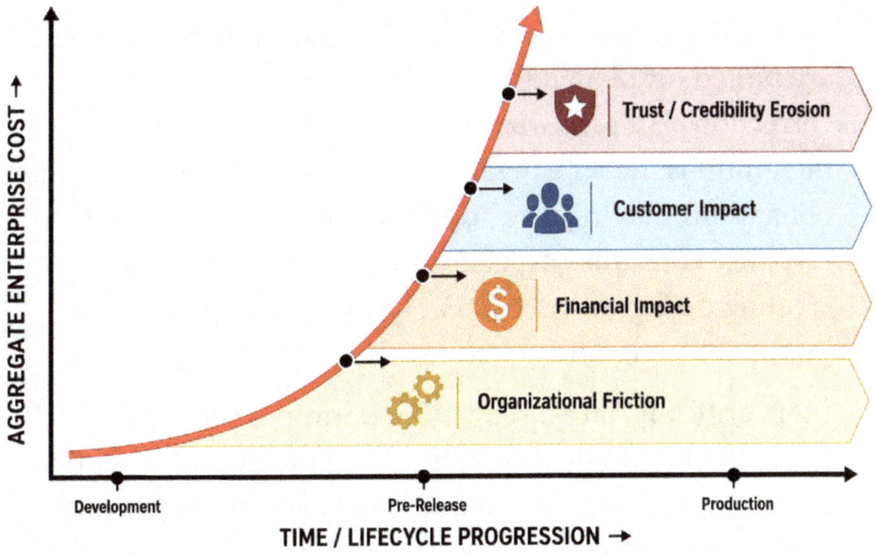

The cost of late quality discovery increases nonlinearly as issues are identified later in the lifecycle, compounding financial impact, customer impact, organizational friction, and trust erosion.

What makes late discovery particularly damaging is not the defect itself, but the timing. When quality signals emerge only after commitments have been made—after features are promised, timelines communicated, and dependencies locked—the organization is forced into reactive decision-making. At that point, even technically minor issues carry disproportionate cost and risk.

The Financial Compounding Effect

The financial impact of late quality discovery is rarely linear. Direct remediation costs represent only the most visible portion of the loss. (Boehm, 1981)

Once a defect or systemic issue is revealed late in the lifecycle, rework is no longer isolated. It cascades across schedules, contracts, and resource plans. Enterprise teams are pulled off planned initiatives to address urgent corrections. Release windows are missed. Downstream integrations must be revalidated. Regulatory or contractual obligations may require additional review cycles. Each response consumes capacity already allocated elsewhere, creating opportunity cost that is difficult to quantify but impossible to ignore.

More critically, late discovery undermines financial predictability. Budgets assume a certain level of execution efficiency and delivery confidence. When quality failures surface after those assumptions have been operationalized, forecasts become unreliable. Leaders are forced to choose between absorbing unplanned cost, deferring value delivery, or accepting elevated risk.

Over time, organizations normalize this volatility. Contingency buffers grow. Approval layers increase. Delivery commitments become conservative to compensate for uncertainty. What began as isolated quality issues becomes a structural drag on enterprise performance.

Trust and Credibility Erosion

Trust operates as an invisible control system within the enterprise. It governs how quickly decisions are made, how much autonomy teams are granted, and how confidently leadership communicates commitments.

Late quality discovery degrades this system incrementally but relentlessly. When quality issues emerge after assurances have been given—whether to executives, regulators, partners, or customers—confidence in those assurances weakens. Even when teams resolve the immediate issue effectively, the memory persists. The next commitment is questioned. Additional evidence is demanded. Oversight increases.

This erosion is not limited to external stakeholders. Internally, repeated late discoveries signal that existing reporting, metrics, and review mechanisms cannot be relied upon to surface risk early. Leaders begin to discount quality indicators altogether, viewing them as lagging or incomplete.

In response, they introduce parallel checks, redundant reviews, or escalation protocols. Paradoxically, these controls further delay signal flow. Teams spend more time justifying decisions and less time improving outcomes. Trust is not restored through effort alone; it requires sustained evidence of early, credible insight—something traditional quality models struggle to provide.

Customer Churn and Support Impact

From the customer's perspective, late discovery is indistinguishable from unreliability. End users do not evaluate organizations based on internal root cause analyses or remediation narratives. They experience impact: degraded functionality, interrupted service, inconsistent behavior, or delayed resolution.

When quality issues reach customers, support organizations become the front line of quality failure. Call volumes increase. Case resolution times lengthen. Knowledge bases expand reactively rather than strategically. In many enterprises, support teams are measured on efficiency—yet late quality discovery forces them into exception handling, eroding both performance metrics and morale.

More damaging still is the cumulative effect on customer confidence. A single incident may be forgiven. A pattern is not. Customers adapt by limiting usage, seeking alternatives, or building workarounds that reduce dependence on the platform.

Over time, churn increases—not always visibly or immediately, but measurably. Once customers begin making decisions based on anticipated quality failure rather than expected value, recovery becomes exceedingly difficult. Marketing and customer success efforts cannot compensate for systemic uncertainty. Trust, once lost externally, requires sustained reliability over time to rebuild.

Organizational Friction and Decision Drag

Late quality discovery introduces friction not because people resist change, but because the organization is forced into conflict under pressure. When issues emerge late, tradeoffs must be made quickly, often without sufficient context.

Engineering teams may advocate for technical remediation. Product teams may push to preserve scope or timelines. Legal or compliance functions may raise concerns about exposure. Leadership is left arbitrating between incomplete viewpoints, under time constraints, with limited confidence in available data.

These moments harden into patterns. Functions become defensive. Information is withheld until it is "safe." Metrics are optimized locally rather than shared holistically. Decision cycles slow as stakeholders seek to protect themselves from downstream consequences they can no longer predict.

Over time, the organization adapts to this environment by adding gates, committees, and approvals. While these mechanisms may reduce immediate risk, they also suppress learning. Signals that could have informed earlier decisions are filtered or delayed, ensuring that discovery remains late. Teams expend energy navigating friction rather than resolving root causes. Transformation efforts stall because the organization lacks confidence in its own ability to see clearly.

The Structural Implication

Across financial performance, trust, customer experience, and organizational cohesion, a common pattern emerges: late quality discovery converts uncertainty into cost. It forces enterprises to operate in a constant state of response rather than anticipation. This is not a failure of effort. In most cases, organizations invest heavily in quality activities, metrics, and controls.

The failure lies in the inability to convert those activities into early, actionable intelligence that informs decisions before commitments are made. As long as quality remains something organizations measure after execution rather than understand during decision-making, the costs described here will persist—regardless of tooling, staffing levels, or process maturity.

The implication is unavoidable: addressing late quality discovery requires more than improving testing efficiency or expanding coverage. It requires rethinking the role quality plays in how enterprises perceive risk, allocate resources, and make decisions.

That shift—from quality as a reactive function to quality as a source of enterprise intelligence—is not optional at scale. It is the prerequisite for sustainable delivery, credible leadership, and durable customer trust.

1.6 Real-World Failure Patterns

Across industries, across technology stacks, and across organizational models, major quality failures almost never begin as sudden catastrophes. They emerge slowly, quietly, and often invisibly—embedded within everyday delivery practices that appear functional until they are no longer tolerable. By the time failure reaches executive attention, the conditions that produced it have usually been present for months or years.

Figure 1.5 – Systemic Quality Failure Pattern Loop

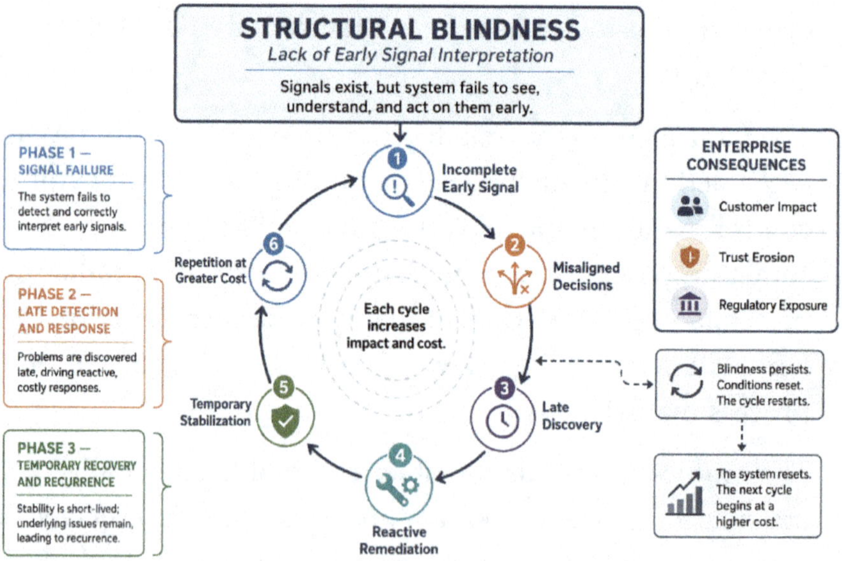

Late discovery, leadership surprise, reactive remediation, and temporary stabilization form a repeatable loop that preserves underlying quality blindness.

This section does not describe isolated incidents, tools, or organizations. It examines recurring systemic patterns observed across large enterprises—patterns that explain why quality breakdowns are consistently detected late, why leadership is often surprised by their severity, and why consequences escalate beyond engineering into customer trust and regulatory exposure.

Late Discovery as the Default Condition

Late discovery is not an anomaly in modern delivery organizations; it is the expected outcome of how quality is currently measured, monitored, and governed. (Reason, 1997) Most enterprises do not lack testing activity. They lack signal (activity vs. insight – signal vs. interpretation). Quality data is abundant but fragmented, retrospective, and decoupled from decision-making. Defects are logged after the fact. Metrics are aggregated after releases. Root causes are examined only once there is failure to explain.

As a result, early indicators of degradation rarely surface as risks. Instead, they appear as routine noise:

- Minor defects deferred to protect delivery timelines
- Intermittent failures labeled "flaky" or "environmental"
- Customer support tickets categorized as edge cases
- Performance regressions masked by infrastructure elasticity

Each signal is rationalized in isolation. None are evaluated as part of a cumulative pattern. Quality risk accumulates horizontally across teams and vertically across layers of the system—but visibility remains local. By the time impact becomes undeniable, the failure is already baked into production behavior. The system did not suddenly break. It simply reached the point where compensating mechanisms—manual workarounds, support interventions, operational heroics—could no longer contain it. Late discovery, in this sense, is not about timing. It is about structural blindness [[GL:Structural Blindness]]: organizations lack mechanisms to observe quality drift while it is still reversible.

Leadership Blind Spots and the Illusion of Control

When major quality failures surface, executives often react with genuine surprise. Dashboards were green. Delivery metrics were strong. Investments in tooling, automation, and process maturity appeared substantial. From a leadership perspective, the system was functioning. This disconnect is not caused by inattentive leadership. It is produced by misaligned abstractions.

Leadership visibility is commonly derived from summary indicators optimized for reporting, not diagnosis: release frequency, throughput, defect counts post-release, or SLA compliance. These metrics reflect activity and output—not structural health. They describe what happened, not what is forming. As systems scale, quality risk does not rise linearly. It compounds across dependencies, integrations, and operational contexts. Yet reporting models flatten this complexity into averages and thresholds that mask localized collapse. A small number of severely degraded paths can coexist with statistically acceptable overall performance.

At the same time, responsibility for quality is often distributed in ways that obscure ownership. Engineering teams own delivery. QA teams own testing. Operations own stability. Product owns prioritization. Each function optimizes locally, but no role is accountable for the quality of the system as a system. This fragmentation produces leadership blind spots:

- Quality risk appears contained within delivery teams
- Structural issues are framed as execution problems
- Escalations arrive without early context or lineage
- Accountability discussions happen after impact, not before
- When leadership is finally engaged, the failure is already reframed as a crisis rather than a detectable trend. The question becomes "What went wrong?" instead of "Why did we not see this forming?"

The Escalation Path into Customer Impact

Quality failures that escape internal detection rarely fail quietly once exposed to real users. Customer impact is usually the first visible consequence—but it is rarely the last. Initial signs often appear as subtle friction: inconsistent behavior, degraded performance, or confusing workflows. These issues erode confidence before they trigger formal complaints. Customers adapt briefly—retrying actions, contacting support, or abandoning features altogether. As degradation persists, adaptation turns into attrition. Trust decays faster than metrics can capture. Net promoter scores lag reality. Usage analytics describe symptoms but not causes. By the time impact is undeniable, customers have already formed judgments that are difficult to reverse.

Critically, customer-visible failures often illuminate systemic weaknesses that were already present internally:

- Missing validation paths
- Unmonitored decision logic
- Uncontrolled feature interactions
- Inconsistent data assumptions across services

What reaches the user is the final manifestation of longstanding internal fragility—not an unexpected edge case. Once customer impact is public, response timelines compress. Decision-making shifts from deliberative to reactive. Fixes are expedited under pressure, often without full diagnostic clarity—introducing further risk.

Regulatory Exposure as a Secondary Consequence

In regulated environments, customer impact is only the beginning. When failures intersect with compliance obligations, data handling, financial accuracy, accessibility, or safety requirements, regulatory exposure follows rapidly. Here, late discovery carries compounding risk. Regulations typically assume that organizations have preventive controls, not just corrective responses. When incidents occur, regulators examine not only what failed, but what was known, when it was known, and what governance mechanisms existed to detect and address it.

Organizations that discover issues late often struggle to demonstrate:

- Continuous oversight rather than periodic inspection
- Traceability between decisions and outcomes

- Evidence of proactive risk identification
- Clear accountability pathways

The absence of these artifacts transforms technical failures into governance failures. At that point, remediation is no longer limited to fixing software. It expands into audits, reporting obligations, consent decrees, or operational restrictions. Importantly, regulatory escalation is rarely about novel defects. It is about systemic neglect—patterns that show quality was treated as an operational afterthought rather than a governed discipline.

Why These Patterns Persist

These failure patterns reappear not because organizations are careless, but because prevailing quality models were designed for environments that no longer exist. Modern systems evolve continuously. They integrate third-party services, deploy changes incrementally, and operate across heterogeneous environments. Yet quality oversight mechanisms remain episodic, siloed, and retrospective. In this gap, organizations confuse motion with control. Activity replaces insight. Effort substitutes for intelligence. Late discovery, leadership surprise, customer harm, and regulatory intervention are sequential outcomes of a single condition: quality recognized only after it manifests as failure.

Until organizations develop the ability to observe, interpret, and govern quality as an evolving system characteristic—not a phase or function—these patterns will continue to recur, regardless of investment level or intent. This is the terrain in which Q-Intelligence becomes necessary—not as an optimization layer, but as a response to a structural incapacity that traditional quality models can no longer overcome.

1.7 Why Optimization Will Never Be Enough

For decades, organizations have pursued a familiar promise: if every process is optimized, the system will eventually behave. Waste removed, cycle time reduced, variance smoothed—control would emerge as a byproduct of efficiency.

The logic felt sound, the results measurable, and the tooling abundant. Yet across industries, the same pattern repeats. Despite unprecedented investment in optimization, leaders feel less—not more—in control.

This is not because organizations have failed to optimize. Optimization improves performance inside known boundaries. Modern organizations no longer operate inside such boundaries.

Figure 1.6 – Why Optimization Fails Without Intelligence

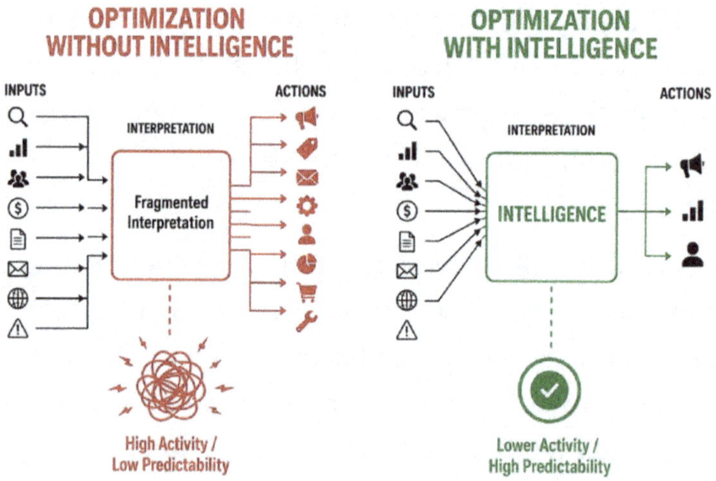

Optimization alone increases activity without improving control; intelligence enables fewer, more deliberate decisions that produce predictable outcomes.

More Tools Do Not Equal More Control

Every new operational challenge seems to invite the same response: add another tool. Dashboards are layered on top of dashboards. Risk registers coexist with compliance trackers, audit logs, performance heat maps, and workflow automations. The proliferation fragments understanding rather than consolidating it. Each system captures a partial view, defined by its local logic and metrics rather than a coherent system perspective.

Leaders are left to reconcile conflicting signals: performance indicators improving while risk accumulates elsewhere, compliance scores rising while customer trust erodes, velocity accelerating while resilience declines. Control requires coherence. Tools typically optimize islands.

The deeper problem is not tool quantity, but tool logic. Most operational tools are designed to measure activity, not meaning. They track whether steps were completed, thresholds met, or resources consumed, but not whether the system is moving toward a stable, sustainable outcome.

Organizations become highly instrumented yet poorly oriented. They measure extensively, but lack a coherent understanding of what those measurements mean. Because everything is measured, leaders assume it is understood. But measurement without interpretation becomes noise. Teams optimize to visible metrics even when the metrics no longer represent underlying reality. When outcomes diverge, the response is predictable: add another tool, refine another KPI, introduce another control layer. Complexity compounds. Control recedes.

Conceptual Interpretation: An environment with many dashboards but no synthesis behaves like a control room filled with readings but no operator capable of determining whether the system is stable or drifting.

In human, sociotechnical systems, variables change their meaning as conditions change. What worked yesterday becomes harmful tomorrow. Tools persist; context does not.

Speed Without Intelligence Is Force, Not Progress

Optimization tooling delivered something alongside efficiency: speed. Decisions happen faster. Workflows compress. Feedback cycles shorten—until speed outruns understanding.

Organizations often celebrate velocity improvements without asking a more uncomfortable question: faster toward what? When intelligence lags speed, risk does not only increase—it changes form and becomes harder to detect. Small misjudgments propagate faster than corrective signals. Weak assumptions embed themselves more deeply before they are questioned. Decision authority collapses downward into automated rules that no longer reflect reality but continue to execute flawlessly.

Optimization trains systems to execute correctly; intelligence is required to decide whether execution remains appropriate. Without that distinction, speed converts efficiency into exposure.

Consider how often organizations respond to emerging risk after acceleration has locked in a trajectory. By the time anomalies surface in reports, the system has already scaled the behavior. Rollbacks become costly, politically charged, and reputationally dangerous.

Leaders then mistake the cost of reversal for evidence of inevitability. This is why crises in optimized systems rarely arrive suddenly. Warning signals were present, but filtered out by performance logic that prioritized throughput over meaning. The system was blind not because it lacked data, but because it lacked interpretive capacity.

Optimization Solves the Wrong Problem

At its core, optimization asks a narrow question: How do we do this faster, cheaper, or more consistently? Intelligence asks a different question: Should we be doing this at all, and under these conditions? Modern organizations are facing environments where the second question matters more than the first.

Regulatory landscapes shift mid-cycle. Technologies change stakeholder expectations faster than governance updates. Social trust becomes a variable that cannot be engineered through efficiency.

Optimization cannot answer these questions because it presumes stability. It assumes goals are fixed, risks enumerable, and cause-and-effect relationships legible. When those assumptions break, optimization becomes self-reinforcing blindness.

This is why leaders feel trapped inside systems they helped design. Metrics say "success" while intuition says "danger." Formal controls report compliance while informal workarounds proliferate. The organization becomes highly optimized against yesterday's understanding. Adding optimization pressure in such conditions does not restore control—it accelerates misalignment.

Modern Reflection: AI Changes the Scale, Not the Problem

Organizations can now generate requirements, code, tests, documentation, and analysis at unprecedented speed. What once required weeks of effort can be produced in minutes.

Yet generation is not understanding.

Thousands of requirements do not guarantee alignment. Thousands of test cases do not guarantee confidence. Thousands of recommendations do not guarantee effective decisions.

As AI increases the volume of activity, the need for intelligence becomes more—not less—important. Organizations that mistake generated output for understanding risk accelerating the very conditions that created the modern quality paradox.

The fundamental challenge remains unchanged: how do organizations determine whether what was generated represents the right understanding, the right decision, and the right outcome?

Control Emerges From Sensemaking, Not Efficiency

True control is not the absence of variance; it is the capacity to detect, interpret, and respond to change without system collapse.

That capacity does not come from more tools or faster execution. It comes from intelligence embedded above and across optimized processes—an ability to recognize when efficiency metrics no longer correspond to reality. Without that layer, organizations confuse predictability with safety and repeatability with reliability. They become excellent at doing wrong things consistently.

This is the paradox at the heart of modern operations: the more optimized a system becomes, the more dangerous it is to operate without intelligence. Optimization reduces slack. Slack once absorbed uncertainty. Remove it without replacing interpretive capacity, and small shocks become systemic failures. Leaders often attribute these failures to "complexity" as if it were an external force. In truth, complexity was manageable. The breakdown occurred because optimization stripped away the organization's ability to think about its own behavior.

Why This Matters Now

The limits of optimization were tolerable when environments changed slowly and errors remained local. That era has ended. Today, decisions cascade globally, reputational impact is instantaneous, and system failures rarely stay contained. Efficiency multiplies reach. Automation multiplies consequence.

In such conditions, optimization alone is no longer just insufficient—it is unsafe. The question is no longer how to optimize better. It is how to operate intelligently in systems where speed, scale, and uncertainty are inseparable. Until organizations confront that shift, they will continue to add tools, increase velocity, and wonder why control keeps slipping further away.

1.8 The Inevitable Shift

For more than a century, quality has been treated as a secondary function—important in principle, but marginal in practice. It has lived at the edges of organizations: after design, after production, after delivery, after failure.

When systems break, quality is summoned to explain what went wrong. When auditors arrive, quality is asked to produce evidence. When leaders speak about improvement, quality is acknowledged politely and then set aside for what is perceived as the "real work" of strategy, growth, and innovation.

That model is no longer viable. Modern organizations operate in environments defined by speed, complexity, regulation, interdependence, and public visibility. Decisions propagate instantly. Failures scale before they can be contained. Assumptions that once remained local now echo across supply chains, platforms, and ecosystems.

In this reality, quality cannot remain a reactive discipline, nor can it survive as a compliance artifact. It must evolve into something more fundamental: an intelligence discipline embedded in how organizations see, decide, and act. This shift is not ideological. It is structural.

From Control to Cognition

Historically, quality emerged to manage variation in industrial systems. Statistical tools, inspection regimes, and later process models enabled organizations to stabilize outcomes. These methods delivered value in environments where systems were relatively bounded and change occurred incrementally. But as organizations became more software-driven, data-saturated, and interconnected, the assumptions that sustained traditional quality approaches eroded.

Control-based quality assumes that the system is sufficiently understood, that variation is observable after the fact, and that corrective action can be meaningfully applied before consequences compound. Today's systems violate all three assumptions. Causality is diffuse. Signals arrive late or distorted. Corrections applied in one area produce unintended consequences elsewhere.

Under these conditions, inspection and compliance are no longer safeguards; they are lagging indicators. What organizations increasingly require is not more control, but better awareness.

Intelligence disciplines exist to solve exactly this class of problem. They do not wait for failure; they help systems perceive emerging conditions. They do not rely on single metrics; they synthesize weak signals across domains. They do not promise certainty; they enable judgment under uncertainty.

When quality remains framed as a function rather than an intelligence capability, it cannot fulfill these roles. The shift, then, is not about abandoning rigor. It is about redirecting rigor toward sensemaking rather than policing.

The Pressure for Integration

Another force driving this shift is organizational fragmentation. Strategy is developed in one arena, operations optimized in another, risk managed elsewhere, and quality assessed after the fact. Each function claims rigor, yet the organization as a whole often lacks coherence. Decisions are locally rational and globally destabilizing. Quality, when elevated to an intelligence discipline, occupies a unique position in this landscape. It naturally intersects with design intent, operational reality, regulatory constraint, customer expectation, and ethical obligation.

But only when quality is permitted to operate upstream—before commitments are locked in—can it serve as connective tissue rather than scoreboard.

Without this shift, organizations grow increasingly dependent on escalations, heroics, and post-incident reform. Learning becomes episodic rather than continuous. Memory fragments. Institutional knowledge erodes as experience is lost to turnover and reorganization. In such environments, quality teams are often blamed for not preventing failure, even though they were never empowered to influence the conditions that produced it. An intelligence discipline does not suffer this paradox. Its mandate is not enforcement, but illumination.

What the System Now Demands

Modern systems demand capabilities that traditional quality structures were never designed to provide. These demands are not abstract; they are operational and unavoidable.

First, organizations must be able to perceive quality-relevant signals early—long before they manifest as defects, incidents, or nonconformities. This requires sensitivity to patterns across processes, technologies, behaviors, and decisions, not just outputs. Second, those signals must be interpretable by decision-makers. Data alone does not confer understanding. Quality insight that cannot be translated into strategic or operational judgment is functionally inert.

Third, organizations must be able to retain and evolve their quality knowledge over time. Lessons must accumulate rather than reset with each reorganization or crisis. This implies continuity, traceability, and disciplined memory—qualities rarely emphasized in compliance-oriented environments. Fourth, quality intelligence must operate at multiple temporal scales. Some signals require immediate response; others indicate structural drift that unfolds over months or years. A discipline fixated only on short-term metrics cannot support long-term resilience.

Finally, and perhaps most critically, quality must inform action without prescribing it. Intelligence enables choice; it does not replace leadership. When quality attempts to dictate solutions, it invites resistance. When it clarifies consequences, tradeoffs, and trajectories, it earns legitimacy. These are not enhancements to the existing quality paradigm. They are incompatible with it unless quality is fundamentally repositioned.

The Cost of Delay

Organizations that resist this shift often do so unintentionally. They invest in tools, frameworks, and certifications under the belief that surface modernization equates to systemic change. But adding dashboards does not create intelligence. Instituting new standards does not repair fragmented cognition. Without rethinking the role quality plays in organizational sensemaking, these investments produce diminishing returns.

The cost of delay is cumulative. Each failure treated as an isolated anomaly reinforces reactive habits. Each improvement initiative launched without institutional memory weakens trust.

Over time, leaders begin to perceive quality as overhead rather than guidance, and quality professionals retreat further into defensive postures. By the time an organization recognizes the need for deeper change, the gap between decision velocity and organizational awareness may already be dangerous.

An Unavoidable Transition

The shift toward quality as an intelligence discipline is not optional for organizations that wish to remain viable in complex environments. It is not driven by fashion, nor by theoretical elegance, but by the basic mismatch between how modern systems behave and how traditional quality models attempt to govern them. This transition does not require abandoning the past, but it does require moving beyond it. The tools of quality remain necessary, but they are no longer sufficient.

What matters now is how those tools contribute to organizational understanding—how they help leaders navigate uncertainty, balance competing pressures, and act with foresight rather than hindsight.

Q Intelligence™ [[GL:Quality Intelligence]] must therefore move from the perimeter to the center: from compliance to cognition, from after-action to anticipation, from functional specialization to systemic intelligence. The organizations that make this shift deliberately will discover that quality ceases to be a cost of doing business and becomes a way of seeing it. Those that do not will continue to manage complexity with instruments designed for a simpler world—until that world finally disappears.

1.9 Transition — Why the Old Model Persists

If the old quality model were merely ineffective, it would already be gone. It has not survived because it works well. It has survived because it explains failure in familiar ways, distributes responsibility comfortably, and offers the illusion of control without demanding change. What persists here is not a system so much as a set of stories—myths that allow organizations to keep doing the same things while convincing themselves they are improving.

These myths are durable because they are useful. They allow leaders to point to compliance instead of capability, activity instead of outcomes, and certifications instead of understanding. They make underperformance legible, manageable, and—most importantly—excusable.

When defects recur, delays compound, or customer trust erodes, the model already contains the language needed to explain why: more rigor is needed, more training, more enforcement. The diagnosis is always that the rules were not followed well enough, not that the rules themselves are misaligned with reality.

Over time, this reinforces the model rather than challenges it. Each failure becomes further evidence that quality must be tightened, centralized, or automated, even when those same moves have repeatedly failed to produce durable results. The organization does not learn; it rationalizes.

The model persists because it absorbs contradiction without changing its core assumptions. The myths also persist because they protect institutional comfort.

They separate "quality" from decision-making, allowing leaders to delegate accountability downward while retaining authority upward. Quality becomes something assessed after the fact rather than something embedded in how choices are made. This separation is critical to the model's longevity: it ensures that quality functions can expand, tools can proliferate, and metrics can multiply without threatening how decisions are actually governed.

In this way, the old model is self-sealing. It survives not by being right, but by being resilient to critique. It offers just enough explanatory power to avoid scrutiny, and just enough ceremony to signal seriousness.

Organizations don't abandon it because doing so would require confronting a more unsettling possibility—that quality failures are not execution mistakes layered atop a sound system, but symptoms of how the system itself thinks.

Yet something has shifted. The accumulation of exceptions, overrides, rework, and reconciliation has reached a level that can no longer be managed quietly. The gap between what organizations document and what they actually do is no longer incidental; it is structural.

Leaders increasingly sense this, even if they lack the language to describe it. They feel the drag, the brittleness, the way decisions slow as complexity rises. They sense that quality has become something to get through rather than something that guides.

This is where the myths begin to weaken—not because they are disproven, but because they can no longer carry the weight placed on them. They were designed for environments where variability could be contained, knowledge was stable, and authority flowed cleanly through hierarchies.

They strain under conditions where decisions must be made faster, accountability is distributed, and insight emerges from signals rather than rules. Dismantling these myths is therefore not an act of criticism; it is an act of recognition.

This is uncomfortable work, because myths do more than explain systems—they stabilize identities. They tell professionals what their role is, where responsibility begins and ends, and how success is recognized. Letting go of them feels less like upgrading a model and more like relinquishing a worldview.

But without that dismantling, no meaningful shift is possible. New language cannot take root in a landscape still governed by old assumptions. New approaches cannot function when they are forced to coexist with myths that quietly override them.

The persistence of the broken model is not due to lack of innovation, but to the failure to release what no longer fits. This marks the threshold of the argument. Up to this point, the case has been diagnostic: not to propose a replacement, but to make the hidden visible.

To show that what is often framed as a tooling problem, a skills gap, or a compliance shortfall is, at its core, a problem of how organizations understand quality itself.

What must come next is not another layer of process, but a shift in orientation—away from myth maintenance and toward sensemaking. Crossing that threshold requires abandoning the comfort of inherited explanations.

It means accepting that quality cannot be bolted on, audited in, or enforced into existence. It must be understood as something that emerges from how decisions are made, how signals are interpreted, and how responsibility is distributed across the system.

That realization does not yet tell us what to do. It tells us why the old answers keep failing—and why continuing to rely on them is no longer viable. The next step is not construction, but clearance: making room for a different way of thinking by finally letting the myths go.

A new discipline is required—one that connects quality signals across the lifecycle, transforms activity into insight, and enables informed action before failure becomes inevitable. That discipline is Q-Intelligence™ [[GL:Q Intelligence™]]. The chapters that follow will examine why prevailing assumptions obscure this reality, and how a structured, intelligence-driven approach redefines what quality can achieve at enterprise scale.

Summary

This chapter establishes that the limitations of traditional quality models are structural, not operational, and that increasing activity without intelligence exacerbates rather than resolves systemic risk. Together, these concepts form the foundation for understanding quality not as a function of execution or measurement, but as an organizational capability centered on interpretation, sensemaking, and early decision support. The next chapter builds on this by examining the underlying assumptions that sustain outdated quality models and identifying why they persist despite consistent failure at scale.

Key Takeaways

- Quality investment does not guarantee quality control.
- Enterprise scale turns activity into noise without interpretation.
- Late discovery is a symptom of missing quality intelligence.

- Q Intelligence™ is needed to convert distributed signals into decision-ready insight.
- Optimization cannot replace organizational sensemaking.
- Quality must move from reactive function to intelligence discipline.

Questions for Reflection

- What does this concept reveal about how your organization currently interprets quality signals?
- How would the intelligence gap manifest within your enterprise systems, processes, and decision structures?
- What signals would indicate that quality activity is increasing while actual understanding and control are declining?

Chapter 2 — The Five Myths of Quality Engineering

Chapter Introduction

Chapter 1 showed that quality failures at enterprise scale are systemic, not accidental. This chapter examines why those conditions persist by exposing the belief structures that reinforce them.

In complex organizations, simplifying assumptions [[GL:Quality Myth]] emerge to make uncertainty manageable. Over time, these assumptions harden into professional common sense. They shape how quality is discussed, measured, and defended—often without scrutiny. When outcomes degrade, they redirect attention toward activity, optimization, and compliance instead of the beliefs guiding those responses.

Outcomes are interpreted through the same simplifying belief, preventing contradiction and reinforcing the belief system rather than challenging it.

These assumptions persist because they reduce cognitive load in environments where full understanding is not achievable. By narrowing the range of questions considered necessary, they allow organizations to act with confidence even when underlying dynamics remain unclear.

In an enterprise setting, this typically appears as recurring language patterns, standardized reporting constructs, and accepted narratives that frame what "good" looks like without revalidation. Over time, teams optimize within these narratives rather than reassessing them.

When this capability is absent, organizations lose the ability to distinguish between assumptions and evidence. Simplifications harden into unquestioned truths, and alternative interpretations of system behavior are excluded from consideration.

This directly affects decision quality, as leadership actions become anchored to incomplete or outdated interpretations of reality, increasing the likelihood of delayed recognition and systemic misalignment.

Figure 2.1 – The Effect of Simplifying Myths on Interpretation

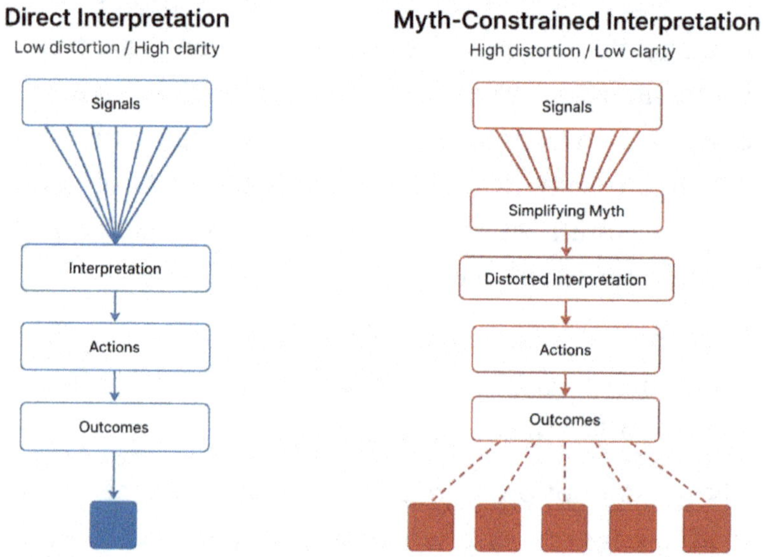

Simplifying myths do not remove signals—they distort interpretation, leading to increased activity but reduced clarity and stability of outcomes.

The five myths in this chapter are those stabilizing beliefs. Each feels reasonable. Each offers short-term reassurance. Together, they sustain late discovery [[GL:Late Discovery]], fragile systems, and recurring surprise. This chapter makes those beliefs visible so they can be examined—before any redefinition of quality can take hold.

To understand their influence, we must first define what a quality myth is and how it operates within complex systems.

2.1 — What a Quality Myth Really Is

Quality myths persist not because organizations lack data, but because they simplify responsibility. In complex systems, they function as cognitive shortcuts. They reduce ambiguity, diffuse accountability, and create the appearance of control [[GL:Illusion of Control]].

This simplification shifts attention away from how outcomes are produced toward who appears accountable. As a result, responsibility becomes abstracted rather than examined at the level where system behavior originates.

In an enterprise setting, this typically appears as broad accountability statements without corresponding visibility into decision pathways. Responsibility is declared, but causal relationships remain obscured.

When this capability is absent, accountability structures fail to map to actual system dynamics. Decisions that introduce risk remain unchallenged, and corrective action is misapplied to downstream symptoms.

This directly affects predictability, as organizations become unable to trace outcomes back to their originating conditions, increasing variability and reducing confidence in future performance.

Most quality myths began as truths under different conditions. Manual testing worked when systems were small. Automation improved consistency when change was slow. Metrics provided feedback when cause and effect were tightly coupled. Maturity models stabilized chaotic practices. Context changed faster than these beliefs adapted.

At scale, these inherited ideas become unsafe abstractions because they no longer reflect system behavior. They narrow the questions leaders feel required to ask. Activity replaces inquiry. Compliance replaces understanding. When results worsen, quality myths absorb contradictory evidence by demanding more of the same response.

Conceptual Interpretation: When outcomes degrade, organizations increase activity within the same belief system rather than questioning it, reinforcing the conditions that produced the failure.

Because they are socially reinforced, myths become invisible. Questioning them feels riskier than repeating them. The result is systemic degradation [[GL:Systemic Degradation]] that appears unconnected until it is too late to intervene.

> **Concept Insight: Quality myths function as cognitive shortcuts that simplify responsibility while obscuring how outcomes are produced. Their persistence is not due to lack of data, but because they reduce uncertainty and stabilize decision-making under complexity.**

Myth 1 — More Testing Equals Better Quality

The belief that more testing improves quality persists because testing is visible. It produces artifacts, metrics, and schedules. When confidence erodes, the response is to add tests. Activity creates the perception of progress.

This belief is reinforced by how quality is reported. Test counts and coverage percentages offer reassurance. They signal diligence even when underlying risk remains unchanged. Over time, activity is mistaken for assurance [[GL:Activity as Assurance]].

Coverage metrics sustain the myth. Coverage shows what was exercised, not what the system can withstand. Tests are written to meet targets, not to surface uncertainty. Shallow and redundant tests accumulate while critical assumptions remain unexamined.

This distinction is critical because exercising behavior does not validate resilience. Systems may perform as expected under known conditions while remaining vulnerable to unexamined interactions or edge conditions.

In an enterprise setting, this typically appears as increasing coverage percentages alongside persistent production issues. Test suites expand, yet incident patterns remain unchanged or grow more complex.

When this capability is absent, organizations equate execution completeness with system readiness. Testing activity increases without improving insight into failure conditions, allowing risk to accumulate undetected.

This directly affects performance predictability, as stable test results mask underlying fragility, increasing the likelihood of unexpected failure in live environments.

As long as tests pass, concern is deferred, which delays recognition of accumulating risk. Risk accumulates beneath stable metrics. When failure surfaces—often in production—it appears sudden. In reality, signals were present but invisible to a regime optimized for volume. This is the pattern of late discovery (see Glossary: Late Discovery).

More testing does not improve quality when it is disconnected from understanding. Without a way to separate signal from noise, increased testing accelerates execution, not insight.

Concept Insight: Testing activity can create the illusion of assurance without improving system understanding. True quality improvement depends on uncovering uncertainty, not increasing execution volume.

Myth 2 — Automation Solves the Quality Problem

Automation promises speed and scale. When manual processes feel slow or costly, automation appears curative. Investment looks like progress; dashboards turn green.

Automation increases execution speed. It does not determine whether the right conditions are examined or whether emerging risk is recognized in time. Applied without understanding, it scales existing assumptions. Weak tests run faster. Incomplete mental models propagate efficiently.

Speed amplifies whatever assumptions are embedded in the system. Without improving the quality of those assumptions, faster execution only accelerates the reinforcement of existing blind spots.

In an enterprise setting, this typically appears as highly efficient pipelines producing consistent outputs that nevertheless fail to detect emerging issues. Execution quality appears high, while situational awareness remains low.

When this capability is absent, organizations mistake throughput for intelligence. Automated systems scale incomplete understanding, making it more difficult to identify where insight is missing.

This directly affects decision quality, as leaders rely on signals produced by systems that execute efficiently but fail to represent actual risk conditions.

Tool proliferation compounds the problem. Each system reports local success while no mechanism integrates signals into a coherent view of risk. The organization becomes highly instrumented and poorly oriented—rich in data but weak in sensemaking [[GL:Sensemaking]].

Conceptual Interpretation: Sensemaking is the process by which signals are interpreted into insight. Without it, data accumulation does not improve understanding.

Leaders then ask why failures persist despite automation. The belief itself goes unexamined. Effort increases; judgment does not. Automation increases execution speed but does not improve awareness.

Myth 3 — Quality Is a QA Responsibility

Assigning quality to a QA function simplifies accountability. It makes quality someone else's job.

This framing treats QA as a downstream validator of decisions it did not make. Risk is introduced early—through scope, architecture, and timelines—but remains invisible to the function tasked with assuring outcomes.

The separation creates structural blindness [[GL:Structural Blindness]]. Upstream decisions escape feedback, and downstream teams inherit consequences. Responsibility fragments into functional silos, producing fragmented accountability [[GL:Fragmented Accountability]]. When quality degrades, attention shifts to execution gaps rather than the systemic conditions that produced them.

This blindness is not a lack of effort but a consequence of misaligned visibility. When the point of assurance is disconnected from the point of decision, critical system conditions remain outside the scope of evaluation.

In an enterprise setting, this typically appears as recurring defects traced back to early-stage decisions that were never subject to meaningful feedback. Downstream teams detect issues but cannot influence their origin.

When this capability is absent, organizations repeatedly address symptoms rather than causes. Quality interventions occur too late to alter outcomes, reinforcing cycles of rework and escalation.

This directly affects outcome reliability, as systemic risks introduced upstream persist through delivery, increasing the frequency and severity of downstream failures.

The myth persists because it avoids discomfort. Failures are framed as misses, not inevitabilities. Prevention is deferred; response becomes the norm.

Myth 4 — Metrics Provide Control

Metrics feel authoritative because they are numerical and repeatable. Over time, reporting substitutes for understanding. Visibility is treated as a substitute for judgment.

Metrics describe what has happened, not what is emerging. As measurement expands, interpretation lags. Organizations become data-rich and insight-poor [[GL:Data Rich, Insight Poor]].

This temporal limitation constrains their usefulness in dynamic systems. While metrics can confirm past performance, they do not inherently reveal changing conditions or future risk.

In an enterprise setting, this typically appears as stable dashboards coexisting with shifting system behavior. Reported performance remains consistent even as underlying dependencies and risks evolve.

When this capability is absent, organizations rely on lagging indicators to guide forward-looking decisions. Emerging signals are overlooked, and critical shifts go unrecognized until impact occurs.

This directly affects decision timing, as actions are based on outdated representations of system state, increasing the likelihood of delayed or misaligned responses.

Stable numbers preserve confidence while system dynamics shift. Dependencies densify. Assumptions age quietly. Work optimizes toward what is measured, not what is uncertain.

This produces the illusion of control: leaders feel governed by evidence while remaining disconnected from the forces shaping outcomes.

> **Concept Insight: Metrics provide visibility into past behavior but do not inherently reveal emerging risk. Without interpretation and context, measurement reinforces confidence without improving understanding.**

Myth 5 — Process Maturity Equals Readiness

Maturity models promise order through stages and compliance. Advancing levels feels like progress, and readiness is inferred from certification [[GL:Readiness (beliefbased)]].

At scale, the assumptions break. Linear progression and predictable feedback no longer hold. Processes mature faster than systems evolve. Documentation improves while dependencies multiply.

This divergence creates a false sense of alignment. While documented practices improve, the underlying system complexity continues to grow in ways that those practices cannot fully capture.

In an enterprise setting, this typically appears as strong audit outcomes alongside increasing operational instability. Compliance signals progress, while systemic risk continues to accumulate.

When this capability is absent, organizations interpret process adherence as evidence of readiness. Critical gaps between documented practice and actual system conditions remain unexamined.

This directly affects risk exposure, as confidence grows independently of system robustness, increasing the likelihood of failure under real operating conditions.

Compliance increases alongside fragility. Risk remains unseen until impact occurs. Late discovery becomes structural, not accidental.

Maturity fails when it is used to signal readiness in conditions it cannot observe. Confidence accumulates without understanding.

Figure 2.2 – What Each Myth Produces Instead of Capability

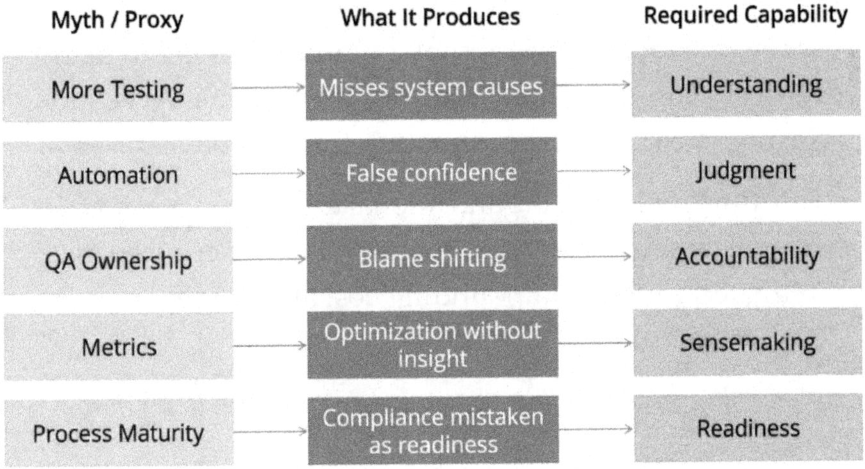

Each myth produces a misleading outcome that replaces the capability required, creating confidence without understanding, judgment, accountability, sensemaking, or readiness.

2.2 — The Cost of Myth Retention

The five quality myths simplify decisions while compounding risk. Together, they create an operating model that appears disciplined yet fails under pressure.

Costs begin with delay. Quality myths replace inquiry with reassurance. Discovery arrives only when options have narrowed.

At this stage, the system has already committed to a constrained set of outcomes. The ability to influence direction is reduced, and corrective actions become more costly and less effective.

In an enterprise setting, this typically appears as late-stage escalations where teams must choose between delay, rework, or risk acceptance. Strategic flexibility has already been lost.

When this capability is absent, organizations fail to detect early signals that would allow for lower-cost intervention. Response becomes reactive rather than adaptive.

This directly affects organizational efficiency, as resources are consumed in resolving issues that could have been mitigated earlier, compounding cost and eroding confidence.

Figure 2.3 – The Cost Gradient of Myth Retention

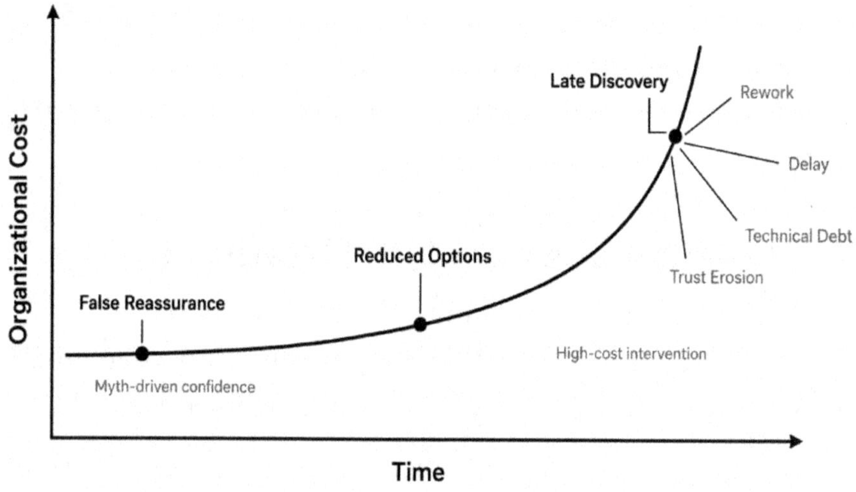

Cost escalation is structural: early reassurance delays discovery, reduces available options, and drives late-stage cost amplification that spreads across the system.

As shown in Figure 2-3, the reinforcing interaction of the myths causes organizational costs to compound over time, even as perceived confidence increases.

The deepest cost is cognitive. Organizations adapt their thinking to avoid confronting uncertainty. Failures recur under new names. Effort increases; outcomes degrade. The bill is paid in rework, delay, debt, eroding trust, and attrition—losses rarely visible on dashboards.

2.3 — A System-Level Shift

With the myths exposed, the problem is no longer a lack of activity, tooling, metrics, or process maturity.

The problem is the model itself.

Quality is not produced by isolated practices operating independently.

Testing, automation, AI, and organizational roles do not function as competing approaches—they function as interdependent capabilities within a larger system.

When these capabilities are treated separately, organizations optimize fragments of behavior while losing visibility into how outcomes are actually produced.

What is required instead is coordination.

Not coordination as process alignment, but as a system-level capability that continuously integrates:

- understanding (functional testing)
- execution stability (automation)
- augmented insight (AI)
- lifecycle participation (quality assistance)

This coordination is not manual.

It is not periodic.

It is not implicit.

It must be explicit and continuous.

This is the role of system orchestration.

Figure 2.4 – System orchestration integrates quality capabilities.

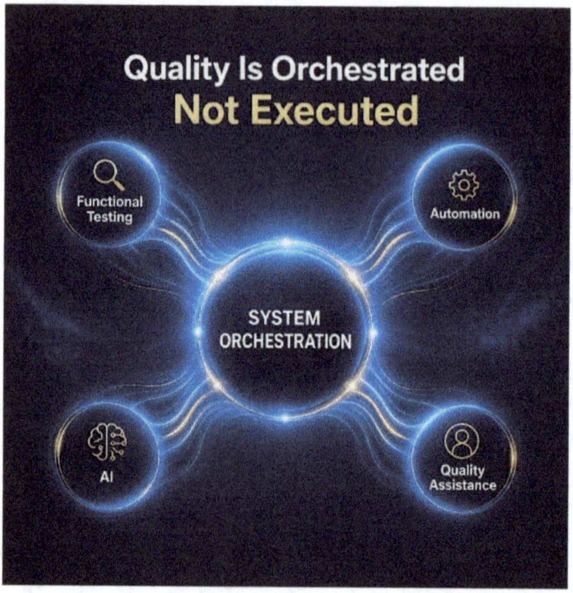

Quality, at scale, does not emerge from the strength of any single practice.

It emerges from how effectively these capabilities are orchestrated across the system.

Without orchestration, activity increases while understanding degrades.

With orchestration, signals become connected, interpretable, and actionable.

This distinction marks the transition away from myth-driven execution—and toward a system capable of producing quality intentionally.

2.4 — From Myth to Definition

Removing a myth creates uncertainty. That discomfort is necessary.

The resulting uncertainty reflects the removal of previously stabilizing assumptions. Without those assumptions, organizations must confront the complexity they had abstracted away.

In an enterprise setting, this typically appears as hesitation or resistance when established interpretations are challenged. Teams may struggle to operate without familiar reference points.

When this capability is absent, organizations revert to previous beliefs to regain stability. Myths re-emerge, and the opportunity for deeper understanding is lost.

The inability to tolerate uncertainty directly limits transformation potential, preventing adoption of more accurate, system-aligned definitions of quality.

This chapter establishes the structural role of belief systems in sustaining enterprise quality failure. Together, these concepts form a diagnostic lens for identifying how organizations reinforce misunderstanding through seemingly rational practices. The next chapter builds on this by redefining quality in a way that reflects actual system behavior rather than inherited assumptions.

Summary

This chapter surfaced the beliefs that make failure repeatable. Without naming them, any redefinition would inherit old meanings and measures.

Chapter 3 begins from this cleared position—where quality myths are visible but not yet replaced—so quality can be defined in terms that match how modern systems behave, not how organizations wish they did.

Key Takeaways

- Quality myths simplify uncertainty while hiding system causes.
- More testing increases activity, not necessarily assurance.
- Automation scales assumptions as quickly as it scales execution.
- Metrics require interpretation before they can support control.
- Process maturity does not prove enterprise readiness.
- System orchestration is required to replace myth-driven quality behavior

Questions for Reflection:

- What does this concept reveal about system behavior?
- How would this appear in an enterprise context?
- What signals would indicate this is not functioning correctly?

Chapter 3 — When Scale Breaks Judgment

Chapter Introduction

By the time organizations confront recurring quality failure at scale, they have usually corrected the obvious explanations. Myths have been challenged, language modernized, and responsibility redistributed across governance structures designed to manage complexity. And yet the failures persist.

Although the myths examined in the previous chapter have been exposed, their influence does not disappear. Organizations continue to operate through these assumptions long after evidence has shown their limitations.

This chapter argues that what breaks under scale is not effort, intent, or even execution discipline, but judgment itself. As systems scale, the organization's ability to perceive its own condition degrades in predictable ways. Signals weaken, meaning fragments, and recognition occurs only after commitment has already been made. Control is not lost because people believe the wrong things; it is lost because the system can no longer perceive early enough to act.

What follows does not propose remedies. It establishes a boundary: the point at which correct beliefs, mature process, and experienced leadership are no longer sufficient to govern quality. Beyond that boundary, failure is not aberrant. It is structural.

This chapter builds on the prior examination of quality myths by addressing what persists after those myths are removed—specifically, how perception and judgment degrade under scale even when understanding improves.

It focuses on the structural limits of perception, the distortion introduced by scale, and the transition from execution failure to judgment failure.

This is critical because it establishes the point at which traditional improvements no longer restore control, clarifying that failure at scale is not accidental but inherent to how the system perceives itself.

3.1 Why Exposing Myths Does Not Restore Control

Organizations often respond to repeated quality failures by correcting beliefs. They challenge outdated assumptions, retire familiar myths, and adopt more modern language about complexity, risk, or systems. These efforts are necessary, but they do not restore control. Failure persists even after the myths are gone. If myths do not restore control, the next question is why perception itself degrades as systems scale.

The reason is structural. Myths operate at the level of explanation, not perception. This distinction is critical because explanation occurs after events have already unfolded, while perception determines whether those events can be anticipated at all. An organization may develop increasingly accurate narratives about failure without improving its ability to detect that failure in formation, leaving underlying conditions unchanged despite greater conceptual clarity. Removing them improves how organizations narrate failure after it occurs, but it does not change how early signals are detected, interpreted, or acted upon while systems are still in motion. The organization may now know that quality does not emerge automatically from good intentions or documented process, yet still fail to see deterioration until consequences are unavoidable.

This gap explains a recurring pattern in mature enterprises: retrospectives become more accurate while outcomes remain unchanged. Leaders describe failures with greater sophistication, but discovery still arrives late, framed as surprise rather than anticipation. The problem is no longer ignorance about what should be true, but incapacity to perceive what is becoming true in time to matter.

Correct beliefs do not compensate for degraded perception. In an enterprise setting, this typically appears as improved post-incident analysis paired with unchanged operational trajectories. Reports become more refined and aligned, yet the timing of recognition remains constant, with issues continuing to surface at points of high commitment rather than early formation. They only make the absence of control more visible.

When this capability is absent, the organization develops a pattern of retrospective precision without prospective awareness. Teams become increasingly skilled at explaining failure conditions after escalation, while remaining unable to identify those same conditions while they are still forming within active work.

This directly affects decision quality by reinforcing confidence in understanding that is temporally misaligned with action. It also increases risk exposure, as interventions occur only after constraints have hardened, reducing the organization's ability to respond effectively.

Concept Insight: Correcting myths improves how organizations explain failure but does not improve their ability to detect it early. As scale increases, the critical breakdown shifts from misunderstanding to degraded perception. Without restoring perception, improved insight only exposes the absence of control rather than correcting it.

From Orchestration to Perception Breakdown

Chapter 2 established that quality is produced through the orchestration of interdependent capabilities rather than isolated practices. This reframing resolves the limitations of competing approaches by positioning functional testing, automation, AI, and quality assistance as coordinated sources of signal within a unified system.

However, orchestration alone does not restore control.

As systems scale, the conditions required for effective orchestration begin to degrade. Signals that were previously clear, localized, and interpretable become distributed, transformed through layers of aggregation, and increasingly detached from their originating context. The system continues to operate, and orchestration remains structurally present, but the integrity of the signals it depends on begins to fail.

This creates a critical distinction: coordination persists, but understanding does not.

At this point, the organization is no longer limited by incorrect beliefs or insufficient activity. It is limited by its ability to perceive. Orchestration depends on the continuous flow of meaningful signals, and when those signals fragment or distort, the system cannot interpret its own condition in time to act.

The result is a system that remains active and coordinated while becoming progressively less aware.

Figure 3.1 – Orchestration–Perception Gap Under Scale

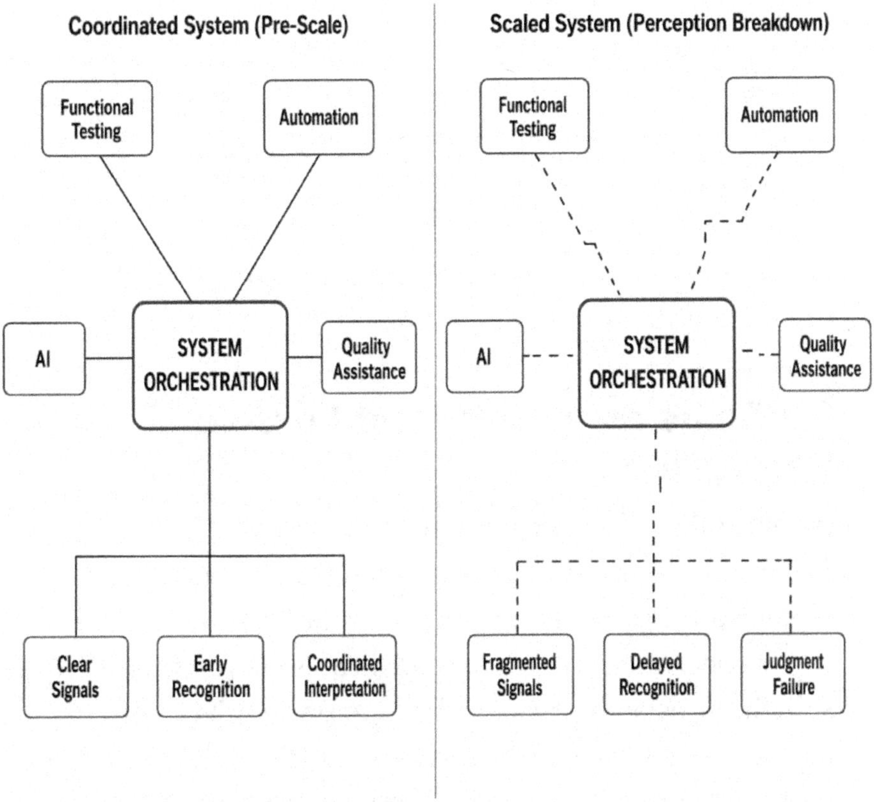

As scale increases, the system's ability to integrate signals into coherent understanding degrades. Orchestration remains present as a structural capability, but its effectiveness declines as signal clarity, coherence, and timing are lost. This leads to delayed recognition, fragmented interpretation, and ultimately degraded organizational judgment.

Figure 3.2 – Perception vs Explanation Gap

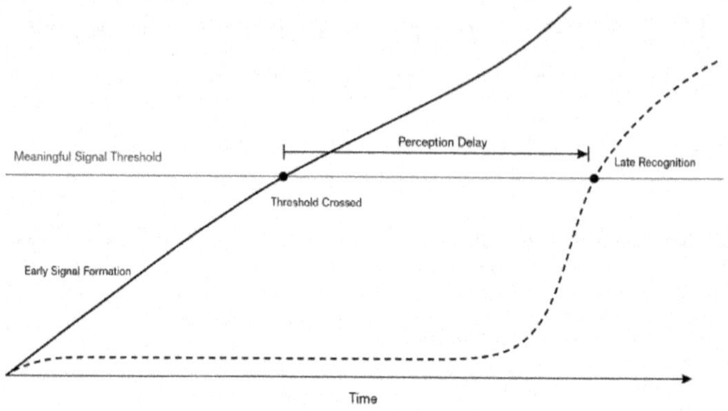

Perception delay: meaningful conditions form before organizational recognition occurs.

3.2 Scale as a Distorting Force on Perception

As organizations scale, they rely on intermediaries to perceive and report on reality. As scale increases, metrics replace direct observation and summaries replace firsthand experience, and governance substitutes for proximity. These substitutions are not flaws; they are prerequisites of coordination at scale. Yet each substitution alters what can be perceived. This alteration is not simply a reduction in detail, but a transformation of signal meaning. As perception moves further from direct interaction with work, the organization becomes increasingly dependent on abstractions that represent conditions rather than reveal them, shifting awareness from observation to inference.

In an enterprise setting, this typically appears as heavy reliance on aggregated metrics and normalized reporting structures that show stability while masking localized disruption. Teams operate within environments where reported performance appears consistent, even as underlying conditions diverge.

When this capability is absent, anomalies lose their distinctiveness before they can be interpreted. Local signals are absorbed into broader categories, preventing early differentiation between normal variation and emerging risk patterns.

This directly affects predictability by reducing the organization's ability to distinguish between stable and deteriorating conditions. It also weakens confidence calibration, as leadership decisions are based on representations that no longer reliably correspond to execution reality.

Signals that are sharp and unambiguous in small systems become diffuse as they pass through layers of aggregation. Local variation is averaged away. Context is stripped to achieve comparability. Anomalies are normalized to preserve stability in reporting. The organization continues to measure quality, but it increasingly measures representations of conditions rather than the conditions themselves.

This distortion is cumulative. Each additional layer introduced to manage scale adds latency, filtering, and incentives that shape what can be perceived. Over time, the organization becomes highly confident in reports that grow increasingly detached from the underlying state of execution. The very mechanisms designed to provide oversight begin to soften the signals oversight depends on.

At this point, scale does not merely complicate perception; it reshapes it. The organization no longer experiences quality directly. It infers quality from artifacts whose reliability declines as complexity increases.

Concept Insight: Scale introduces structural distortion by replacing direct observation with abstraction, aggregation, and reporting. This transformation weakens signal clarity and shifts perception from reality to representation. As a result, organizations become increasingly confident in views that are progressively detached from actual conditions.

Figure 3.3 – Scale-Induced Signal Distortion [[GL:Signal Distortion]]

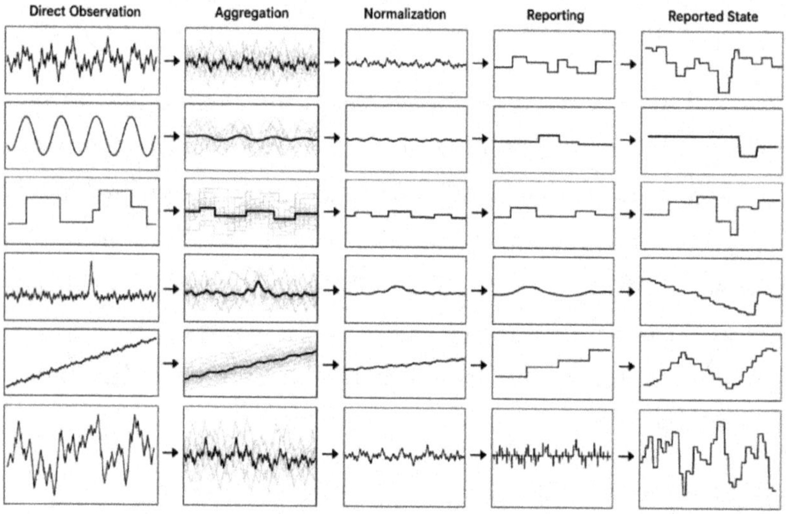

Scale distorts direct observation through aggregation, normalization, and reporting, producing outputs that no longer preserve the underlying reality.

Recognizable Situation:

> *Every quality leader has seen a program that "looked green" across ten dashboards suddenly fail at production. The reports were accurate. The reviews happened. Standards were followed. And yet — at scale — no one could see the failure forming. The system had grown beyond the reach of the judgment being applied to it. In an AI-enabled environment, this dynamic accelerates — because the system can now grow faster than the judgment can adapt.*

3.3 Late Discovery Is Structural (Not Late)

When failures surface late, they are often attributed to timing: insufficient testing, delayed reviews, or missed checkpoints. These explanations imply that discovery could have occurred earlier if attention had been sharper or discipline more rigorously applied.

In scaled systems, this assumption no longer holds. Discovery occurs when the system is structured to recognize it—typically after signals have been aggregated into thresholds visible to reporting. This reframes timing as a function of system design rather than attentiveness. The moment of recognition reflects the point at which dispersed signals achieve sufficient coherence within existing structures, not the point at which those signals first emerged. Early signals exist, but they are weak, distributed, and often not interpretable outside their local context. By the time those signals cohere into something recognizable at the enterprise level, the system has already committed.

In an enterprise setting, this typically appears as issues becoming visible only when they breach predefined thresholds, such as performance limits, defect counts, or compliance triggers, even though earlier indicators were present but fragmented across teams.

When this capability is absent, early signals remain isolated and uninterpreted, creating a condition where meaningful patterns exist but cannot be assembled into actionable insight before escalation occurs.

This directly affects response effectiveness by compressing the available window for intervention. It also increases the perceived abruptness of failure, reinforcing the false impression that issues emerge suddenly rather than accumulate over time.

Labeling this condition "late discovery" obscures its structural cause (as introduced in Chapter 2). Nothing arrives late relative to how the organization is designed to perceive. What appears as delay is actually alignment between system structure and what the organization is capable of perceiving. The system discovers issues precisely when it is capable of discovering them—and not before.

This makes escalation feel abrupt and disproportionate. Leadership experiences failure as a sudden event, even though deterioration has been underway for some time. The surprise is not the presence of failure, but the realization that governance has been operating without timely perception.

Concept Insight: Late discovery is not a timing issue but a structural outcome of how systems are designed to perceive. Signals emerge early but remain fragmented until they reach thresholds defined by reporting structures. What appears as delay is actually the system recognizing issues at the earliest point it is capable of doing so.

Figure 3.4 – Structural Nature of Late Discovery

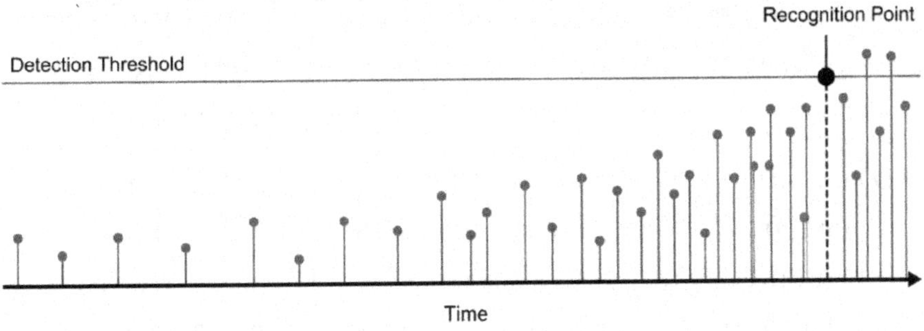

Signal Emergence vs Signal Recognition

Recognition occurs at the system's detection threshold, not at signal origin.

3.4 From Execution Failure to Judgment Failure

Historically, quality breakdowns were treated as failures of execution. Work was incomplete, controls were bypassed, defects escaped. Responsibility could be traced to actions taken—or not taken—by identifiable teams.

At scale, the failure shifts. Teams may execute correctly within their local constraints, adhere to process, and satisfy reported criteria, while the organization as a whole makes decisions based on an incomplete or distorted picture of reality. The breakdown occurs not in activity, but in organizational judgment. This shift reflects a change in where correctness resides within the system. Individual actions may remain aligned with defined expectations, yet the collective interpretation of system state becomes insufficient to guide appropriate decisions at the organizational level.

In an enterprise setting, this typically appears as widespread compliance with process alongside declining alignment between decisions and actual outcomes. Teams fulfill requirements, but the organization continues to move in directions that do not reflect underlying conditions.

When this capability is absent, the system produces decisions that are internally consistent but externally misaligned. Confidence remains high because actions conform to expectations, even as those expectations no longer correspond to reality.

This directly affects governance effectiveness by decoupling authority from accurate perception. It also amplifies systemic risk, as each successive decision reinforces conditions built on incomplete understanding.

This transition is subtle but consequential. When judgment fails, corrective measures aimed at execution have diminishing returns. More rigor at the edges does not restore clarity at the center. Decisions continue to be made with confidence, but that confidence is no longer proportional to actual understanding of system conditions.

The organization is not failing to act—it is failing to see. And because judgment governs where attention, resources, and authority are directed, this failure compounds. Each decision made on degraded perception further entrenches the conditions that produced it.

Figure 3.5 – From Execution Failure to Judgment Failure

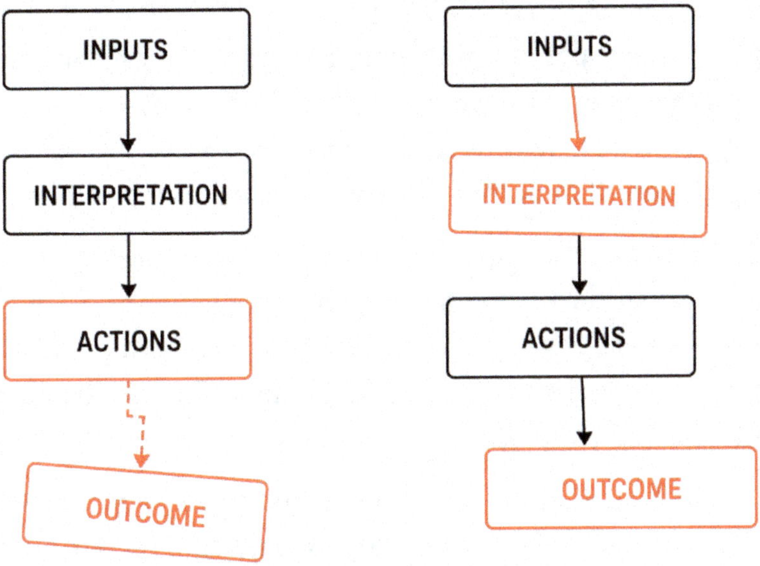

Failure shifts from incorrect action to incorrect system interpretation.

3.5 The Threshold Moment

There is a point at which accumulated distortion crosses a threshold. Beyond it, the organization cannot reliably perceive quality early enough to govern it, regardless of intent, investment, or experience. This point represents a structural ceiling rather than a temporary limitation. The organization's existing mechanisms for sensing and interpreting conditions no longer scale proportionally with system complexity, establishing a persistent gap between reality and recognition. Past success offers no immunity. Established controls provide diminishing assurance.

In an enterprise setting, this typically appears as repeated investments in tooling, process refinement, or leadership intervention that fail to improve the timing of issue detection, despite increasing effort and sophistication.

When this capability is absent, the organization continues to operate under the assumption that incremental improvements will restore control, leading to cycles of investment that do not materially change perception fidelity.

This directly affects strategic risk by increasing the cost of recovery and reducing the reliability of forward planning. It also deepens the separation between perceived control and actual system behavior, making future failures harder to anticipate and contain.

This moment is rarely acknowledged when it occurs. It is often mistaken for a temporary lapse, a tooling gap, or a leadership transition issue. In reality, it marks a structural limit: the point at which existing mechanisms of judgment no longer scale with the system they are meant to oversee.

Crossing this threshold does not immediately produce collapse. Systems can continue to operate, sometimes for years, under conditions of delayed recognition. What changes is the nature of risk. Failure becomes less predictable, recovery more costly, and confidence increasingly decoupled from actual control.

At this boundary, the organization is no longer deciding with present reality, but about it—after the fact. A different kind of intelligence is now required, not as an enhancement, but as a constraint imposed by scale itself. Crossing this threshold establishes the condition that necessitates a new discipline—one concerned with how judgment is formed under scale.

Figure 3.6 – The Threshold Moment

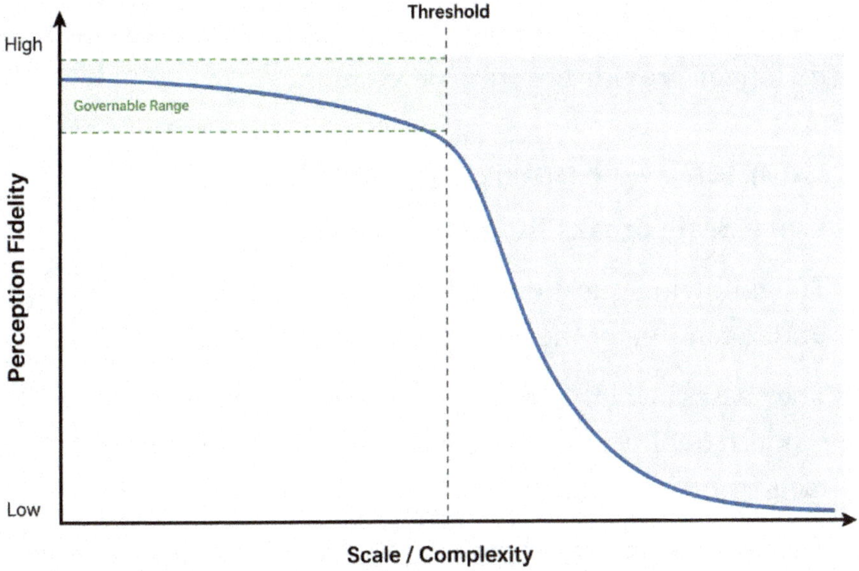

A structural threshold beyond which perception can no longer support timely governance.

Summary

Enterprise quality systems eventually reach a structural threshold where their ability to perceive and interpret conditions no longer scales with system complexity. At this point, existing mechanisms—tooling, process, and expertise—fail to provide timely and reliable insight, creating a persistent gap between reality and recognition.

Beyond this threshold, organizations continue to operate, but with increasing uncertainty. Failure becomes less predictable, recovery more costly, and confidence increasingly disconnected from actual system behavior. This condition reflects a limit of judgment, not effort, and cannot be resolved through incremental improvement.

Crossing this boundary establishes the need for a new form of intelligence—one designed to govern how judgment is formed under scale, rather than relying on mechanisms that no longer provide accurate perception.

Chapter 3 — Knowledge Check

When Scale Breaks Judgment

The following questions are designed to verify conceptual understanding of the material in this chapter.

They assess whether the reader has internalized why modern quality systems fail at scale, rather than recalling facts or proposing solutions.

These questions are diagnostic and reflective. They are not intended to evaluate implementation knowledge.

Knowledge Check 3.1 — Why Insight Is Not Enough

Question

Why does correcting quality myths, as discussed in Chapter 2, fail to restore control in large, complex organizations?

Knowledge Check 3.2 — Structural Late Discovery

Question

What does it mean to say that late discovery is structural rather than simply late?

Knowledge Check 3.3 — The Threshold Condition

Question

What condition must the reader accept before progressing from this chapter to the next?

Knowledge Check 3.4 — Judgment Failure Recognition

Question

How does execution failure differ from judgment failure in the context of this chapter?

Guidance for the Reader

If you can clearly explain why quality breakdowns persist even after beliefs are corrected—and why this condition is inevitable at scale—you are ready to proceed to the next chapter, which formally defines the discipline required to address this problem.

This chapter establishes that failure at scale is not driven by lack of effort, discipline, or understanding, but by structural limits in perception that degrade organizational judgment. It defines the boundary where traditional approaches to quality cease to be effective.

Together, these concepts form the foundation for understanding why control cannot be restored through incremental improvement alone, and why a different form of intelligence becomes necessary as systems grow in complexity.

The next chapter builds on this by formally defining the discipline required to operate within these constraints and restore the conditions necessary for effective judgment under scale.

Key Takeaways

- Correct beliefs do not restore degraded perception.
- Scale distorts quality signals through abstraction and aggregation.
- Late discovery reflects system recognition limits, not simple delay.
- Judgment failure occurs when decisions outpace accurate perception.
- The threshold moment marks the limit of traditional quality control.
- A new intelligence discipline becomes necessary when perception no longer scales.

Questions for Reflection:

- What does this concept reveal about system behavior as complexity increases?
- How would degraded perception manifest in an enterprise you are familiar with?
- What signals would indicate that judgment—not execution—is failing within the system?

Chapter 4 — Q-Intelligence™ Defined

Chapter Introduction

This chapter builds on the concept established in Chapter 3 that failure at scale is a breakdown of judgment by defining the discipline required to stabilize that judgment.

It focuses on establishing Q Intelligence™ as the governing layer that ensures quality signals become intelligible, comparable, and actionable across the enterprise.

This is critical because without a defined intelligence discipline, organizations cannot achieve consistent, reliable judgment at scale, regardless of execution effectiveness or measurement maturity.

Chapter 3 established that failure at scale is a breakdown of judgment. This chapter defines the discipline required to address that condition.

4.1 What Q Intelligence™ Is

Q Intelligence™ is an enterprise discipline that treats quality as a problem of intelligence. It governs how quality is perceived, interpreted, and judged under conditions of scale.

This definition emphasizes that quality is not inherent in artifacts or outcomes alone, but emerges through interpretation structures that make those artifacts meaningful. The discipline therefore centers on how meaning is constructed, not on how outputs are produced.

In an enterprise setting, this typically appears as multiple teams evaluating the same signals differently, where interpretations drive differing conclusions about quality despite shared data.

When this capability is absent, quality becomes defined by local perception, leading to conflicting judgments, fragmented conclusions, and an inability to reconcile differing views of the same system.

This directly affects decision consistency, reduces confidence in enterprise-level conclusions, and increases risk as actions are based on incompatible interpretations rather than shared understanding.

Figure 4.1 – The Domain of Q Intelligence™

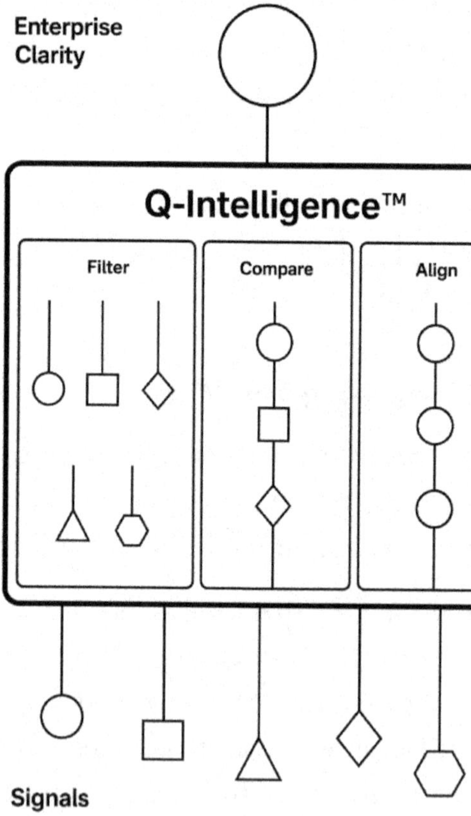

Q-Intelligence™ operates as the governing layer that stabilizes how quality signals are interpreted across the enterprise.

Formally defined, Q Intelligence™ is the structured capability through which an organization establishes and governs the intelligibility [[GL:Intelligibility]] of quality signals across systems, teams, and decision layers. It concerns the organization's capacity to render quality legible, comparable, and actionable for enterprise judgment.

Q Intelligence™ operates at the level of judgment formation, not task execution. This distinction clarifies that the discipline governs how decisions become valid, not how work is performed. It operates upstream of execution, shaping the conditions under which outcomes are interpreted.

In an enterprise setting, this typically appears as decision forums, governance layers, or review bodies relying on synthesized signals rather than direct observation of work.

When this capability is absent, judgment defaults to execution artifacts, causing decisions to rely on incomplete, localized, or misinterpreted evidence.

This directly affects decision accuracy, increases rework and contradiction across layers, and reduces predictability in enterprise outcomes.

This discipline is not a methodology, maturity model, or compliance artifact. It does not replace existing quality activities. Instead, it defines the intelligence architecture required to govern those activities coherently at scale, where fragmentation, abstraction, and signal distortion emerge.

The boundaries of Q-Intelligence™ are explicit:

- It defines what must be true for quality judgment to be reliable at enterprise scale.
- It does not define how any organization implements those conditions.
- It establishes the canonical frame within which quality governance becomes possible, without specifying governance mechanisms.

Concept Insight: Q Intelligence™ defines the enterprise capability required to make quality judgment reliable by governing how signals are interpreted, not how work is executed. It establishes the conditions under which quality becomes meaningful and decision-ready at scale.

4.2 Why Existing Frameworks Cannot Do This

Existing quality frameworks are designed to certify conformance, standardize practice, or optimize localized execution. These functions operate under the assumption that quality meaning remains stable as it moves across contexts, which is not sustained at enterprise scale.

In an enterprise setting, this typically appears as consistent adherence to process producing divergent interpretations at higher decision layers.

When this capability is absent, organizations rely on process compliance as a proxy for judgment integrity, masking underlying incoherence.

This directly affects the reliability of enterprise decisions, creating false confidence and increasing systemic risk despite apparent operational success.

If existing frameworks cannot sustain judgment, the constraints governing valid judgment must be defined explicitly.

Figure 4.2 – Category Separation: Framework Functions

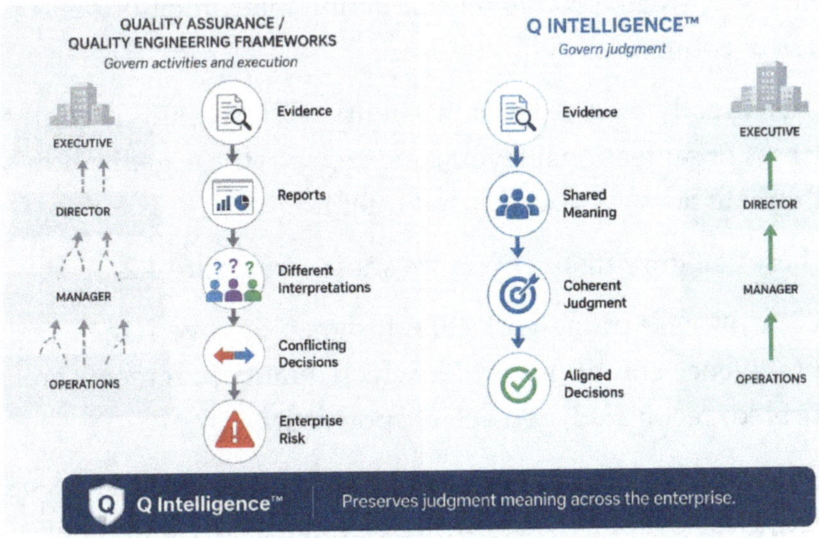

Q Intelligence™ occupies a distinct discipline category focused on governing judgment, not certifying activity or optimizing execution.

Q-Intelligence™ occupies a different category.

Quality assurance and quality engineering frameworks operate primarily as compliance systems and production safeguards. Their artifacts—plans, cases, metrics, certifications—presume that quality meaning is stable, observable, and transferable across organizational boundaries.

At enterprise scale, this presumption fails. The failure occurs because evidence is no longer directly observed but mediated through layers of abstraction, where interpretation becomes the determining factor.

In an enterprise setting, this typically appears as dashboards, summaries, and aggregated metrics becoming the primary basis for decision-making.

When this capability is absent, signal meaning degrades as it moves upward, producing conflicting interpretations and loss of context.

This directly affects decision fidelity, increases misalignment across organizational layers, and reduces the organization's ability to act with coordinated intent.

These category distinctions are shown in Figure 4.2.

None of these frameworks are designed to govern the intelligence conditions under which quality judgments are formed, reconciled, and acted upon at scale.

Q Intelligence™ does not compete with these frameworks. It defines a separate discipline that explains why judgment failure can occur even when those frameworks function correctly.

4.3 The Core Axioms of Q-Intelligence™

The axioms of Q Intelligence™ are nonnegotiable. They function as constraints on what must be true for valid judgment, independent of organizational preference or implementation choice.

In an enterprise setting, this typically appears as persistent limits on judgment accuracy regardless of tooling, process maturity, or measurement sophistication.

When this capability is absent, organizations attempt to compensate for structural limitations with increased measurement, control, or procedural rigor.

This directly affects system efficiency, increases operational overhead, and fails to resolve the underlying constraints that degrade judgment quality.

Figure 4.3 – The Axiomatic Constraint Model

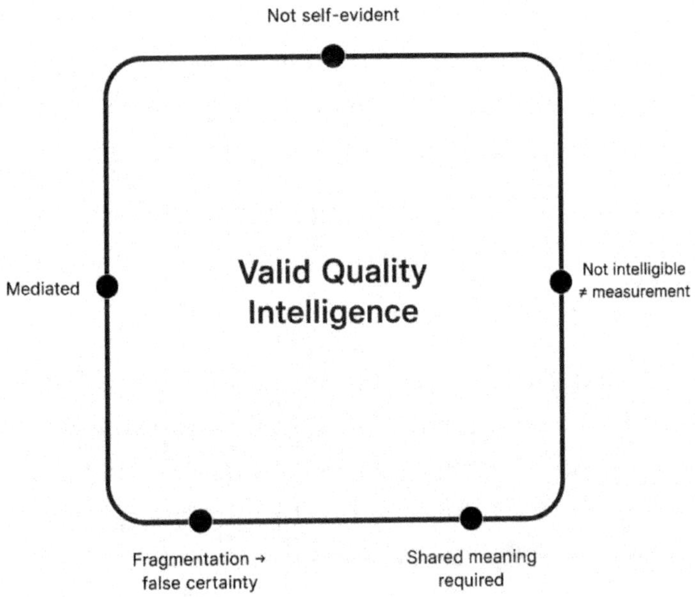

The core axioms define nonnegotiable constraints that bound all valid quality intelligence.

Axiom 1: Quality is not self evident at scale. As systems, teams, and interfaces increase, quality cannot be inferred from local observation alone.

Axiom 2: Quality judgments are mediated by intelligence structures. Every enterprise judgment about quality depends on signal selection, aggregation, interpretation, and trust.

Axiom 3: Measurement without intelligibility weakens judgment. Data volume or metric precision does not guarantee decision fidelity without a coherent interpretive structure.

Axiom 4: Fragmented intelligence produces false certainty. When quality signals are locally valid but globally incoherent, organizations develop confidence without control.

Axiom 5: Governance is impossible without shared quality meaning. Authority over quality cannot be exercised when interpretive frames diverge across decision layers.

These axioms do not suggest implementation strategies. They define immovable constraints that any enterprise scale quality system must respect.

> **Concept Insight: The axioms define nonnegotiable constraints that bound all valid quality judgment, independent of tools, processes, or organizational design. They make explicit the structural limits that cannot be overcome through increased measurement or procedural control.**

4.4 The Principles That Operationalize Intelligence

Principles translate axioms into orientation. They define how an organization must think about intelligence conditions, establishing a consistent stance without prescribing actions.

In an enterprise setting, this typically appears as shared expectations about how signals should be interpreted, trusted, and used in decision-making.

When this capability is absent, interpretations diverge across teams and layers, even when principles are nominally defined.

This directly affects governance effectiveness, weakens coherence in decision-making, and increases the likelihood of conflicting actions across the enterprise.

Figure 4.4 – Axioms to Principles: Orientation, Not Action

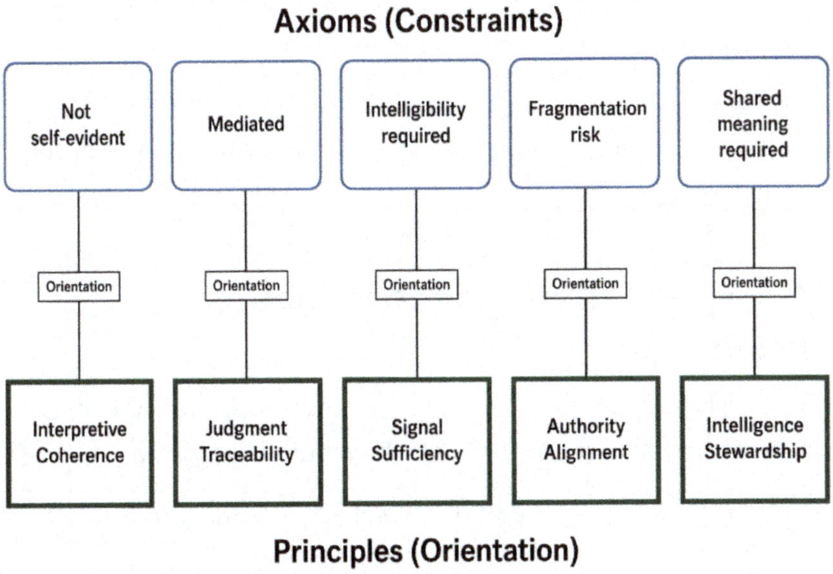

Principles translate axioms into orientation without prescribing action, mechanism, or implementation.

Principle of Interpretive Coherence
Quality signals must be interpretable in a consistent manner across organizational boundaries.

Principle of Judgment Traceability
Enterprise decisions about quality must be traceable to their originating intelligence conditions.

Principle of Signal Sufficiency
Only signals sufficient to support bounded judgment should be treated as decision bearing.

Principle of Authority Alignment
Decision rights over quality must align with the level at which quality meaning is synthesized.

Principle of Intelligence Stewardship
Quality intelligence must be actively governed as a first class organizational asset.

These principles describe orientation, not practice. They define the posture required to treat quality as intelligence rather than output.

4.5 The Q-Intelligence™ Master Framework

The Q-Intelligence™ Master Framework is the canonical conceptual structure that organizes the discipline.

Figure 4.5 – The Q Intelligence™ Master Framework

Enterprise Context

Local Evidence Enterprise Clarity

Intelligence Layer (Core)

Signal Interpretation Decision Readiness

Signal Layer

Signal Production Data Presence

The Q Intelligence™ Master Framework provides a conceptual structure for reasoning about quality intelligence without operational detail.

The framework provides a common language for discussing quality intelligence without collapsing into metrics, tools, or workflows. Its role is to preserve conceptual clarity across contexts, enabling consistent reasoning without prescribing how that reasoning is executed.

In an enterprise setting, this typically appears as different stakeholders referencing the same conceptual structure to interpret signals, even when operating in different domains.

When this capability is absent, discussions default to tool-specific or metric-specific interpretations, fragmenting understanding.

This directly affects alignment, reduces the ability to form coherent enterprise judgments, and increases the risk of disconnected decision-making.

The Master Framework is intentionally abstract. Its purpose is to stabilize meaning, not to prescribe operation. It serves as the reference architecture against which quality intelligence can be evaluated for coherence.

Operational mechanics, diagnostic usage, and executional structures related to this framework are explicitly deferred. Those concerns are addressed separately and do not belong to the definitional role of this chapter.

> **Concept Insight: The Master Framework provides a stable conceptual structure for reasoning about quality intelligence without introducing operational detail. Its purpose is to preserve clarity and coherence in how quality is understood across contexts.**

4.6 The Q-Intelligence™ Manifesto

Figure 4.6 – The Q Intelligence™ Manifesto: Institutional Posture

Quality is an intelligence problem before process

Judgment failure is structural, not personal

Data does not create clarity – interpretation does

Scale changes the meaning of evidence

Governance requires shared intelligibility

Confidence without coherence is risk

Quality authority rests on intelligence integrity

The Q-Intelligence™ Manifesto establishes the institutional stance of the discipline, not operational guidance or promised outcomes.

Q-Intelligence™ asserts the following declarations:

These declarations establish a fixed interpretive stance, defining how quality must be understood before any operational consideration is introduced.

In an enterprise setting, this typically appears as a shared institutional mindset that shapes how signals are interpreted and how decisions are justified.

When this capability is absent, interpretations revert to local assumptions, and the declarations are treated as abstract statements rather than governing truths.

This directly affects organizational coherence, weakens the integrity of quality judgments, and increases systemic risk as decisions lose alignment with shared intelligence principles.

- Quality is an intelligence problem before it is a process problem.
- Judgment failure is a structural condition, not a personnel deficiency.
- Data does not create clarity; interpretation does.
- Scale changes the meaning of evidence.
- Governance requires shared intelligibility.
- Confidence without coherence is risk.
- Quality authority must be earned through intelligence integrity.
- Enterprise quality is governed, not inspected into existence.

Summary

Q-Intelligence™ establishes a fixed interpretive stance for understanding quality at enterprise scale, defining how signals must be interpreted before any operational decisions are made. Unlike frameworks that prescribe activity, it governs how meaning is derived from system behavior.

In the absence of this shared interpretive foundation, organizations revert to local assumptions, fragmenting judgment and reducing coherence across decisions. As a result, quality outcomes become inconsistent, and risk increases as signals lose their ability to support reliable interpretation.

The Q-Intelligence™ Manifesto formalizes this stance, ensuring that quality is treated as an intelligence problem requiring shared understanding, disciplined interpretation, and alignment across the enterprise.

Chapter 4 — Knowledge Check

Q Intelligence™ Defined

The following questions are designed to verify accurate understanding of the definitions, boundaries, and conceptual structure introduced in this chapter. They assess whether the reader can clearly distinguish what Q Intelligence™ is from what it is not, and whether the foundational elements of the discipline have been understood precisely.

These questions are non procedural. They do not assess implementation knowledge.

Knowledge Check 4.1 — Definition Precision

Question
Define Q Intelligence™ in a single, complete sentence.

Knowledge Check 4.2 — Boundary Recognition

Question
Which of the following is not a function of Q Intelligence™?
A. Producing decision ready quality insight
B. Enabling enterprise quality governance
C. Defining testing techniques and execution practices
D. Treating quality as an intelligence problem

Knowledge Check 4.3 — Discipline Differentiation

Question

Why does Q Intelligence™ represent a different category of discipline than traditional quality frameworks?

Knowledge Check 4.4 — Axioms versus Principles

Question

What is the conceptual difference between axioms and principles within Q Intelligence™?

Knowledge Check 4.5 — Framework Scope

Question

What role does the Q Intelligence™ Master Framework play in the chapter, and what does it intentionally avoid prescribing?

Knowledge Check 4.6 — Manifesto Interpretation

Question

What is the purpose of the Q Intelligence™ Manifesto, and why is it presented separately from operational guidance?

Guidance for the Reader

If you can state the definition of Q Intelligence™ precisely, explain its boundaries clearly, and distinguish its foundational elements without describing how it is implemented, you are prepared to proceed to the next chapter, which introduces the architectural system that operationalizes the discipline.

This chapter establishes Q Intelligence™ as a distinct enterprise discipline that governs how quality is understood, interpreted, and judged under conditions of scale.

Together, these concepts form the definitional foundation required to separate quality intelligence from execution activity, measurement practices, and traditional frameworks.

The next chapter builds on this by introducing the architectural system that operationalizes these constraints, translating definition into structured enterprise capability.

Key Takeaways

- Q Intelligence™ governs how quality signals become reliable judgment.
- Existing frameworks do not govern enterprise interpretation conditions.
- Axioms define fixed constraints on valid quality intelligence.
- Principles translate those constraints into organizational orientation.
- The Q Intelligence™ Master Framework preserves conceptual coherence.
- Shared intelligibility is required before quality can be governed.

Questions for Reflection:

- What does this concept reveal about system behavior when quality meaning is not shared?
- How would this appear in an enterprise context where multiple decision layers rely on abstracted signals?

- What signals would indicate that quality judgment is being formed without sufficient intelligibility?

Chapter 5 — QOS™ — The Quality Operating System

Chapter Introduction

This chapter builds on the preceding foundation of Q Intelligence™ by introducing the architectural system required to sustain that discipline at enterprise scale. It focuses on how a structured operating system enables distributed quality activity to function as a coherent whole without collapsing variation or imposing uniformity. This is critical because, without a formal coordinating structure, enterprise quality cannot maintain consistent meaning, alignment, or predictability as complexity increases.

5.1 Why Quality Requires an Operating System

At enterprise scale, quality rarely breaks down because people lack effort, tools, or expertise. Most organizations have all three. What they often do not have is a formal architectural construct capable of coordinating quality as an enterprise concern. The result is familiar: quality work is happening everywhere, yet coherence [[GL:System Coherence]] remains difficult to sustain.

What exists in many enterprises is not a system, but an accumulation. Practices, functions, measurements, and platforms all contribute something important, but they typically do so from within local contexts and with local aims. Over time, these contributions can become extensive without ever becoming integrated. The more complex the organization becomes, the more visible that distinction becomes as well.

This distinction matters because accumulation does not inherently produce coherence. Individual capabilities may function effectively within their local context, yet still fail to contribute to a unified understanding of quality at the enterprise level. The absence of a coordinating structure means that integration is incidental rather than intentional.

Quality is inherently cross cutting. It spans products, services, processes, suppliers, customers, and time horizons at the same time. As scale increases, this creates a structural tension. Quality activity becomes more distributed across the enterprise, while the expectation of coherence remains. Without a coordinating structure to manage that distribution, alignment depends on interpretation, negotiation, and local accommodation rather than on structure.

Seen this way, fragmentation is not a sign of weak intent or poor execution. It is the predictable outcome of trying to sustain a system-level concern without a [[GL:SystemLevel Architecture]]. The issue is architectural before it is operational.

This structural gap—between distributed activity and required coherence—defines the need for an operating system.

An operating system [[GL:Enterprise Operating System]], in enterprise terms, is not a metaphor and not a convenience layer. It is a coordinating structure that allows multiple components to function coherently while remaining independently evolvable. It does not replace the components it coordinates. Instead, it establishes how they relate, how they interact, and how meaning is preserved as those interactions occur. This treatment of structural decomposition follows established architectural principles that emphasize separation of concerns as the basis for system coherence rather than procedural control. (Parnas, 1972)

That distinction matters. Tools, frameworks, and practices all contribute capability. They enable action, describe patterns, or shape behavior. Individually, they do not create [[GL:EnterpriseScale Coherence]]. They can improve local performance without resolving systemic fragmentation. Without an operating system, coordination remains dependent on human effort rather than maintained through design.

In an enterprise setting, this typically appears as parallel quality efforts progressing simultaneously without shared interpretation. Teams optimize locally, metrics evolve independently, and decisions are made based on partial or context-specific views of quality rather than a consistently understood system-level signal.

When this capability is absent, quality becomes increasingly dependent on informal alignment mechanisms such as meetings, escalations, or personal expertise. Patterns of rework, conflicting priorities, and inconsistent decision outcomes begin to emerge, particularly as the organization scales or diversifies.

This directly affects the enterprise's ability to sustain predictable performance. Decision quality degrades as signal meaning diverges, and the organization becomes more reactive, increasing operational risk and reducing confidence in quality-related outcomes.

Quality depends on sustained coherence over time. Intent needs to remain recognizable as the enterprise changes. Signal needs to preserve meaning as it crosses organizational boundaries. Response needs to remain aligned with purpose even when execution differs by environment or context. Those conditions cannot be secured through process alignment alone. They require [[GL:Architectural Coordination]].

[[AC:QOS™]] (Quality Operating System) exists to fulfill that requirement. It provides the operating system through which quality can function as an integrated enterprise capability, rather than as a set of well-intentioned but disconnected activities.

> **Concept Insight: Enterprise quality challenges are structural rather than operational. QOS™ addresses the gap between distributed activity and required coherence by providing a coordinating architecture that preserves meaning across the system. Without such a structure, alignment remains dependent on individual effort rather than being sustained by design.**

5.2 QOS™ at a Glance (Conceptual Overview)

QOS™ is the [[GL:Quality Operating System]] that operationalizes Q Intelligence™ at enterprise scale. Q Intelligence™ establishes the discipline; QOS™ provides the architectural system that allows that discipline to function coherently across domains, layers, and time horizons.

Figure 5.1 – QOS™ as the Enterprise Quality Operating System

QOS™ structures intent, intelligence, and response while preserving coherence across diverse enterprise elements operating across those layers.

At a conceptual level, QOS™ does not introduce a new category of quality work. Its role is different. It creates the structural conditions within which existing and future quality capabilities can coexist without fragmenting the enterprise's understanding of quality. Its purpose is to preserve cohesion, not to prescribe activity.

This reinforces that the role of QOS™ is not additive in terms of activity, but structural in terms of coherence. Its value is realized not by increasing the volume of quality work, but by ensuring that existing efforts contribute to a consistent and interpretable system of meaning.

In an enterprise setting, this typically appears as previously disconnected quality efforts becoming mutually intelligible.

Signals generated in one domain can be understood and used in another without reinterpretation, and intent established at the enterprise level remains visible across diverse execution environments.

When this capability is absent, initiatives intended to improve quality often introduce additional fragmentation. New tools and methods create localized improvements, but also increase divergence in interpretation and response, weakening overall system coherence.

This directly affects the enterprise's ability to scale quality reliably. Gains achieved in one area fail to translate elsewhere, limiting the durability of improvements and increasing the risk of systemic inconsistency over time.

That distinction is easy to overlook, especially in environments where new systems are often introduced as mechanisms for control, standardization, or transformation. QOS™, however, is not designed to compete with methods, tools, or existing practices. It is designed to make coherence possible across them. It does not ask every part of the enterprise to operate in the same way. It ensures that quality intent, intelligence, and response remain structurally connected, even when the enterprise itself is varied and uneven.

This is why QOS™ is explicitly an enterprise architecture construct. It assumes variation in organizational models, execution environments, and operating forms. It does not eliminate that variation. It creates a stable system within which variation does not automatically become fragmentation. This treatment reflects the formal definition of architecture as the fundamental organization of a system embodied in its components, their relationships, and the principles governing their design. (ISO/IEC/IEEE 42010, 2011)

At a high level, QOS™ integrates three domains often treated separately: quality intent, quality intelligence, and organizational response. Without an operating system, these domains drift apart—intent becomes abstract, intelligence becomes localized, and response becomes disconnected from both. QOS™ preserves their relationship without collapsing them into a single layer or function.

QOS™ is therefore architecture, not execution. It does not define actions, decisions, or controls. It defines the shape of the enterprise quality system so that intelligence can persist without distortion and purpose can endure without continual manual reinforcement.

When functioning well, an operating system is rarely the most visible part of an enterprise. Its value is often clearest in what it prevents: fragmentation, signal decay, and the gradual loss of meaning that otherwise accompanies scale.

To sustain this coherence, QOS™ must be structured in a way that preserves separation while enabling interaction.

Concept Insight: QOS™ does not add new quality activity—it creates the structural conditions that allow existing efforts to coexist coherently. Its value lies in preserving shared meaning across domains, ensuring that quality intent, intelligence, and response remain connected without forcing uniform execution.

Recognizable Situation:

Consider the organization where every team runs its own test strategy, its own definition of "done," and its own dashboard. Nothing is technically broken. Every team can defend its practices. Yet leadership cannot answer a single question consistently: What is our quality state right now? The absence is not a tool gap — it is the absence of a shared operating system beneath the activity.

5.3 The QOS™ Layer Model

QOS™ is structured as a [[GL:Layered Architecture]]. This layering should not be understood as an organizational recommendation or as a sequence of activities. It is an architectural separation of responsibilities intended to preserve coherence while managing complexity. Layered architectural models are commonly used to preserve separation of responsibility while allowing coordinated interaction across system boundaries. (Richards & Ford, 2020)

Figure 5.2 – The QOS™ Layer Model

QOS™ is organized as a layered architecture that separates intent, intelligence, and response to preserve enterprise-scale coherence.

Layered architectures are useful because they prevent meaning from collapsing into a single point of responsibility. They isolate concerns so that one part of the system can evolve without destabilizing another. In the case of QOS™, that separation is especially important because quality depends not only on action, but on the continued intelligibility of the relationships among intent, intelligence, and response.

This highlights that separation is not about dividing work, but about preserving clarity. Each layer maintains a distinct role in sustaining coherence, ensuring that meaning is not prematurely reduced to action, interpretation, or enforcement.

In an enterprise setting, this typically appears as clear distinctions between strategic intent, observed conditions, and operational activity. These distinctions allow different parts of the organization to evolve independently while remaining aligned through preserved relationships.

When this capability is absent, layers begin to collapse into one another. Intent becomes embedded in operational directives, intelligence becomes inseparable from interpretation, and response becomes constrained by assumptions that limit adaptability.

This directly affects system clarity and adaptability. The organization becomes less able to distinguish between what it intends, what it observes, and how it acts, increasing the likelihood of misaligned decisions and reducing responsiveness to changing conditions.

The first layer is the [[GL:Intent and Direction Layer]]. Its role is to express enterprise-level quality intent—to make explicit what the enterprise seeks to preserve, optimize, or protect with respect to quality. This layer establishes orientation, not mechanism. It does not interpret, measure, or act. Its role is to ensure that quality intent is structurally present in the system rather than left implicit.

The second layer is the [[GL:Intelligence and Signal Layer]]. This layer represents the state of quality across the enterprise. It serves as the system's intelligence surface, preserving fidelity between observed conditions and their systemic meaning. Its purpose is not to define how observations are gathered or how intelligence is interpreted. Its purpose is to hold quality-related signal in a form that remains legible across boundaries.

The third layer is the [[GL:Operational Response Layer]]. This layer enables the enterprise to respond coherently to quality intelligence. It provides the structural interface through which intelligence can influence action, without prescribing how work must be performed. That neutrality matters. It allows different execution models to coexist while preserving alignment at the architectural level.

The effectiveness of this model depends on the deliberate [[GL:Structural Separation of Responsibilities]] among these layers. Once the layers begin to collapse into one another, the system loses clarity. Intent moves too quickly into prescription. Intelligence becomes inseparable from interpretation. Response begins to absorb concerns that belong elsewhere. QOS™ protects coherence by preventing that collapse before it occurs.

The result is not rigidity, but clarity. Each layer has a distinct architectural responsibility, and the integrity of the system depends on those distinctions remaining intact.

Once defined structurally, the relationship between layers determines how intelligence moves through the system.

> **Concept Insight: The layered architecture of QOS™ preserves clarity by separating intent, intelligence, and response. This separation enables each to evolve independently while maintaining coherent relationships, preventing the collapse of meaning that typically occurs in complex enterprise systems.**

5.4 Layer Interaction and Intelligence Flow

Each QOS™ layer has a clearly defined architectural role, but the operating system derives its value not from those roles in isolation, but from how they relate to one another. The system is designed to support interaction without collapse, alignment without entanglement, and coherence without control.

This emphasizes that coherence emerges from the preservation of meaning as it moves in both directions across those relationships, not from the optimization of individual layers. The integrity of the system depends on how these layers interact while maintaining their separation.

In an enterprise setting, this typically appears as the consistent flow of quality-related meaning across boundaries without distortion. Signals retain their relevance as they move through the system, and actions reflect both local context and enterprise-level intent.

When this capability is absent, intelligence loses fidelity as it moves through the organization, even though interaction between layers continues. Signals are reinterpreted at each boundary as bidirectional interaction continues without a shared coherence-preserving intelligence layer, leading to divergence in understanding and inconsistent responses to similar conditions.

This directly affects the enterprise's ability to coordinate effectively. Predictability decreases as actions become increasingly dependent on local interpretation, and systemic risk increases as misalignment accumulates across the system.

Figure 5.3 – Layer Interaction and Intelligence Flow

QOS™ enables bidirectional intelligence flow across layers, allowing context to move downward and operational learning to move upward while preserving shared signal meaning.

The intent and direction layer provides orientation rather than instruction. Its role is to establish what the enterprise seeks to preserve or protect with respect to quality, not to dictate how activity should unfold. That orientation shapes the system by giving other layers context, allowing quality intelligence to be interpreted and acted upon without constant reinterpretation.

The intelligence and signal layer represents observed conditions without modifying their meaning. It does not judge or prioritize. Its purpose is to preserve meaning as signals traverse organizational boundaries, ensuring that intelligence remains legible across domains and time horizons.

The operational response layer sits where intelligence encounters action. Its structure allows intelligence to shape response without prescribing execution. Alignment emerges from preserved meaning rather than standardized behavior. From a systems-theoretic perspective, system behavior emerges from structural relationships rather than component-level optimization, reinforcing the need for architectural coherence over isolated improvement. (Leveson, 2012)

This interaction functions because authority, interpretation, and execution are intentionally excluded from the operating system. When they are introduced too early, architecture collapses into governance or process. QOS™ maintains coherence by preserving [[GL:Architectural Neutrality]] across these relationships.

Feedback within QOS™ is architectural rather than procedural. Learning occurs because relationships are preserved over time, not because pathways are enforced.

Intelligence can inform intent because meaning remains intact. Response can evolve because architecture does not constrain execution.

In this way, QOS™ enables enterprise-scale intelligence flow without defining workflows, pipelines, or control paths. Coherence emerges from structure, continuously rather than through intervention.

5.5 What QOS™ Is Not

By this point in the chapter, QOS™ should be recognizable as a specific kind of architectural construct. It introduces coordination where fragmentation would otherwise persist, and it does so without prescribing behavior or embedding authority. Precisely because that role is uncommon, QOS™ can be easily mistaken for categories that are more familiar to enterprise readers.

Clarifying what QOS™ is not is therefore not a side note. It is part of protecting the architecture from misclassification. Once the operating system is mistaken for a framework, a compliance model, or a transformation initiative, the boundaries established in this chapter begin to weaken. Later chapters then have to compensate for confusion that should have been prevented here.

This clarification strengthens the boundaries of the architecture by reducing the likelihood of misinterpretation. Clear distinctions prevent the system from being assigned responsibilities that would compromise its structural role.

In an enterprise setting, this typically appears as disciplined use of QOS™ strictly as a coordinating structure, while tools, frameworks, and governance mechanisms operate within their appropriate domains without being conflated.

When this capability is absent, QOS™ is often repurposed as a control mechanism or implementation framework. This introduces expectations that conflict with its architectural nature, leading to erosion of its intended boundaries.

This directly affects the sustainability of the system. Misclassification leads to overextension, reducing clarity and ultimately weakening the enterprise's ability to maintain coherence over time.

Figure 5.4 – Failure State: Distorted Intelligence Flow

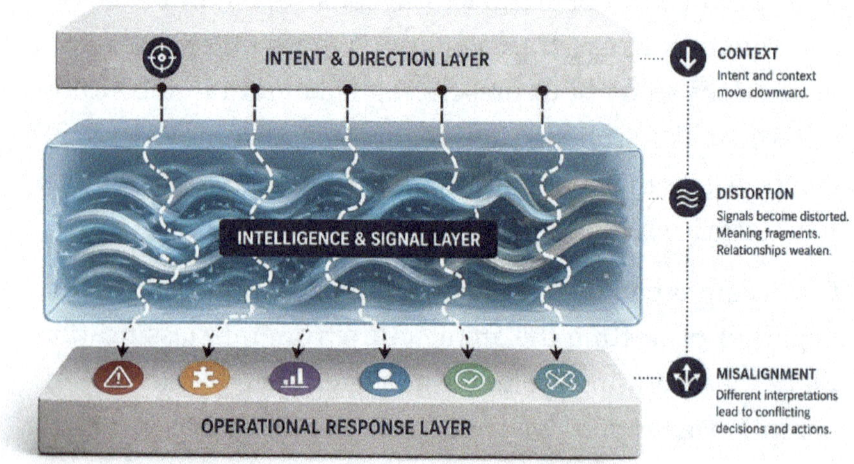

When shared meaning is not preserved, intelligence loses coherence—context and operational learning continue to move across layers, but their relationship becomes unstable, leading to signal distortion and misalignment.

With that boundary in place, QOS™ should not be understood as any of the following:

- **A toolchain**
  Tools provide capability. Operating systems provide

coordination. QOS™ remains independent of any specific technology or platform.

- **A framework**
  Frameworks offer conceptual guidance or reference models. QOS™ defines system architecture within which frameworks may operate.
- **A maturity model**
  QOS™ does not assess progression, readiness, or organizational state. It exists whether or not it is being used effectively.
- **A compliance system**
  Architecture can enable alignment, but it does not enforce behavior or define obligations.
- **An operating model or transformation initiative**
  QOS™ is not a program. It persists beyond initiatives and remains stable even as execution strategies change.

These distinctions are not rhetorical. They preserve the architectural integrity of the system by preventing it from being overloaded with expectations it is not designed to meet. QOS™ does not replace tools, frameworks, governance, or execution models. It creates the conditions under which those elements can operate without undermining coherence.

With these boundaries established, the remaining responsibility—decision authority—becomes explicit.

5.6 The Architectural Handoff

QOS™ establishes the architectural conditions necessary for enterprise-scale quality intelligence to function coherently. It defines how intent, intelligence, and response relate as a system. What it intentionally does not define is who decides, who is accountable, or how authority is exercised.

That separation is deliberate.

This reinforces the importance of maintaining a clear boundary between architecture and governance. The durability of the operating system depends on its ability to remain focused on coordination rather than decision-making.

In an enterprise setting, this typically appears as a clear distinction between the structural system that enables quality coherence and the governance mechanisms that guide decisions and accountability.

When this capability is absent, architectural structures begin to absorb governance responsibilities. Decision-making becomes embedded within the system itself, reducing flexibility and increasing the likelihood of rigid or misaligned outcomes.

This directly affects organizational adaptability and decision quality. The system becomes less capable of supporting diverse execution models, and governance becomes constrained by structures that were not designed to carry decision authority.

An operating system can remain durable only if it does not absorb responsibilities that belong to governance. The moment architecture begins to decide, prioritize, or enforce, it ceases to be an enabling system and becomes a control mechanism. QOS™ therefore concludes precisely where governance must begin. This distinction aligns with the foundational separation of policy from mechanism in operating system design, where architectural mechanisms enable coordination without embedding decision authority. (Brinch Hansen, 1973) This view is consistent with systems-theoretic approaches that treat organizations as complex systems whose effectiveness depends on structural relationships rather than procedural intervention.

The chapters that follow build on this foundation by addressing how quality intent is governed, how intelligence is formally interpreted, and how organizational authority operates over the system that QOS™ makes possible. Those mechanisms depend on the architectural clarity established here, but they are not part of it.

This chapter establishes QOS™ as the architectural operating system required to coordinate quality across a distributed enterprise without imposing uniformity or control. Together, these concepts form a structural foundation that preserves the relationships between intent, intelligence, and response, enabling coherence to persist as the organization evolves. The next chapter builds on this by addressing how governance operates over this architecture, defining how decision authority, interpretation, and accountability interact with the system QOS™ makes possible.

Summary

QOS™ defines the architectural foundation required for enterprise-scale quality intelligence by structuring the relationship between intent, intelligence, and response. It enables coordination and coherence across distributed systems without prescribing decision-making authority.

Maintaining a strict boundary between architecture and governance is essential. When this separation breaks, architectural systems begin to absorb decision responsibilities, reducing flexibility and increasing the risk of rigid or misaligned outcomes.

The architectural model must therefore conclude where governance begins. This boundary ensures that QOS™ remains a durable enabling system, while governance defines how decisions are made, interpreted, and enforced across the enterprise.

Chapter 5 — Knowledge Check

QOS™ – The Quality Operating System

The following questions are designed to verify accurate understanding of the architectural concepts introduced in this chapter. They assess whether the reader can distinguish between accumulation and system-level coherence, understand the role of QOS™ as a coordinating architecture, and correctly interpret the separation of intent, intelligence, and response within an enterprise quality system.

These questions are nonprocedural. They do not assess implementation mechanics or execution techniques.

Knowledge Check 5.1 — Architectural Purpose

Question

What problem does QOS™ solve at enterprise scale?

Knowledge Check 5.2 — System vs Accumulation

Question

What is the difference between an accumulation of quality capabilities and a coordinated quality system?

Knowledge Check 5.3 — Operating System Concept

Question

Why is QOS™ described as an operating system rather than a framework, toolset, or methodology?

Knowledge Check 5.4 — Layer Model Clarity

Question

What are the three layers of QOS™, and what distinct role does each perform?

Knowledge Check 5.5 — Structural Separation

Question

Why is the separation of intent, intelligence, and response critical to maintaining coherence at scale?

Knowledge Check 5.6 — Architectural Role vs Execution

Question

Why does QOS™ avoid defining execution practices, decision authority, or governance mechanisms?

Knowledge Check 5.7 — Intelligence Flow

Question

What happens to system behavior when signal meaning is not preserved as it moves across layers?

Guidance for the Reader

If you can explain why enterprise quality requires a coordinating architecture, distinguish between accumulation and system-level coherence, and describe how QOS™

preserves relationships across intent, intelligence, and response, you are prepared to proceed.

This chapter establishes QOS™ as the architectural system required to coordinate quality across a distributed enterprise without imposing uniformity or control. It defines how structural separation and interaction enable coherence to persist as complexity increases.

The next chapter builds on this foundation by introducing how governance operates over this architecture, defining how decision authority, interpretation, and accountability interact with the system QOS™ enables.

Key Takeaways

- • Enterprise quality requires architecture, not accumulated activity.
- • QOS™ preserves coherence across distributed quality capabilities.
- • Intent, intelligence, and response must remain structurally separate.
- • Intelligence flow depends on preserved meaning across layers.
- • QOS™ coordinates quality without prescribing execution or governance.
- • Architecture ends where decision authority begins.

Questions for Reflection:

- What does the need for an operating system reveal about the limits of process and tooling in sustaining enterprise quality?

- How would the absence of architectural coordination appear in a large-scale organizational environment?
- What signals would indicate that intent, intelligence, and response are no longer coherently connected within a system?

Chapter 6 — The Governance Pillars

Chapter Introduction

Quality, when viewed from within delivery, often appears as the outcome of disciplined execution. Teams work within structured methodologies, align to defined practices, and produce artifacts that reflect rigor and intent. Chapter 5 established that this execution environment does not operate in isolation. It is supported by QOS™, which organizes and surfaces the intelligence required to understand the state of quality across the enterprise. With this foundation in place, a different question emerges—one that cannot be answered by execution or intelligence alone. Once quality can be observed, understood, and reasoned about, how is it [[GL:Governance]] governed?

This chapter builds on the transition established in Chapter 5, where QOS™ made quality visible as enterprise intelligence, by addressing how that intelligence is governed.

It focuses on how decision authority, accountability, and constraints are structured to guide quality outcomes across the enterprise.

This is critical because without governance, intelligence remains descriptive rather than actionable, leaving quality outcomes subject to inconsistency despite increasing visibility.

To understand governance, it is first necessary to examine the conditions that emerge in its absence.

The transition from Chapter 5 to Chapter 6 marks a shift in focus from visibility to authority. QOS™ provides the conditions under which quality can be known; [[GL:Governance]] establishes how that knowledge is used to make decisions. Without this second step, intelligence remains descriptive rather than directive. The enterprise may understand its risks, constraints, and trade-offs with increasing clarity, yet still act inconsistently if [[GL:Decision Authority]] is not aligned with that understanding. Governance is therefore not an extension of execution, nor a refinement of measurement. It is the structural layer that determines how intelligence is translated into accountable decision-making (Weill & Ross, 2004).

This distinction is essential because it reframes quality as something that must be governed, not merely produced. In many organizations, quality is treated as the outcome of effective delivery practices. While those practices are necessary, they are not sufficient. Decisions about what to prioritize, what risks to accept, and how to balance competing objectives shape quality outcomes in ways that execution alone cannot resolve. These decisions occur continuously, often across boundaries defined by roles, teams, or methodologies. Without a governing structure, they remain fragmented, influenced by local context rather than guided by enterprise coherence.

The Governance Pillars define how these decisions are authorized, constrained, reviewed, and corrected across the enterprise. They do not replace delivery frameworks or prescribe operational models. Whether work is performed within Agile teams, scaled coordination structures, or formal testing disciplines, governance operates above these contexts. It establishes a consistent basis for how decisions are made that allows diverse methods of execution to coexist without producing inconsistent quality outcomes. In this way, governance does not compete with existing methodologies; it aligns them by ensuring that the decisions shaping quality are made deliberately and with clear [[GL:Accountability]].

This chapter establishes how decision authority, [[GL:Accountability]], and constraints operate over QOS™. It defines what governance governs, how decision authority is made explicit, and how accountability is maintained—without reducing governance to control.

By the end of this chapter, the reader should arrive at a clear outcome: quality can now be governed deliberately because decision authority is aligned to intelligence, not activity. This alignment does not emerge naturally from execution or measurement. It must be established through a defined set of governing principles—what this chapter introduces as the Governance Pillars (ISO, 2021). Each section that follows develops this structure, beginning with the conditions that arise when governance is absent, and moving toward the mechanisms that make quality decisions explicit, accountable, and coherent across the enterprise.

Figure 6.1 Governance aligns enterprise intelligence.

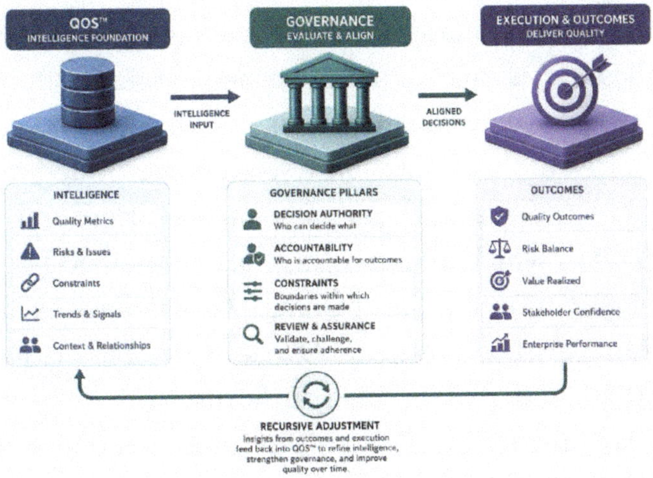

QOS™ provides the intelligence foundation, governance evaluates and aligns that intelligence, and recursive adjustment progressively improves quality outcomes.

6.1 Why Quality Fails Without Governance

Quality does not fail in the absence of effort, capability, or intent. In most enterprises, the people responsible for delivery are experienced, disciplined, and supported by well-established methodologies. Teams operate within structured frameworks, whether iterative delivery models, scaled coordination approaches, or formal testing disciplines. These systems organize work, enable collaboration, and provide visibility into progress. Yet even in environments where execution appears well managed, quality outcomes remain inconsistent. The underlying issue is not a lack of activity, but the absence of a governing structure that determines how decisions about quality are made.

At its core, quality is the result of a sequence of decisions made over time. Every trade-off, every acceptance of risk, and every constraint applied to delivery shapes the outcome. When these decisions are not governed explicitly, they do not disappear—they become implicit. They are made by default, often at the point where work is performed rather than where understanding is greatest. Over time, this creates a condition in which quality outcomes are shaped less by intention and more by circumstance. Governance exists to prevent this drift by ensuring that decisions are made deliberately, under recognized authority, and with appropriate awareness of their implications (Weill & Ross, 2004).

Quality therefore reflects not a single act of execution, but an accumulation of decisions that interact over time. Each decision establishes conditions for the next, creating a compounding effect where early trade-offs shape later possibilities. What appears as a delivery issue at the surface is often the downstream expression of earlier, ungoverned decisions that were never made explicit or examined.

In an enterprise setting, this typically appears as localized decision-making where teams independently resolve trade-offs based on immediate context. Patterns such as divergent risk tolerances, inconsistent acceptance criteria, and uneven prioritization of defects emerge, even when teams follow similar processes.

When this capability is absent, decision-making defaults to convenience or proximity rather than alignment. Decisions cluster around where work occurs rather than where understanding resides, leading to duplicated effort, conflicting outcomes, and increased uncertainty across the system.

This directly affects the enterprise's ability to produce consistent outcomes. Decision quality becomes variable, predictability decreases, and risk accumulates in ways that cannot be easily identified or managed.

A persistent condition in many organizations is the separation between execution and authority. Delivery teams are empowered to move work forward, but not always to define the conditions under which that work is accepted. Conversely, authority to make broader decisions often resides outside the immediate context of delivery, where the practical implications of those decisions are less visible. This separation produces a structural gap. Decisions are made, but the line between who understands the impact and who holds authority over the outcome is unclear. In such conditions, quality becomes uneven not because individuals act unpredictably, but because the system itself does not align decision rights with relevant intelligence.

Two distinct failure modes emerge from this misalignment. In the first, authority exists without sufficient intelligence. Decisions are made at levels where visibility into risk, dependency, or consequence is incomplete. These decisions may be well intentioned, but they lack the context required to produce reliable outcomes. In the second failure mode, intelligence exists without authority. Insights into risk, constraint, or system behavior are generated within execution contexts, but they do not influence decision-making. The information is present, sometimes in considerable detail, but it is not empowered to alter direction. Both conditions produce structural instability.

These failure modes are not isolated conditions but recurring structural patterns. They reflect a system that has separated the capacity to decide from the capacity to understand, creating a persistent imbalance that cannot be corrected through execution improvements alone.

In an enterprise setting, this typically appears as decisions being escalated without sufficient context or, conversely, critical insights remaining unused because they lack formal authority. The system oscillates between centralized decisions lacking fidelity and localized insights lacking influence.

When this capability is absent, organizations compensate by introducing additional controls or escalation paths, which further distance decisions from relevant intelligence and reinforce the underlying misalignment.

This directly affects decision effectiveness and system stability. The enterprise becomes slower to respond, less accurate in its trade-offs, and increasingly dependent on reactive interventions rather than coherent decision-making.

What often masks these conditions is the visible presence of process. Organizations invest heavily in defined workflows, standardized practices, and governance artifacts that appear to establish control. However, process organizes activity but does not assign decision authority or ensure that those decisions are informed by the right intelligence (Pierre & Peters, 2000).

This distinction becomes particularly evident when examining how trade-offs are handled. In delivery environments shaped by methodologies such as Agile, scaled coordination approaches, or formal testing disciplines, trade-offs are continuous and unavoidable.

Scope, time, risk, and quality are constantly negotiated. Without governance, these negotiations occur locally, often driven by immediate pressures rather than systemic considerations. Decisions that appear reasonable in isolation can accumulate into broader instability when viewed across the enterprise. Governance does not remove the need for trade-offs; it ensures that such decisions are made within a structure that aligns decision authority with understanding and maintains enterprise coherence across contexts.

It is also important to recognize that execution, regardless of its discipline or maturity, operates within constraints it does not define. Teams can optimize processes, refine practices, and increase efficiency within those constraints, but they do not determine their legitimacy or adequacy. When [[GL:Constraint | constraints]] remain implicit, they cannot be examined or adjusted in a controlled way. As a result, execution may become highly efficient at delivering outcomes that do not align with intended quality. Governance introduces a mechanism for making constraints explicit and subject to decision, rather than inherited without examination.

Over time, the absence of governance produces a predictable pattern. Decisions become decentralized without clarity, accountability becomes diffuse, and outcomes become difficult to attribute. When issues arise, organizations often respond by increasing controls—adding reviews, expanding documentation, or tightening process gates. While these actions may improve oversight, they do not address the underlying structural issue. Without clear alignment between authority and intelligence, additional controls can increase friction without improving decision quality. The system becomes heavier, but not necessarily more coherent.

The consequence is a form of operational ambiguity in which quality appears to be managed but is not consistently governed. Work progresses, artifacts are produced, and milestones are met, yet the basis on which key decisions have been made remains unclear. This ambiguity limits the enterprise's ability to reason about outcomes, adapt effectively, or sustain consistent quality over time. Governance addresses this condition not by adding more activity, but by establishing a structure in which decisions are made consciously, with defined decision authority and visible accountability.

From this perspective, the failure of quality in many enterprises is not a failure of discipline, methodology, or intent. It is a failure of alignment. Specifically, it is the failure to align decision authority with the intelligence required to exercise it. Without this alignment, quality remains contingent—dependent on circumstance rather than governed by design. Establishing governance is therefore not an administrative exercise, but a structural one. It defines how decisions are authorized, how they are informed, and how their outcomes are owned.

> **Concept Insight: Quality fails not due to lack of effort or discipline, but due to misalignment between decision authority and intelligence. Governance ensures that decisions are made deliberately, preventing fragmentation and restoring coherence to quality outcomes across the enterprise.**

These failure modes point to a more precise question: what, specifically, is being governed?

6.2 What Quality Governance Actually Governs

Governance operates over decisions, not activity. Activity is visible and measurable; decisions occur at points of trade-off, risk acceptance, and constraint definition. Governance establishes how those decisions are shaped.

This distinction shifts the focus from what is being done to why it is being done. Activity can be observed and measured, but the intent and rationale behind decisions that shape that activity remain unseen unless explicitly surfaced. Governance brings this underlying layer into view.

In an enterprise setting, this typically appears as a need to clarify moments of decision within workflows that otherwise appear continuous. Events such as scope adjustments, defect acceptance, or prioritization shifts reveal where decisions occur, even if they are not formally recognized as such.

When this capability is absent, decisions are absorbed into activity and become indistinguishable from execution. This obscures accountability and makes it difficult to trace outcomes back to the decisions that produced them.

This directly affects transparency and traceability. The enterprise loses the ability to understand how outcomes are formed, limiting its capacity to learn, adapt, or improve decision quality over time.

To define what governance governs, it is necessary to make the surface of decision-making explicit. This surface consists of those moments where alternatives exist and a choice must be made. These include decisions about prioritization, where competing objectives must be balanced; decisions about risk, where uncertainty must be accepted or mitigated; and decisions about constraints, where boundaries are set on acceptable outcomes. Each of these decisions carries consequences that extend beyond the immediate context in which they are made. Governance ensures that these consequences are understood and that authority over such decisions is clear.

This focus deliberately excludes the mechanisms of execution. Governance does not determine how testing is conducted, how artifacts are produced, or how work is organized within delivery teams. Those concerns belong to the domain of execution and are supported by the structures established in earlier chapters. Similarly, governance does not operate at the level of tools, environments, or technologies. These elements can influence how work is carried out, but they do not define how decisions are authorized or how accountability is assigned. By maintaining this boundary, governance avoids becoming entangled in operational detail and retains its role as a structural layer.

One of the most important effects of defining this governance surface is the transition from implicit to explicit decisions. In many organizations, decisions are embedded within activity. They occur as part of execution, often without being recognized as distinct events. When a team adjusts scope, accepts a defect, or reallocates effort, a decision has been made. If these decisions remain implicit, they cannot be examined, traced, or governed. Governance requires that such decisions be acknowledged as decisions, with defined authority and [[GL:Accountability]] attached to them. This does not change the fact that decisions must be made, but it changes how they are understood within the system.

In this sense, governance functions as a layer that operates over the intelligence provided by QOS™. The system established in Chapter 5 ensures that relevant information about quality, risk, and system behavior is available. Governance determines how that information informs action. It does not recreate or reinterpret the intelligence; it establishes the conditions under which intelligence can influence decision-making. This separation is essential. Without it, governance risks becoming another form of analysis rather than a structure for decision authority.

By clarifying what governance governs, the enterprise gains a more stable foundation for decision-making. Decisions are no longer dispersed across activities without definition. They are recognized as points where authority must be exercised and where accountability must be assigned. This clarity does not simplify decisions; it makes their complexity visible. It acknowledges that quality outcomes are shaped not by isolated actions, but by a consistent pattern of choices made under varying conditions.

For governance to operate consistently, it must be structured across defined dimensions.

6.3 The Governance Pillars

Figure 6.2 – The Governance Pillars Model

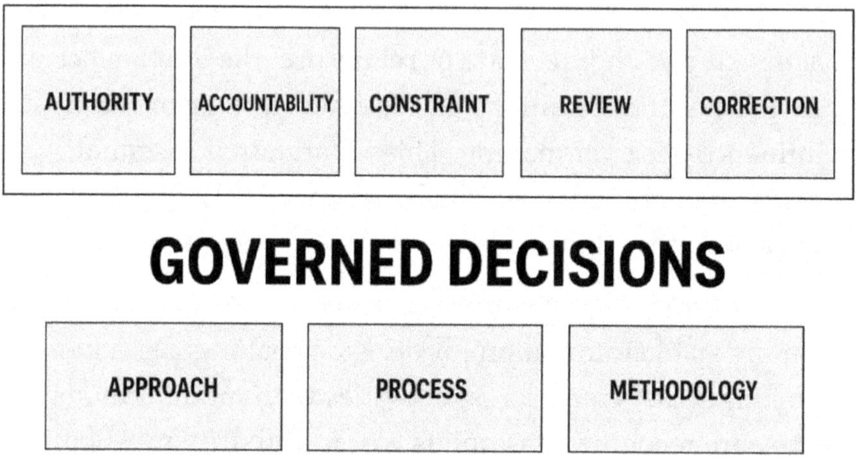

The Governance Pillars define the complete and non-overlapping structural dimensions through which enterprise quality decisions are governed, producing governed decisions that shape execution approach, process, and methodology.

If governance is to operate consistently across the enterprise, it cannot remain implicit or situational. Decisions about quality occur in varied contexts—across delivery teams, coordination layers, and oversight functions—and yet they must exhibit a degree of coherence that transcends those contexts. Without structure, governance risks becoming either centralized and brittle, or distributed and inconsistent. The enterprise therefore requires a way to organize governance itself, not as a set of procedures, but as a stable conceptual framework. This is the role of the Governance Pillars.

The pillars do not prescribe how governance is performed. They define the dimensions through which governance exists. Each pillar represents a distinct aspect of decision control, and together they form a complete structure for how quality decisions are authorized, constrained, reviewed, and corrected. Their purpose is not to introduce additional activity, but to ensure that governance is understood as a coherent system rather than a collection of disconnected practices. In this way, the pillars provide consistency across different delivery models and organizational forms, allowing governance to operate with stability even as execution varies.

Instead, they define the structural completeness of governance. Each pillar addresses a necessary dimension of decision control, ensuring that governance is not partial or skewed toward a single aspect such as authority or review.

In an enterprise setting, this typically appears as different organizational units emphasizing certain aspects of governance while neglecting others. For example, strong authority structures may exist alongside weak accountability, or rigorous constraints may be present without effective correction mechanisms.

When this capability is absent, governance becomes uneven. Certain decisions may be well controlled in one dimension while remaining undefined in another, creating gaps that introduce inconsistency and ambiguity.

This directly affects coherence across the enterprise. Decisions become difficult to align, and accountability becomes fragmented, reducing the overall effectiveness of governance as a system.

For this structure to be meaningful, each pillar must be clearly defined and non-overlapping. If boundaries between pillars are unclear, governance itself becomes ambiguous. Decisions may be made, but without clarity as to whether they are being authorized, constrained, or evaluated. The result is a diffusion of responsibility that undermines accountability. The design of the pillars therefore emphasizes conceptual separation. Each pillar addresses a distinct question about decision-making, and together they ensure that no aspect of governance is left undefined.

- **Decision authority**
  The first of these pillars is [[GL:Decision Authority|decision authority]]. Decision authority establishes who has the right to make a decision and under what conditions that right is exercised. It is not synonymous with influence or expertise. While both may inform decisions, decision authority determines where the decision formally resides. Without clear decision authority, decisions tend to default to those closest to execution or those with the greatest informal influence. This may produce outcomes in the short term, but it does not create a stable basis for governance. Decision authority must be explicit if decisions are to be made deliberately rather than by circumstance.
- **Accountability**
  Closely related, but distinct, is the pillar of [[GL:Accountability]]. Accountability defines who owns the outcome of a decision once it is made. It extends beyond the act of deciding to include the consequences that follow. In many organizations, responsibility for execution is well defined, but accountability for decisions is less clear. This creates a condition in which decisions are made collectively, but outcomes are owned diffusely. Accountability restores clarity by linking decisions to

ownership in a way that persists beyond the moment of action. It ensures that decisions are not only made, but also carried forward in terms of their impact.

- **Constraint**
  The third pillar, [[GL:Constraint|constraint]], addresses the boundaries within which decisions are made. Constraints are often present in delivery environments, but they are frequently implicit or inherited without examination. Governance requires that constraints be defined as part of the decision structure itself. By doing so, it ensures that decisions are not made in an unconstrained space where trade offs are undefined. Instead, constraints establish the limits within which decisions must operate, shaping what is considered acceptable and what lies outside tolerance. This provides a necessary frame for consistent decision-making across contexts.
- **Review**
  The fourth pillar, review, introduces the evaluation of decisions after they have been made. Review is not an approval mechanism, nor is it an inspection of execution detail. It operates at the level of decisions, examining whether they were made with appropriate authority, informed by relevant intelligence, and aligned with defined constraints. In this way, review reinforces governance by ensuring that decisions remain visible and subject to examination. It does not redecide, but it clarifies whether the original decision aligns with the structure established by governance.
- **Correction**
  The fifth pillar, correction, completes the structure by addressing how decisions evolve over time. No decision exists in a static environment. Conditions change, new information emerges, and outcomes develop in ways that may differ from initial expectations. Correction allows the system to adapt by revisiting decisions when necessary. It

is not only reactive to failure; it is a structural capability that acknowledges the dynamic nature of enterprise systems. By incorporating correction as a pillar, governance ensures that decisions are not fixed beyond reconsideration, but remain part of a coherent and adaptable system.

Together, these pillars create a complete and non-redundant structure. Authority determines who decides, accountability defines who owns the outcome, constraint bounds what is allowable, review evaluates the decision, and correction enables adaptation. Each operates independently, yet none is sufficient on its own. Their interaction produces a governance system that is both stable and responsive, capable of supporting consistent decision-making without imposing rigidity.

The completeness of this structure ensures that governance addresses all necessary aspects of decision-making without overlap or omission. Each pillar contributes a distinct function, and their interaction forms the basis for stable and adaptable decision control.

In an enterprise setting, this typically appears as decisions that can be consistently understood regardless of where they occur. Authority is clear, accountability is assigned, constraints are known, and both review and correction operate as part of the ongoing system rather than as external interventions.

When this capability is absent, organizations experience fragmented governance where decisions lack consistency in how they are authorized, evaluated, or adjusted over time.

This directly affects the enterprise's ability to maintain stability while adapting to change. Decision inconsistency increases risk and reduces the reliability of outcomes across different contexts.

This structure is intentionally independent of any specific delivery methodology. Whether work is organized through iterative teams, coordinated at scale, or governed within formal testing disciplines, the same questions of authority, accountability, constraint, review, and correction apply. The pillars do not replace these methods; they provide a governing layer that ensures decisions made within them are coherent at the enterprise level. In doing so, they align diverse execution practices without requiring them to conform to a single operational model.

Once defined structurally, governance must function coherently across decisions.

Concept Insight: The Governance Pillars define a complete structure for decision control, ensuring that authority, accountability, constraint, review, and correction operate coherently. Together, they transform governance from fragmented practices into a stable and adaptable system.

6.4 Decision Authority and Accountability Flow

Figure 6.3 – Governed Decisions Produce Traceable Change

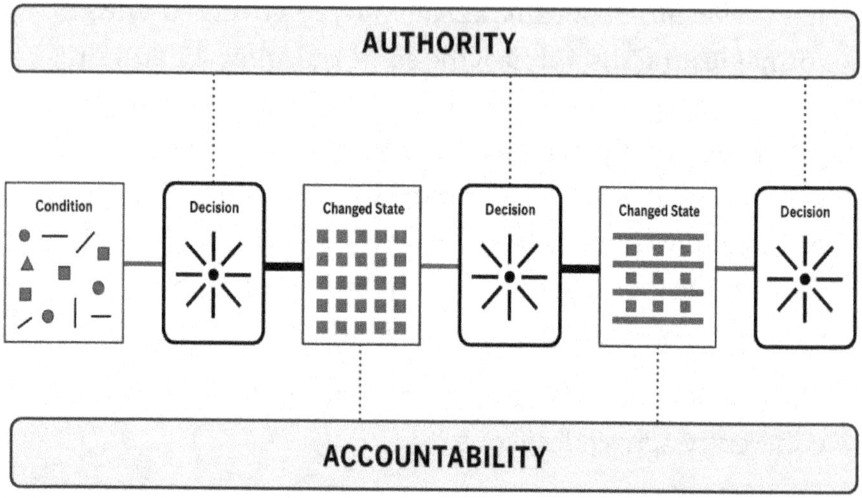

Decisions create system states that are carried forward through accountability, enabling traceable continuity across the enterprise.

Governance becomes tangible through the continuity of authority and accountability across decisions. This continuity connects decisions across contexts, ensuring that governance remains coherent in practice.

To understand this flow, it is necessary to begin with the principle of traceability. A governed [[GL:Decision | decision]] is one whose decision authority can be clearly identified and whose [[GL:Decision Traceability | lineage]] can be understood. This does not require extensive documentation or formal escalation. It requires that, at any point, it is possible to determine who held the decision authority to make a decision and under what constraints that decision authority was exercised. Traceability ensures that decisions are not isolated events, but part of a connected structure in which each decision can be understood in relation to others.

Traceability transforms decisions from isolated actions into components of a connected system. It ensures that decisions can be understood not only individually, but also as part of a broader sequence that shapes enterprise outcomes.

In an enterprise setting, this typically appears as the ability to identify who made a decision, under what conditions, and how it relates to other decisions. This visibility enables coordination across teams and functions without requiring centralized control.

When this capability is absent, decisions become disconnected and difficult to reconcile. Conflicts arise without clear resolution paths, and dependencies between decisions remain hidden until they create issues.

This directly affects coordination and decision clarity. The enterprise struggles to align decisions across contexts, leading to inefficiencies and increased risk of conflicting outcomes.

This visibility becomes critical when decisions intersect across organizational boundaries. In environments where multiple teams and functions operate simultaneously, decisions rarely exist in isolation. A decision made in one context may influence, constrain, or depend on decisions made elsewhere. Without traceable decision authority, these interactions become opaque. Conflicts emerge not because decisions are inherently incompatible, but because their origins and conditions are unclear. Governance addresses this by ensuring that decision authority is not only defined, but also visible in how it is exercised across the enterprise.

Accountability operates alongside authority within this flow, but it serves a different purpose. While authority determines who makes a decision, [[GL:Accountability]] determines who carries its outcome forward. This distinction is essential. Without it, accountability tends to collapse into responsibility for tasks or, in adverse conditions, into retrospective blame. Governance requires a different interpretation. Accountability is forward looking. It defines ownership of outcomes in a way that persists as decisions unfold over time. It ensures that decisions remain connected to those who are positioned to understand and manage their consequences.

The separation between accountability and blame is therefore critical to maintaining effective governance. Blame is retrospective and often reactive, emerging after outcomes are known. It tends to focus on identifying fault rather than understanding the conditions under which decisions were made. Accountability, in contrast, is structural. It is established at the point of decision, not after the fact, and it defines ownership in a way that enables outcomes to be managed rather than assigned. When these two concepts are conflated, governance becomes defensive. Decisions are avoided or delayed to mitigate perceived risk of blame, rather than made with clarity and ownership.

Continuity of authority and accountability also requires that decisions remain connected over time. In many organizations, decisions are treated as discrete events. They are made, implemented, and then replaced by subsequent decisions without a clear sense of continuity. This creates fragmentation in which the rationale for earlier decisions is lost, and later decisions are made without full awareness of their context. Governance addresses this by maintaining coherence across decisions. Decision authority is not redefined arbitrarily at each point; it is sustained in a way that allows decision sequences to be understood as part of a broader structure.

It is important to note that this continuity does not imply escalation or hierarchical control. Governance does not require that decisions move upward through levels of approval. Instead, it requires that wherever authority resides, it is exercised with clarity and remains connected to the broader system. Decisions may be distributed across the enterprise, but they are not disconnected. The flow of authority ensures that even decentralized decisions remain part of a coherent structure, while the flow of accountability ensures that outcomes are consistently owned.

This perspective becomes especially relevant in organizations that operate across multiple delivery models. Teams working within iterative frameworks, coordination layers managing broader alignment, and specialized disciplines contributing domain expertise all participate in decision-making. Without governance, the flow between these contexts becomes inconsistent. Decisions are made locally, but their implications extend globally. Governance provides the structure through which these local decisions align with enterprise-level understanding, not by centralizing control, but by maintaining continuity of authority and accountability.

The practical effect of this flow is a system in which decisions can be understood, traced, and managed without reliance on procedural enforcement. Clarity replaces assumption, and structure replaces improvisation. When authority and accountability flow coherently, decisions reinforce each other rather than conflict. This does not eliminate complexity, but it makes it navigable. The enterprise gains the ability to reason about decisions as part of a connected system rather than as isolated outcomes.

Even with this structure in place, governance is often misunderstood. It is frequently associated with control mechanisms that restrict progress or impose checkpoints on delivery. This perception persists because governance is often implemented through such mechanisms when its structural foundations are absent. To fully understand governance as defined in this chapter, it is necessary to distinguish it from these interpretations. This distinction clarifies why governance, properly structured, operates not as a barrier to delivery, but as a condition for consistent and coherent decision-making (ISO, 2021).

6.5 Why Governance Is Not Gatekeeping

Figure 6.4 – Governance vs Gatekeeping

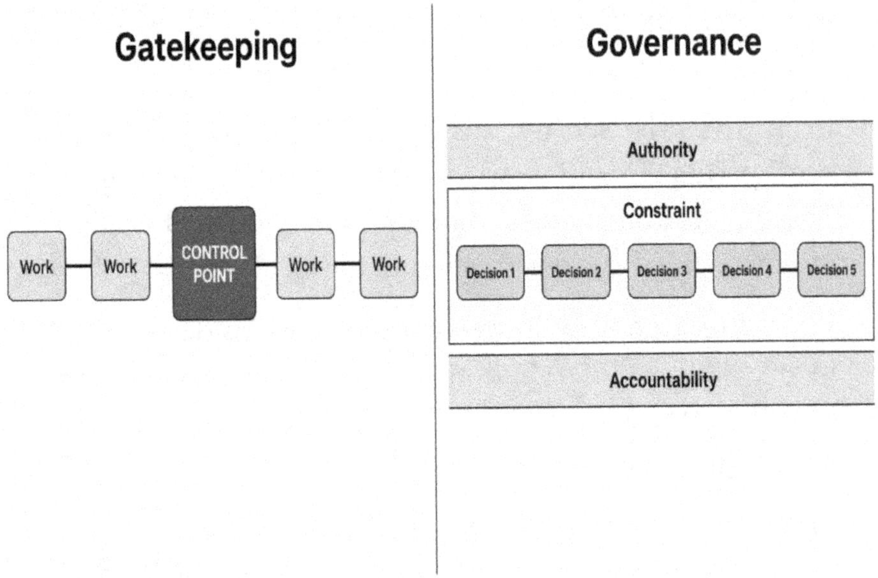

Gatekeeping applies control at discrete checkpoints after work progresses, whereas governance maintains continuous decision coherence by structuring decisions within defined authority, constraints, and accountability.

Governance, when observed from within many organizations, is often associated with control points that regulate the flow of work. These control points—commonly expressed as reviews, approvals, or quality gates—serve a visible function. They create moments where work is examined before proceeding, providing a sense of oversight and assurance. This association is understandable, as such mechanisms are frequently introduced in response to inconsistency or risk. However, they do not represent governance in its structural sense. They are artifacts of an underlying absence rather than expressions of a coherent system.

This association reflects how governance is often implemented rather than what it fundamentally represents. Control points are visible and tangible, making them easy to equate with governance, even though they address only a subset of its purpose.

In an enterprise setting, this typically appears as reliance on checkpoints to validate work after it has been completed. These checkpoints create moments of control but do not influence the decisions that led to the work itself.

When this capability is absent, organizations depend increasingly on intervention to manage outcomes. Decision quality remains inconsistent, and issues are often discovered late in the process.

This directly affects efficiency and cost. Late-stage corrections require more effort, introduce delays, and reduce confidence in delivery outcomes.

The distinction between governance and gatekeeping becomes clear when considering what each seeks to influence. Gatekeeping operates at the level of progression. It determines whether work may move forward based on predefined criteria. Governance operates at the level of decision-making. It determines how those criteria are established, who has the authority to define them, and how accountability for their outcomes is maintained. Where gatekeeping focuses on controlling movement through checkpoints, governance focuses on ensuring that the decisions shaping that movement are coherent, authorized, and aligned with the broader system.

Gatekeeping often emerges in environments where decision authority is ambiguous. In such conditions, organizations introduce checkpoints as a way of compensating for the lack of clarity. These checkpoints centralize decision-making at specific moments, creating the appearance of control. While this may produce short-term stability, it does so by concentrating authority in ways that can become disconnected from the contexts in which work is performed. Decisions are deferred upward or outward, rather than integrated into the ongoing flow of work. The result is a system that relies on intervention rather than coherence.

This reliance introduces structural limitations. Gatekeeping evaluates work after it has been performed, rather than shaping the decisions that guide it from the outset. As a result, it often identifies issues at points where corrective action is more complex and more costly. Moreover, by concentrating decision authority within checkpoints, it can fragment accountability. Those performing the work are responsible for execution, while those enforcing the gate are seen as responsible for quality. This division obscures the fact that quality outcomes are determined by a sequence of decisions made throughout the lifecycle, not only at its boundaries.

Governance addresses these limitations by repositioning control from intermittent enforcement to continuous decision integrity. Instead of asking whether work should proceed at a specific point, governance ensures that the decisions guiding that work are made with appropriate decision authority, informed by relevant intelligence, and bounded by clear constraints, preserving [[GL:Decision Integrity]] across contexts. This shifts the focus from control as restriction to control as coherence. Decisions are not validated only after they occur; they are structured in a way that makes their alignment visible as they are made.

This distinction also changes the perceived relationship between governance and execution. Gatekeeping is often experienced as friction because it introduces interruptions into the flow of work. Governance, properly structured, does not require such interruptions. By aligning authority and accountability with the contexts in which decisions are made, governance enables decisions to occur as part of the natural progression of work. Oversight is maintained not through external intervention, but through the clarity of the decision framework itself. In this way, governance reduces the need for corrective checkpoints without reducing the level of control.

The difference can be understood as one of timing and intent. Gatekeeping reacts to outcomes, seeking to prevent undesirable results after work has been produced. Governance shapes the conditions under which those outcomes are determined. It operates continuously rather than episodically, and its purpose is not to restrict progress but to ensure that progress is guided by coherent and accountable decisions. This does not eliminate the need for review or evaluation, but it integrates them into a broader structure rather than isolating them as control mechanisms.

As organizations move toward governance defined in this way, the function of traditional checkpoints often changes. They become less about approval and more about verification of decision integrity. The emphasis shifts from determining whether work meets criteria, to understanding whether the decisions that produced that work were made within the governing structure. This reframing preserves oversight while removing the dependency on intervention as a primary means of control.

Understanding governance as distinct from gatekeeping is essential because it clarifies its role within the enterprise. Governance is not a barrier that work must pass through; it is the system that ensures decisions guiding that work are consistent, accountable, and aligned. It does not slow execution; it provides the conditions under which execution can proceed with confidence and coherence (Ansell & Torfing, 2021). This clarity prepares the ground for the next consideration. Once governance establishes structured decision-making, it becomes possible to understand how the enterprise evolves in its ability to sustain quality over time.

With governance clarified as continuous decision integrity, its role in shaping capability becomes visible.

> **Recognizable Situation:**
>
> ***Most engineers have experienced the release meeting where a "governance review" was, in practice, a checkpoint where a small group could stop the work but could not improve the decision that produced it. The presence of a gate was mistaken for the presence of governance. Governance is not the ability to say no — it is the structural clarity about who decides what, and on what evidence.***

6.6 Governance as the Precondition for Maturity

The presence of governance transforms not only how decisions are made, but also how the enterprise understands its own capability. Without governance, assessments of quality tend to focus on observable activity—process adherence, artifact completeness, or execution consistency. While these elements provide useful signals, they do not fully capture the structure that produces quality outcomes. They describe what is done, not how decisions shaping those actions are made. As a result, any assessment derived from them remains partial.

Maturity, in its most meaningful sense, reflects the degree to which an enterprise can produce consistent outcomes under varying conditions. This consistency cannot be achieved through execution alone. It depends on the stability of the [[GL:Decision | decision-making]] framework that underpins execution. When decisions are implicit, distributed without clarity, or detached from relevant intelligence, outcomes will vary regardless of how well processes are performed. Governance establishes the conditions under which decisions become stable, explicit, and aligned, making consistent outcomes possible.

Consistency under changing conditions is not achieved through repetition alone. It requires a stable decision framework that ensures similar situations are approached with coherent reasoning and aligned authority.

In an enterprise setting, this typically appears as the ability to handle variation—such as changes in scope, risk, or dependency—without producing disproportionate changes in outcome. Decisions remain anchored in structure rather than shifting with circumstance.

When this capability is absent, outcomes fluctuate significantly even when processes remain the same. The system reacts to variability rather than absorbing it, leading to inconsistent performance.

This directly affects predictability and learning. Without consistent outcomes, the enterprise cannot reliably assess improvement or build upon prior decisions, limiting its ability to mature over time.

This relationship between governance and maturity is structural. Before maturity can be understood, the system that produces outcomes must be defined. Governance provides that definition by making decisions visible and by linking them to authority, accountability, and constraints. Without this structure, the enterprise lacks a stable reference point against which capability can be considered. It becomes difficult to distinguish between variability caused by external factors and variability caused by inconsistency in decision-making itself.

A critical implication of this is that maturity cannot be meaningfully assessed in the absence of governance. If decisions are not explicitly defined, they cannot be evaluated. If authority is unclear, accountability remains diffuse, and outcomes cannot be reliably attributed. In such conditions, any attempt to assess capability risks focusing on surface indicators rather than underlying structure. Governance does not evaluate maturity; it makes evaluation possible by establishing the conditions under which assessment has meaning.

This does not imply that governance replaces capability. The ability to execute effectively, to analyze conditions, and to respond to change remains essential. However, capability operates within the framework that governance defines. Without that framework, capability is applied inconsistently, and its impact becomes difficult to sustain. Governance ensures that capability is directed through a coherent decision structure, allowing its effects to accumulate rather than disperse.

The distinction between governed and unguided systems becomes particularly evident over time. In a governed system, decisions reinforce each other. Authority remains clear, accountability persists, and constraints provide continuity. This creates an environment in which learning can occur in a structured way, because the relationship between decisions and outcomes is visible. In an unguided system, decisions are often disconnected. Outcomes may still be achieved, but their relationship to the decisions that produced them is less clear. Learning becomes fragmented, and improvement is difficult to sustain.

This reinforcement creates a compounding effect where each decision contributes to a more stable and coherent system. Over time, patterns of decision-making become more aligned, enabling the enterprise to operate with greater clarity and confidence.

In an enterprise setting, this typically appears as increasing alignment across teams and functions, where decisions made in different contexts exhibit similar reasoning and adherence to shared constraints.

When this capability is absent, decisions remain isolated and fail to build upon one another. Learning is inconsistent, and improvements in one area do not translate effectively across the system.

This directly affects the sustainability of improvement. Gains are localized and temporary, rather than cumulative and systemic, limiting the enterprise's ability to achieve true maturity.

By establishing governance as the precondition for maturity, the enterprise gains a new point of orientation. Rather than asking how well work is performed in isolation, it can consider how coherently decisions are made across the system. This shift does not diminish the importance of execution; it situates execution within a structure that gives it consistency and meaning. It recognizes that maturity is not a property of individual practices, but of the system that aligns those practices through governed decision-making.

Concept Insight: Maturity is not achieved through execution alone, but through the stability and alignment of decision-making. Governance establishes the structure that allows capability to accumulate, enabling consistent and sustainable improvement across the enterprise.

This chapter has established that governance defines how quality decisions are authorized, constrained, reviewed, and corrected across the enterprise. It has shown that without governance, decisions remain implicit and outcomes become inconsistent, regardless of execution discipline. It has clarified that governance operates not as control over activity, but as structure over decisions, aligning authority with intelligence and accountability with outcomes. It has also demonstrated that governance is distinct from gatekeeping, providing continuous decision integrity rather than intermittent control.

With this foundation in place, the enterprise is positioned to consider a deeper question—how its capability evolves once decision-making is both explicit and governed. [[GL:Governance]] does not measure this evolution, but it creates the conditions under which it can be understood. The next step is to examine how this structured decision environment reveals differences in capability, not as isolated attributes, but as part of a coherent system shaped by governance (ISO, 2021).

This chapter establishes governance as the structural layer that aligns decision authority with enterprise intelligence, ensuring that quality is not only produced but deliberately governed.

Together, these concepts form a coherent system in which decisions are explicit, accountable, and continuously aligned across contexts.

The next chapter builds on this by examining how governed decision environments reveal differences in capability and enable the structured evaluation of enterprise maturity.

Summary

Governance establishes the structural conditions required for consistent decision-making across the enterprise, aligning authority, accountability, and constraints with available intelligence. Without this structure, decisions remain implicit and inconsistent, and quality outcomes vary regardless of execution discipline.

Maturity cannot be achieved or meaningfully assessed in the absence of governance. Consistent outcomes under changing conditions depend on a stable decision framework that ensures alignment across contexts. Without such a framework, variability increases, learning becomes fragmented, and improvement cannot accumulate.

By making decisions explicit, governed, and traceable, governance creates the conditions under which capability can be evaluated and sustained. It does not replace execution, but ensures that execution operates within a coherent system of decision-making, enabling maturity to emerge as a property of the system rather than individual activity.

Chapter 6 — Knowledge Check

The Governance Pillars

The following questions are designed to verify accurate understanding of how governance operates as a structural layer over enterprise quality systems. They assess whether the reader can distinguish governance from execution and control mechanisms, understand how decision authority and accountability function, and recognize the role of governance in enabling coherent enterprise outcomes.

These questions are nonprocedural. They do not assess implementation methods, tools, or process enforcement techniques.

Knowledge Check 6.1 — Governance Purpose

Question
What is the primary purpose of governance within an enterprise quality system?

Knowledge Check 6.2 — Governance vs Execution

Question
Why is governance not an extension of execution or a refinement of measurement?

Knowledge Check 6.3 — Decision Authority and Intelligence

Question
What happens when decision authority is not aligned with the intelligence required to support it?

Knowledge Check 6.4 — Governance Surface

Question

What does governance operate over, and why is this distinction critical?

Knowledge Check 6.5 — The Governance Pillars

Question

What are the five Governance Pillars, and what role does each play in structuring decision-making?

Knowledge Check 6.6 — Authority and Accountability Flow

Question

What is the difference between decision authority and accountability, and why must they remain distinct?

Knowledge Check 6.7 — Governance vs Gatekeeping

Question

Why is governance not equivalent to gatekeeping, and how does each influence quality outcomes differently?

Knowledge Check 6.8 — Governance and Maturity

Question

Why is governance considered a precondition for maturity rather than a measure of maturity?

Guidance for the Reader

If you can explain how governance operates as a structural layer over quality, distinguish between authority and accountability in decision-making, and describe how the Governance Pillars create coherence across enterprise decisions, you are prepared to proceed.

This chapter establishes governance as the system through which quality decisions are made explicit, accountable, and aligned with enterprise intelligence. It defines how authority, constraints, review, and correction operate as a coherent structure over distributed decision-making.

The next chapter builds on this foundation by examining how governed decision environments reveal differences in capability, enabling structured evaluation of enterprise maturity across the system.

Key Takeaways

- Governance aligns decision authority with enterprise intelligence.
- Quality governance operates over decisions, not activity.
- Authority, accountability, constraint, review, and correction form the governance structure.
- Accountability owns outcomes; authority makes decisions.
- Governance maintains decision integrity without becoming gatekeeping.
- Maturity requires governed decision-making before it can be assessed.

Questions for Reflection:

- What does this concept reveal about system behavior?
- How would this appear in an enterprise context?

- What signals would indicate this is not functioning correctly?

Chapter 7 — The QACE Maturity Model

Chapter Introduction

The concept of maturity within enterprise systems is frequently misunderstood. Organizations often describe themselves as either "capable" or "not capable," "compliant" or "non-compliant," as though effectiveness were a binary state. This distinction cannot be understood as a categorical classification—it must be interpreted as a progressive model of capability development. Enterprise performance does not emerge instantaneously, nor does it remain static. This progression reflects the accumulation of structural capability over time rather than isolated improvements. Maturity therefore captures how consistently a system can translate intent into repeatable outcomes, even as conditions change, rather than whether it has demonstrated success in specific instances.

When this capability is absent, performance appears episodic and difficult to explain. Success may occur, but it is not repeatable, and failures are often attributed to external factors rather than understood as indicators of underlying system conditions. This directly affects the organization's ability to make reliable decisions, as outcomes cannot be predicted with confidence. It also increases operational risk, since variability remains unmanaged and system behavior is not consistently aligned with intent. It evolves through progressive stages of capability development. The QACE Maturity Model [[GL:Maturity Model]] is designed to make this progression explicit, observable, and governable.

Figure 7.1 – Binary vs Maturity-Based Capability Model

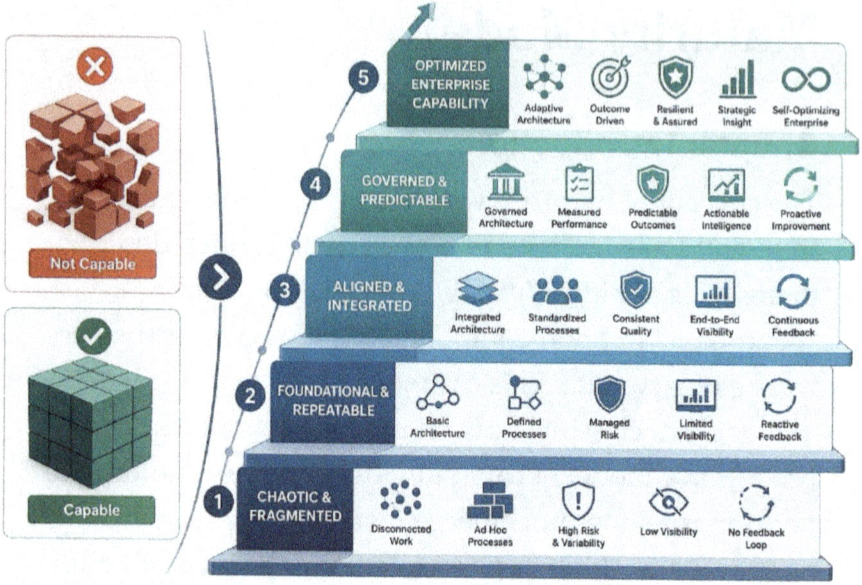

Binary classifications obscure system capability, whereas maturity reflects progressive and observable development of aligned performance.

The critical distinction is not the labels themselves, but the shift from static classification to evolving system capability.

This chapter builds on the preceding discussion of system-level constructs by clarifying how maturity is expressed as observable behavior within an enterprise system.

It focuses on how capabilities evolve from fragmented practices into coordinated and predictable outcomes.

This is critical because maturity determines whether quality efforts produce consistent results or remain dependent on isolated success.

This chapter builds on the foundational QACE system constructs by addressing how capability evolves over time through structured progression. It focuses on making maturity observable, comparable, and governable as a core property of enterprise systems. This is critical because without a clear model of progression, organizations cannot reliably assess capability, interpret system behavior, or make informed decisions about improvement.

At its core, maturity represents the degree to which a system can consistently produce intended outcomes under varying conditions. It is not defined by isolated achievements, individual competencies, or temporary successes, but by sustained system behavior over time. Within the QACE framework, maturity is treated as a structural property of the enterprise system, shaped by the alignment of architecture, execution, governance, and feedback mechanisms.

In an enterprise setting, this typically appears as a clear distinction between teams that consistently deliver stable outcomes and those that rely on individual effort to achieve results. When maturity is low, outcomes fluctuate even when effort increases, because the system lacks the structural alignment required to sustain performance. This directly affects predictability, making it difficult for leadership to rely on quality signals when making decisions.

The need for a maturity model arises from the inherent complexity of enterprise systems. Without a structured method for defining and evaluating maturity, assessments devolve into subjective judgments, inconsistent interpretations, and non-repeatable conclusions. The QACE Maturity Model establishes a common language and a consistent framework through which organizations can assess their capability progression in a disciplined and comparable manner.

This model does not exist to label organizations. It exists to reveal structural realities that are otherwise obscured—enabling informed understanding of system behavior and creating a foundation for deliberate improvement. Maturity progresses through the accumulation of structural capability rather than the occurrence of isolated successes. This progression must be understood as structural accumulation rather than a series of isolated improvements.

Figure 7.2 – Accumulation of Structural Capability [[GL:System Capability]]

System capability develops through the accumulation of aligned structures, not isolated improvements.

What appears as improvement is in fact the result of accumulated alignment within the system structure. This progression occurs because alignment within the system reduces variability in how outcomes are produced. As alignment increases, execution pathways become more consistent, dependencies become explicit, and the system's ability to produce repeatable results improves.

Without this structural accumulation, performance remains dependent on individual effort, resulting in variability that cannot be consistently managed or explained.

At a conceptual level, maturity defines what the system is capable of. At a structural level, it reflects how system components are aligned. At a behavioral level, it is expressed through consistency in outcomes. At a dynamic level, it evolves through progressive reduction of variability across conditions.

Concept Insight: Maturity reflects the system's ability to produce outcomes consistently, not the intensity of effort. Without structural alignment, increased activity does not translate into improved performance.

7.1 — Maturity Model Design and Purpose

The design of the QACE Maturity Model is grounded in the principle that enterprise effectiveness is directly correlated with maturity across defined system dimensions. Rather than focusing on isolated functions or departmental performance, the model considers the enterprise as an integrated system whose outcomes are the product of interdependent components. This perspective reinforces that no single function can be evaluated in isolation without distorting the understanding of system capability. Maturity is therefore determined by how effectively these components operate together rather than how well they perform independently.

In an enterprise setting, this typically appears as cross-functional dependencies influencing outcomes, where changes in one area produce visible effects in others. Alignment across architecture, execution, governance, and feedback becomes observable through coordinated behavior rather than isolated performance improvements.

When this capability is absent, organizations often optimize locally while degrading overall system performance. Improvements in one domain may introduce instability in another, and the absence of integration leads to fragmented and contradictory outcomes. This directly affects the coherence of enterprise operations, reducing the effectiveness of decision-making and increasing the likelihood of unintended consequences. It also limits the organization's ability to sustain improvements, as gains are not reinforced at the system level.

The purpose of the model is therefore twofold. First, it provides a structured definition of maturity that removes ambiguity from the assessment process. Second, it establishes a coherent framework through which progression can be analyzed, compared, and understood.

Maturity, in this context, is not abstract. It is defined through observable patterns of system behavior that reflect the degree of alignment, consistency, and adaptability present within the enterprise. The model organizes these patterns into distinct levels. Each level represents a qualitatively different state of system capability.

Crucially, the QACE Maturity Model is dimensionally integrated. Maturity is not evaluated within isolated domains; it is assessed across core system dimensions, including architecture, execution, governance, and feedback.

These dimensions collectively determine how effectively an organization translates intent into outcomes.

These dimensions are not independent contributors to performance; they are interdependent mechanisms that collectively determine system behavior. This interdependence cannot be interpreted in isolation—it must be understood as a unified system operating through coordinated dimensions.

Figure 7.3 – Maturity as a System Property

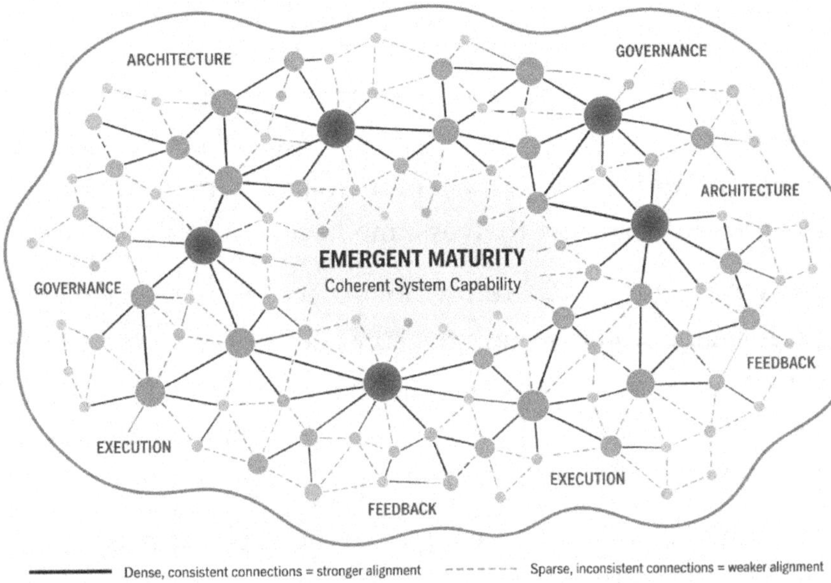

Maturity emerges from the alignment of architecture, execution, governance, and feedback, functioning as an integrated system.

No single dimension determines system capability; maturity emerges only through their continuous alignment. Architecture defines how the system is constructed, execution determines how work is performed, governance establishes how decisions are controlled, and feedback enables the system to adjust over time.

A deficiency in any one dimension introduces variability into the others, preventing the system from achieving consistent alignment and reducing the reliability of outcomes. The model's design ensures that maturity cannot be inferred from partial evidence. A system may demonstrate strength in one dimension while exhibiting weakness in another; true maturity is reflected only when alignment exists across the full system.

This integrated view prevents fragmented assessments and reinforces the systemic nature of enterprise quality. Ultimately, the model provides structure where ambiguity would otherwise persist, enabling maturity to be assessed systematically rather than assumed.

System maturity is therefore not observed through isolated performance, but through the consistency with which these dimensions operate in coordination. When coordination is present, outcomes stabilize; when it is absent, variability persists regardless of localized improvements.

With this structure defined, maturity can be expressed through discrete levels.

> **Concept Insight: The QACE Maturity Model establishes a structured, integrated framework for assessing enterprise capability as a system-wide condition rather than isolated performance. True maturity is only visible when alignment across architecture, execution, governance, and feedback is consistently achieved.**

7.2 — The Five Levels of Enterprise Quality

The QACE Maturity Model defines enterprise quality across five distinct levels, each representing a progressive stage of system capability. These levels are not arbitrary classifications; they reflect observable transitions in how systems are designed, governed, and executed. Each level represents a distinct pattern of system behavior rather than a simple increase in capability. Transitioning between levels reflects a structural shift in how the system operates, not just incremental improvement within the same operating model. Advancement between levels must therefore be interpreted as a change in system structure, not an incremental increase in performance.

In an enterprise setting, this typically appears as clear differences in coordination, predictability, and decision-making. Lower levels show fragmented activity and variable outcomes, while higher levels demonstrate consistency driven by aligned structures and shared operational logic. When this capability is absent, organizations may attempt to improve performance without recognizing the need for structural change. Efforts remain confined to existing patterns, resulting in limited gains and recurring instability. This directly affects progression, as the organization becomes constrained within its current maturity state. Without recognizing these structural transitions, advancement stalls and variability persists despite continued effort.

Figure 7.4 – Structural Shift Between Maturity Levels

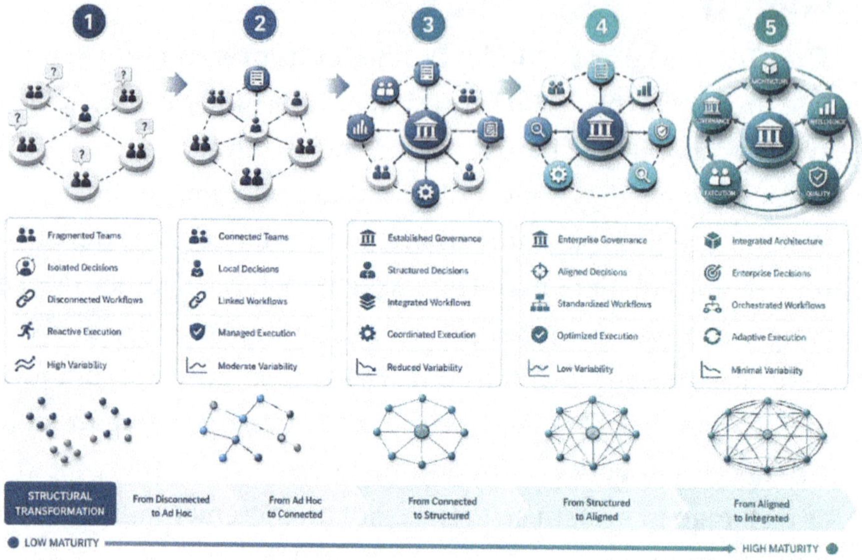

Transition between maturity levels occurs through structural shifts in system coordination, not incremental improvement.

Progression occurs only when the system transitions to a new operating structure, not when existing patterns are extended. Transition between maturity levels is not driven by incremental improvement within existing patterns, but by structural shifts in how the system operates. Each transition reflects a change in coordination, where previously implicit dependencies become explicit, localized decisions become system-informed, and variability is managed through design rather than correction. Without this structural shift, the system remains constrained within its existing level regardless of increased effort or activity.

At the lowest level, system behavior is largely reactive and inconsistent. Outcomes vary significantly, dependencies remain implicit, and coordination is limited. As maturity increases, systems begin to exhibit greater structure, repeatability, and alignment. Processes become more defined, roles more clearly understood, and interactions more predictable. These differences must be understood as distinct patterns of system behavior rather than variations in effort.

Figure 7.5 – Low vs High Maturity System Behavior

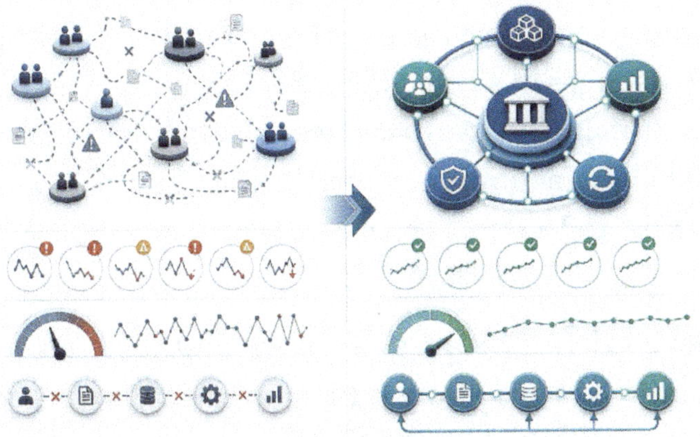

System maturity is reflected in the consistency and predictability of outcomes, not the intensity of effort.

The defining characteristic is not output volume, but the consistency with which outcomes are produced. Mid-level maturity is characterized by increasing coherence across the system. Execution is no longer isolated but begins to align with architectural intent and governance expectations. Feedback mechanisms become more consistent, enabling the system to detect and respond to variation more effectively. At higher levels of maturity, the system demonstrates integrated behavior. Architecture, execution, governance, and feedback operate in a coordinated manner, reinforcing one another rather than acting independently. Decision-making becomes informed by system signals rather than localized judgment, and variability is managed through intentional design rather than reactive correction.

At the highest level, the enterprise functions as a coherent, adaptive system. Outcomes are not only consistent but predictable, and the organization is capable of responding to change without degrading performance. Alignment is sustained not through control alone but through shared structure and systemic clarity. These transitions are visible through changes in system behavior rather than increases in output. As maturity increases, coordination becomes more deliberate, interactions more predictable, and outcomes more stable, reflecting a shift from reactive execution toward intentional system design.

These levels define progression, not a destination. Organizations move through them over time, with each level building upon the structural foundations established in previous stages. To make these levels observable, the model relies on identifiable system signals.

7.3 — Characteristics and Signals by Level

The distinction between maturity levels is made visible through observable signals—those patterns of behavior, interaction, and outcome that reflect the underlying state of the system. These signals are essential because they transform maturity from abstract description into observable system behavior. Signals provide the mechanism by which maturity becomes visible and comparable. Without them, maturity remains interpretive rather than observable, limiting the ability to assess or validate system capability consistently. In an enterprise setting, this typically appears as recurring patterns in outcomes, interactions, and feedback. These patterns are not isolated observations but consistent indicators of how the system operates across conditions and over time. When this capability is absent, organizations rely on anecdotal evidence or subjective interpretation to assess performance. This leads to inconsistent conclusions, misalignment in understanding, and reduced confidence in assessment outcomes. This directly affects the reliability of comparisons and decisions based on those assessments. Without consistent signals, it becomes difficult to distinguish between actual capability and perceived performance, increasing the risk of misinformed actions.

Signals emerge as a direct result of underlying system conditions. System structure influences how work is performed, which produces observable patterns in outcomes, interactions, and feedback. These patterns, when consistently observed, reveal the underlying maturity of the system. In this way, signals do not define maturity; they reflect it, providing a reliable mechanism for interpreting system behavior. At lower levels of maturity, signals often include inconsistency in outcomes, ambiguity in roles, and reliance on informal coordination. Execution varies widely, and success is dependent on individual effort rather than system design. Governance mechanisms exist in limited or inconsistent forms, and feedback loops are weak or delayed.

As maturity increases, signals shift toward greater stability and clarity. Processes become more repeatable, responsibilities more defined, and dependencies more explicitly managed. Variability decreases as the system becomes more structured, and outcomes begin to exhibit greater consistency. At advanced levels of maturity, signals reflect systemic coherence. Interactions between system components are aligned, feedback is timely and actionable, and governance structures are consistently applied. The system demonstrates the ability to anticipate and manage variation rather than simply react to it. At the highest level, signals indicate not only stability but adaptability. The system responds to change without losing alignment, and outcomes remain consistent even as conditions evolve. This level of maturity is characterized by a strong correlation between system design and system behavior, where intended outcomes are reliably achieved.

These signals provide the basis for comparison across teams, functions, and institutions. Because they are observable and repeatable, they enable maturity to be evaluated in a way that is both consistent and meaningful. Assessment therefore follows a consistent pathway: system conditions produce behavior, behavior generates observable signals, and those signals enable interpretation of maturity. This pathway must be interpreted as a causal sequence linking system conditions to observable signals. Without this pathway, assessment becomes subjective, as observations cannot be reliably linked to underlying system capability.

Figure 7.6 – System Conditions to Signals Pathway

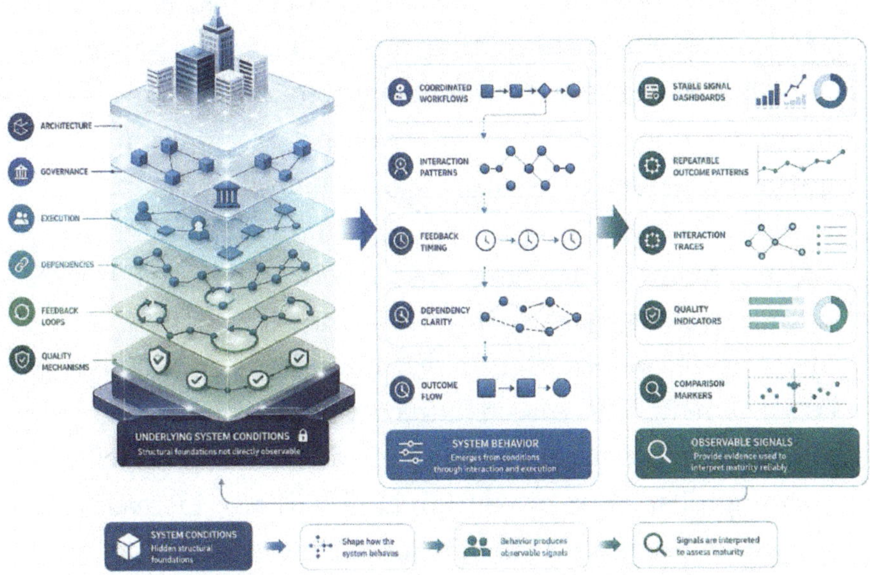

Observable signals reflect underlying system conditions through behavior, enabling reliable interpretation of maturity.

Without this causal linkage, signals cannot be reliably interpreted as indicators of system capability.

> **Concept Insight: Observable signals translate maturity from abstract concept into measurable system behavior. Consistent patterns in outcomes, interactions, and feedback enable reliable assessment and comparison of enterprise capability.**

7.4 — Progression Pathways and Constraints

Progression through maturity levels is neither automatic nor linear. This reinforces that advancement is contingent on structural change rather than the passage of time or isolated improvement efforts. Movement between levels reflects the development of system-wide alignment rather than localized gains. In an enterprise setting, this typically appears as uneven progress across different system dimensions. Improvements in execution may outpace changes in governance or architecture, creating temporary gains without sustained progression. When this capability is absent, organizations often misinterpret activity as progress. Effort increases, but structural constraints remain unchanged, leading to recurring limitations and stalled advancement. This directly affects the organization's ability to evolve, as resources are consumed without producing meaningful shifts in system capability. It also increases frustration, as improvements fail to produce durable outcomes. It is shaped by both enabling conditions and structural constraints that influence how systems evolve over time.

Advancement in maturity requires the strengthening of alignment across system dimensions. Improvements in execution alone are insufficient if architecture remains fragmented, governance inconsistent, or feedback mechanisms underdeveloped. Progress depends on coordinated development across the full system, where changes in one dimension reinforce the others. Progression occurs when alignment across system dimensions increases, enabling the system to operate more coherently. Progression must therefore be understood as the interaction between enabling alignment and limiting constraints.

Figure 7.7 – Maturity Progression Pathway with Constraints

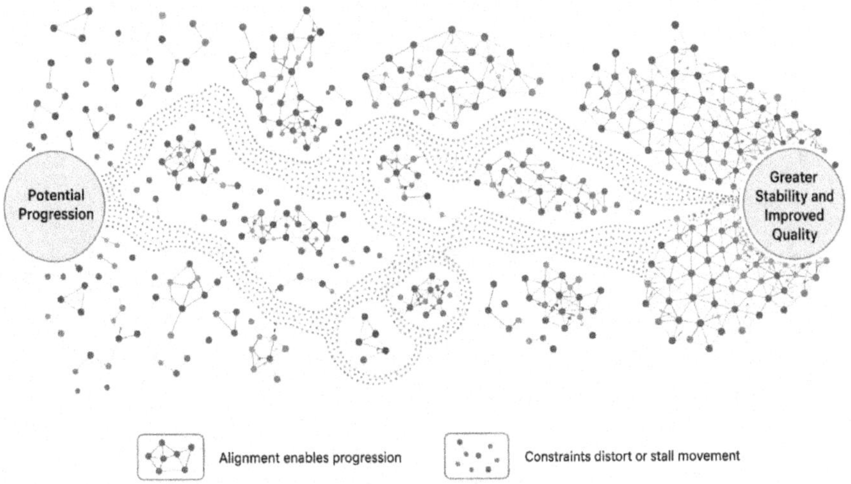

Maturity progression is enabled by alignment and constrained by structural limitations within the system.

Advancement occurs only when constraints are reduced and alignment is strengthened simultaneously. Constraints, by contrast, limit this progression by maintaining fragmentation or inconsistency within the system. Advancement therefore depends on reducing constraints while strengthening alignment, not simply increasing activity within individual dimensions.

At the same time, progression is constrained by existing system conditions. Legacy structures, misaligned incentives, unclear governance, and fragmented communication can all inhibit advancement. These constraints are not external obstacles but intrinsic characteristics of the system itself, reflecting its current maturity state.

Constraints define the current boundary of system capability. These constraints must be understood as structural limits that define the system's current capability.

Figure 7.8 – Constraint Boundary of System Capability

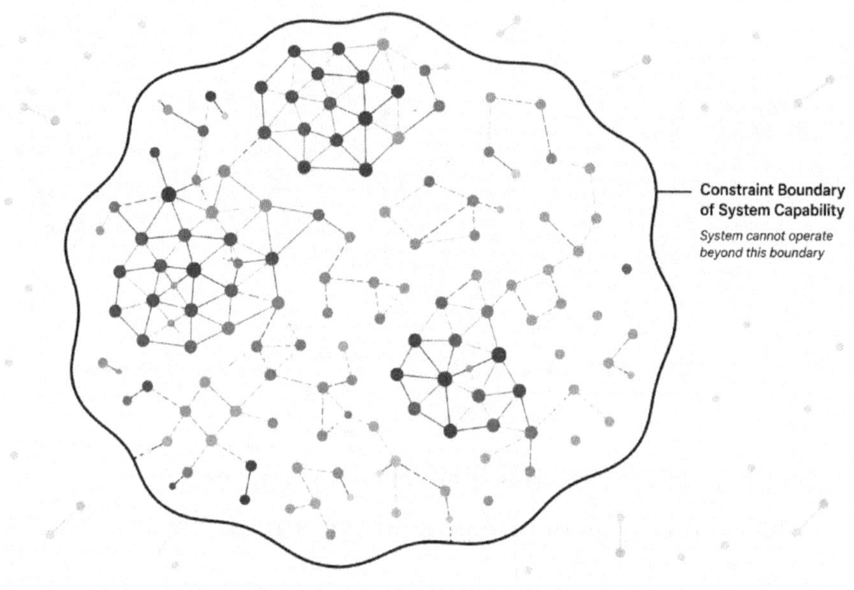

Constraints define the limits of system capability, restricting progression until structural alignment is achieved.

Until these boundaries are altered, the system cannot progress beyond its existing level of capability. They are structural in nature, representing limitations in alignment, clarity, or coordination that prevent the system from operating beyond its current state. Until these constraints are addressed, progression is restricted regardless of effort or intent.

As organizations progress, the nature of constraints changes. Early-stage constraints often stem from lack of structure and clarity, while later-stage constraints may arise from rigidity or over-reliance on established patterns. Recognizing these evolving constraints is essential for understanding how progression occurs. Importantly, maturity progression is not driven by isolated initiatives or episodic improvements. It requires sustained structural evolution, where changes reinforce one another and contribute to overall system coherence. Each level establishes the conditions necessary for progression to the next, creating cumulative effects over time. This progression reflects a transition from reactive to intentional system behavior. As maturity increases, outcomes are shaped by design rather than circumstance. As alignment improves and constraints are reduced, the system transitions from reactive behavior toward intentional operation. This transition must be interpreted as a shift in how system behavior is produced, from reactive response to intentional design. This transition reflects a change in how outcomes are produced, shifting from variability driven by circumstance to consistency driven by design.

Figure 7.9 – Reactive to Intentional System Behavior

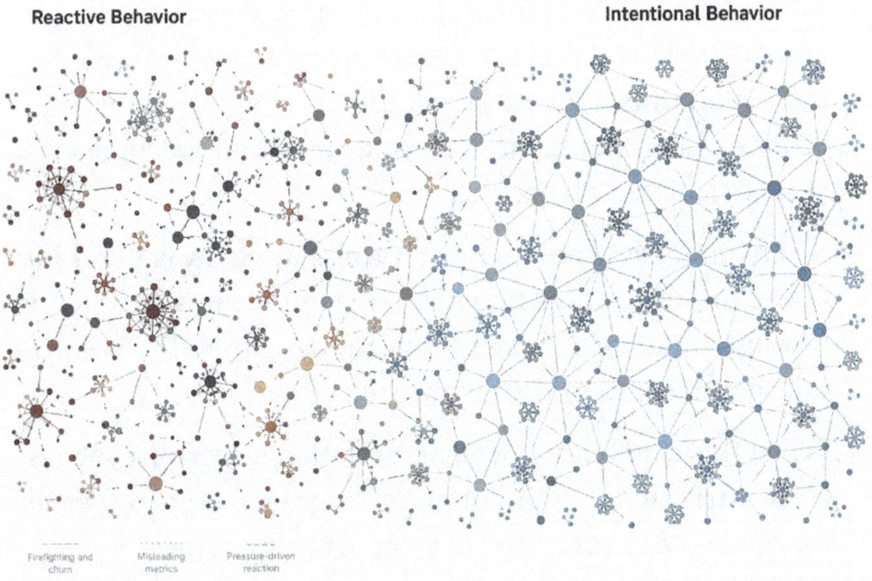

As maturity increases, system behavior transitions from reactive variability to intentional, design-driven consistency.

As this shift occurs, outcomes become a function of system design rather than circumstance.

> **Concept Insight: Maturity progression depends on structural alignment across system dimensions and is constrained by existing system conditions. Advancement requires coordinated evolution rather than isolated improvements or increased effort.**

This progression gains practical meaning when the model is applied within the broader QACE system.

7.5 — Role of the Maturity Model in QACE

Within the broader QACE system, the maturity model serves as a foundational mechanism for understanding enterprise capability. It provides the lens through which system effectiveness is interpreted and the framework through which variation in performance is explained. This emphasizes that the model is not an evaluative tool alone but a mechanism for understanding system behavior. It frames performance variation as a structural outcome rather than an isolated occurrence.

In an enterprise setting, this typically appears as the ability to explain differences in outcomes across teams or functions through underlying system conditions. Variability becomes interpretable rather than ambiguous.

When this capability is absent, variation in performance is often attributed to individuals or external factors rather than recognized as a reflection of system design. This misinterpretation limits the effectiveness of corrective actions. This directly affects decision quality, as interventions may target symptoms rather than causes. It also reduces the organization's ability to improve predictability, since the underlying drivers of variation remain unaddressed.

The diagnostic function of the model enables organizations to interpret current system behavior by linking observed outcomes to underlying structural conditions. The predictive function extends this capability by allowing organizations to anticipate how changes in structure will influence future outcomes. Together, these functions transform maturity from a descriptive concept into a practical instrument for decision-making.

The model's role is not to classify organizations for its own sake. Classification without purpose offers limited value. Instead, the maturity model exists to inform understanding and enable targeted intervention. By revealing the structural state of the system, it allows organizations to identify where and why outcomes vary—and to act accordingly.

This function is inherently predictive because system structure determines outcome reliability. As maturity increases, so does the reliability of outcomes. Higher levels of maturity correlate with greater alignment, reduced variability, and increased predictability of system behavior. This predictive capacity is critical for enterprise decision-making, enabling leaders to anticipate outcomes rather than react to them.

At the same time, the model must be governed. Consistent application is essential to maintain its integrity. Without governance, assessments become inconsistent, comparisons lose validity, and the model's value diminishes. Governance ensures that the maturity model remains a reliable and repeatable framework across contexts.

In this way, the QACE Maturity Model operates as both a diagnostic and a structural instrument. It defines what maturity is, clarifies how it manifests, and establishes a consistent basis for understanding enterprise systems. Through this lens, maturity becomes not an abstract aspiration but a measurable and governable property of the system—one that reflects the organization's ability to produce outcomes with consistency, alignment, and predictability.

By consistently applying this model, organizations can move from interpreting variability as isolated events to understanding it as a reflection of system design. This shift enables more effective intervention, as actions are directed toward structural causes rather than observable symptoms.

This chapter establishes maturity as a system property, not an assessment label. Together, these concepts define how capability evolves through structural alignment rather than isolated improvement. The next chapter builds on this by explaining how diagnostics reveal system behavior and transform data into actionable insight.

Summary

The QACE Maturity Model provides the structural lens through which enterprise capability is understood, explaining variation in performance as a function of system conditions rather than isolated outcomes. It transforms maturity from a descriptive label into a mechanism for interpreting how systems behave.

By linking observed outcomes to underlying structural conditions, the model enables both diagnostic and predictive insight. Organizations can understand not only why performance varies, but how changes in system structure will influence future outcomes.

The model's effectiveness depends on consistent governance. Without it, assessments become unreliable and comparisons lose validity. When applied correctly, the maturity model establishes a consistent basis for evaluating capability, enabling organizations to move from reactive interpretation to structured, system-level understanding of performance and evolution.

Chapter 7 — Knowledge Check

The QACE Maturity Model

The following questions are designed to verify accurate understanding of how maturity is defined, structured, and interpreted within the QACE system. They assess whether the reader can distinguish maturity from performance, understand how capability evolves structurally, and correctly interpret how system alignment influences outcomes over time.

These questions are nonprocedural. They do not assess implementation techniques or tool usage.

Knowledge Check 7.1 — Maturity Definition

Question
What does maturity represent within an enterprise system, and how does it differ from isolated measures of performance?

Knowledge Check 7.2 — Structural Accumulation

Question

Why must maturity be understood as the accumulation of structural capability rather than a series of isolated improvements?

Knowledge Check 7.3 — System Property

Question

Why is maturity considered a system property rather than an attribute of individual teams or functions?

Knowledge Check 7.4 — Dimensional Integration

Question

Which system dimensions determine maturity within the QACE model, and why must they be evaluated together?

Knowledge Check 7.5 — Maturity Levels

Question

Why do maturity levels represent structural shifts in system behavior rather than incremental improvements in performance?

Knowledge Check 7.6 — Observable Signals

Question

How do observable signals enable reliable interpretation and comparison of maturity across the enterprise?

Knowledge Check 7.7 — Constraints and Progression

Question

What role do constraints play in limiting maturity progression, and how must they be addressed for advancement to occur?

Knowledge Check 7.8 — Role of the Model

Question

What is the primary role of the QACE Maturity Model within the broader QACE system?

Guidance for the Reader

If you can explain how maturity reflects structural alignment across enterprise systems, distinguish capability progression from isolated improvement, and interpret how signals, constraints, and system dimensions influence outcomes, you are prepared to proceed.

This chapter establishes the QACE Maturity Model as the structural framework through which enterprise capability is defined, observed, and evaluated. It demonstrates how maturity emerges from alignment across system dimensions and progresses through observable and governed stages.

The next chapter builds on this foundation by introducing how diagnostic systems interpret these conditions, transforming observable system behavior into actionable intelligence.

Key Takeaways

- Maturity is a system property, not a performance label.
- Capability develops through structural alignment over time.
- Architecture, execution, governance, and feedback must be evaluated together.

- Maturity levels represent structural shifts in system behavior.
- Observable signals make maturity assessable and comparable.
- Progression requires reducing constraints while strengthening alignment.

Questions for Reflection:

- What does this concept reveal about system behavior?
- How would this appear in an enterprise context?
- What signals would indicate this is not functioning correctly?

Chapter 8 — Diagnostics as the Engine of Q Intelligence

Chapter Introduction

Diagnostics operationalize Q Intelligence™ by transforming quality data into structured, interpretable insights that support decision-making and continuous optimization.

Diagnostics operate as a continuous transformation system that converts raw data into structured enterprise intelligence. This transformation is not instantaneous; it progresses through a series of interdependent stages in which each step builds on the previous.

This progression follows a consistent flow:

- Data
- Signals
- Interpretation
- Decision
- Action
- Validation
- Integration

Understanding this sequence is essential, as each stage defines how observation evolves into actionable and validated system behavior.

Figure 8.1 – Diagnostics Transformation Chain

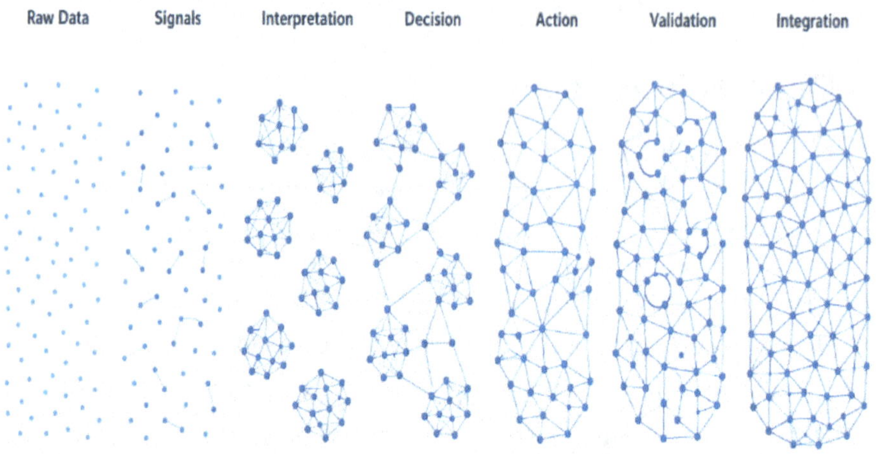

Diagnostics transform data into structured intelligence through a continuous, multi-stage system that connects observation to validated action and enterprise integration.

Rather than functioning as isolated steps, these stages operate as a connected system, ensuring that observation is continuously refined into understanding and coordinated action. (Parnas, 1972)

8.1 — The Role of Diagnostics in Q Intelligence

Diagnostics enable quality to function as intelligence. Without diagnostics, quality remains descriptive—capturing what has occurred while lacking the structural capability to explain why outcomes emerge or how they should influence future decisions. Diagnostics introduce a transformation layer that converts static observation into dynamic insight.

This transformation layer ensures that observation is not treated as an endpoint but as an intermediate state in a broader process of understanding. Diagnostics clarify that data alone does not constitute knowledge; it must be structured and interpreted to reveal meaning aligned with system objectives.

Within Q Intelligence™, diagnostics function as the connective system between measurement and action. This transformation begins with the conversion of data into signals. They establish continuity across the enterprise by ensuring that all observed data contributes to a structured understanding of system behavior. This understanding is not episodic or isolated; it is persistent and continuously evolving as new data enters the system.

Diagnostics do not generate more data; they make existing data meaningful. They elevate quality from a fragmented set of measurements into a coherent intelligence stream that supports enterprise awareness. In doing so, diagnostics establish the foundation for a continuous transformation chain: raw data is not the endpoint of observation but the starting point of intelligence.

Concept Insight: Diagnostics transform measurement into Q Intelligence™ by preserving context, structure, and interpretability across the enterprise.

In an enterprise setting, this typically appears as consistent interpretation of existing performance data across teams and functions, where the same inputs lead to aligned conclusions rather than fragmented or conflicting views. Patterns of performance become recognizable and comparable over time, enabling shared understanding.

When this capability is absent, data accumulates without forming a coherent picture, leading to fragmented interpretations and localized assumptions. Teams may rely on isolated metrics, increasing the risk of misaligned decisions and inconsistent responses across the enterprise.

This directly affects decision quality and system predictability. Without a unified transformation of data into intelligence, the organization experiences variability in judgment, reduced confidence in insights, and weakened ability to anticipate or manage system behavior.

8.2 — From Data to Signals

The transformation from data to signals marks the first critical transition in the transformation chain. Data, in its raw form, reflects discrete observations without inherent meaning. It exists as isolated points—measurements, records, and outcomes—that lack context, direction, or implication.

Diagnostics convert this data into signals by aligning it with outcomes. Signals are not merely aggregated data; they represent patterns, deviations, or consistencies that indicate the state and trajectory of system performance relative to intended outcomes.

Figure 8.2 – Data to Signal Transformation

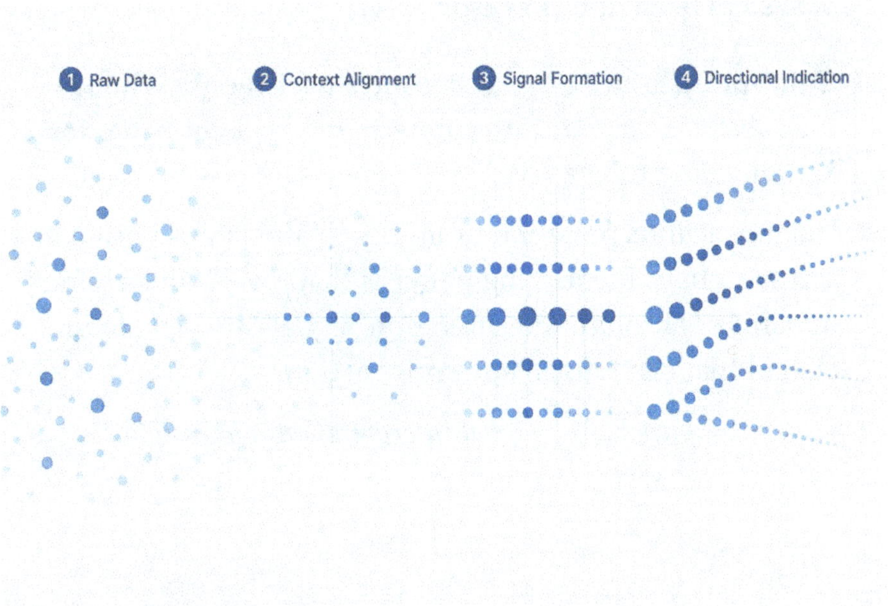

Data becomes meaningful when aligned to outcomes, forming signals that indicate direction and change.

> **Recognizable Situation:**
>
> ***A team reports 94% automated test pass rate week after week. The number is real. The tests are running. But defects continue reaching production – from the same three modules every release. The pass rate is data. The recurrence is a signal. Diagnostics is the discipline of noticing the difference.***

8.3 — Diagnostic Interpretation and Pattern Recognition

Signals alone do not constitute insight. Interpretation is required to translate signals into understanding. This stage introduces analytical reasoning to the diagnostic process, transforming observed patterns into coherent explanations of system behavior. (Leveson, 2012)

> **Concept Insight: A signal becomes useful only when diagnostic interpretation connects it to system behavior and outcome relevance.**

Diagnostic interpretation examines relationships within and across signals, identifying patterns that reveal underlying dynamics. Through interpretation, signals are elevated into insight that can inform enterprise action.

Figure 8.3 – Signal Interpretation into Insight

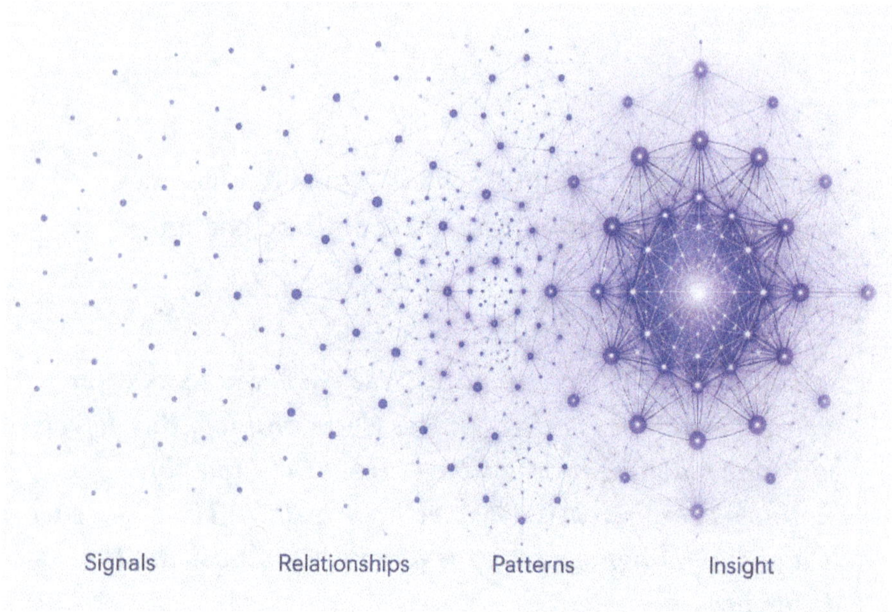

Signals become insight through structured interpretation of relationships and patterns within system context.

8.4 — Diagnostic-Driven Decision Making

Once insight is established, it must be linked to decisions. Diagnostics enable this linkage by providing a structured basis for decision triggers—conditions under which action becomes necessary.

Figure 8.4 – Diagnostic-Driven Decision Triggering

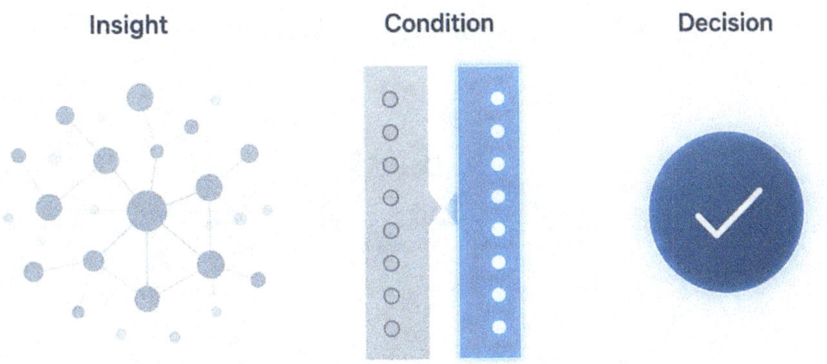

Decisions are triggered by interpreted insight through defined conditions that ensure consistency and alignment.

Diagnostic-driven decision-making ensures that decisions are neither reactive nor arbitrary. Instead, they are directly informed by interpreted insight and aligned with system outcomes.

When this capability is absent, decisions become reactive or inconsistent, often influenced by urgency, perception, or individual interpretation rather than structured insight.

8.5 — Action and Validation Loops

Decision alone does not complete the transformation chain. Action must follow, and its impact must be validated. Diagnostics extend beyond decision-making by establishing feedback loops that confirm whether actions produce the intended outcomes.

> **Concept Insight: Q Intelligence™ is incomplete until action is validated and reintegrated as evidence of system learning.**

Figure 8.5 – Action and Validation Feedback Loop

Validation loops ensure actions are continuously assessed against outcomes, enabling learning and system adaptation.

8.6 — Diagnostic Integration into the QOS

The final stage of the transformation chain is system integration. Diagnostics must not exist as isolated analytical functions; they must be embedded within the enterprise operating model. Within the QOS, diagnostics become a foundational capability that supports continuous intelligence across the organization.

Figure 8.6 – Diagnostics Integrated within the QOS

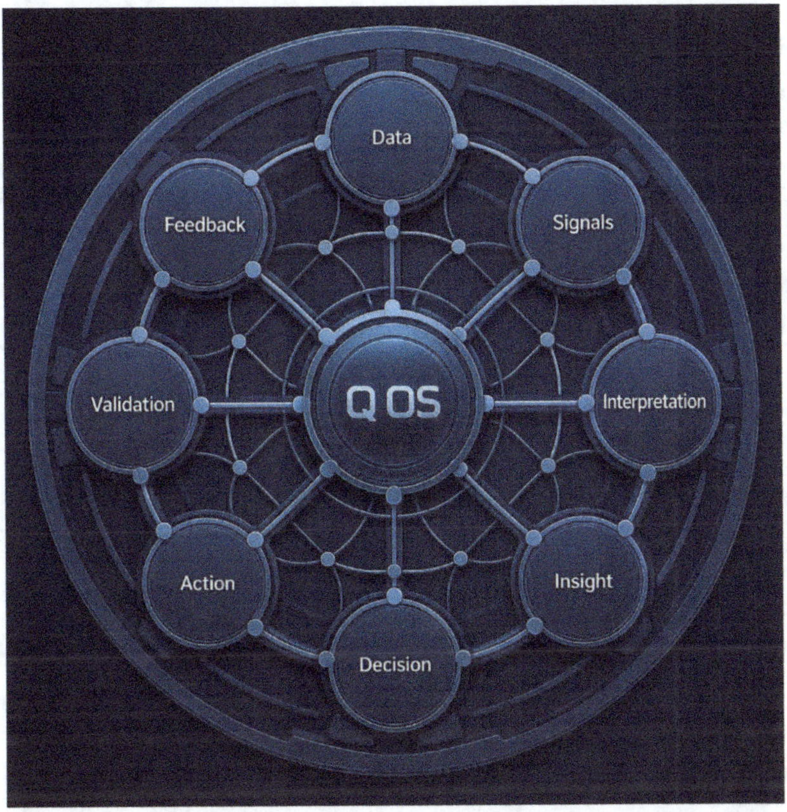

Diagnostics integrate across the [[GL:Enterprise Operating System]] enterprise operating system to create a unified intelligence layer supporting coordinated decision-making.

This chapter establishes diagnostics as the core mechanism that transforms quality from measurement into intelligence. Together, these concepts form a continuous transformation chain that connects data, interpretation, decisions, action, and validation into a unified system of enterprise learning and adaptation.

The next chapter builds on this by positioning automation within the system as a structural capability rather than an execution tool.

Summary

Diagnostics convert observation into structured intelligence by moving data through signals, interpretation, decision, action, validation, and integration. This chapter establishes diagnostics as the mechanism that makes system behavior visible, interpretable, and actionable within Q Intelligence™.

Chapter 8 — Knowledge Check

Diagnostics as the Engine of Q Intelligence

The following questions are designed to verify accurate understanding of how diagnostics transform quality from measurement into structured intelligence. They assess whether the reader can describe the transformation chain, distinguish between data, signals, and insight, and understand how diagnostics enable consistent, evidence-based decision-making and system adaptation.

Knowledge Check 8.1 — Diagnostic Purpose

Question
What role do diagnostics play in transforming quality from measurement into intelligence?

Knowledge Check 8.2 — Transformation Chain

Question
What are the stages of the diagnostic transformation chain, and how does each stage contribute to system understanding?

Knowledge Check 8.3 — Data vs Signals

Question

What is the difference between raw data and signals, and why is this distinction critical?

Knowledge Check 8.4 — Interpretation and Insight

Question

Why do signals alone not constitute insight, and what role does interpretation play in forming understanding?

Knowledge Check 8.5 — Decision Alignment

Question

How do diagnostics ensure that decisions are aligned with system behavior rather than subjective judgment?

Knowledge Check 8.6 — Validation and Learning

Question

What is the role of validation loops in the diagnostic model, and how do they contribute to continuous system improvement?

Knowledge Check 8.7 — Integration into QOS™

Question

Why must diagnostics be integrated into the QOS™ rather than operate as isolated analytical functions?

Knowledge Check 8.8 — System Behavior and Adaptation

Question

What happens to enterprise performance when diagnostics are absent or inconsistently applied across the system?

Guidance for the Reader

If you can explain how diagnostics transform data into structured intelligence, describe the progression from signals to insight, and show how decisions and actions are validated and reintegrated into the system, you are prepared to proceed.

This chapter establishes diagnostics as the continuous transformation mechanism that converts observation into understanding, enabling intelligence to drive decisions, actions, and validated outcomes across the enterprise.

The next chapter builds on this foundation by positioning automation as a structural capability within the system, demonstrating how execution can operate coherently within the intelligence framework established by diagnostics.

Questions for Reflection:

- What does this concept reveal about system behavior?
- How would this appear in an enterprise context?
- What signals would indicate this is not functioning correctly?

Chapter 9 — Automation Architecture

Chapter Introduction

Automation architecture positions execution as a structurally governed expression of system intelligence rather than as an independent source of capability. This chapter clarifies how automation must operate within [[AC:QOS™]] QOS™ (Quality Operating System) to preserve coherence, traceability, and predictable system behavior.

9.1 — The Problem with Automation-as-Tooling

Automation is frequently misunderstood because it is commonly framed as a collection of tools, scripts, or mechanisms intended to make work faster. This framing places automation at the center of attention, where it appears to be responsible for improvement, intelligence, and even decision-making. In this orientation, automation is treated as a capability that can be introduced independently—selected, configured, and deployed to produce outcomes.

This perspective places automation in the wrong role within the system. Automation may appear to act intelligently when it executes quickly and consistently, but without structural grounding, that behavior is not intelligence—it is repetition of instructions. The system must first know what is correct before automation can execute it reliably. (Jois, 2024)

Concept Insight: Automation can execute system intelligence, but it cannot create or validate that intelligence independently.

When treated as tooling, automation is assumed to possess agency. It is expected to determine what actions to take, interpret conditions, and produce results that are meaningful in isolation. As a result, automation becomes conflated with intelligence. Systems rely on automated actions without clearly understanding the structure that defines and constrains them.

The consequence is a drift away from system intelligence. When framed as tooling, automation operates without a governing structure that aligns execution to a coherent system model. It becomes reactive rather than structural, fragmented rather than integrated. Instead of reflecting system intelligence, it introduces behavior that may appear efficient but lacks alignment, which reduces traceability.

This misalignment reveals the core problem: automation-as-tooling substitutes execution in place of structure. It assumes that introducing execution is equivalent to introducing [[GL:System Capability]] system capability. In doing so, it bypasses the requirement that all system behavior must originate from system intelligence. Without that foundation, automation does not enhance the system; it obscures how the system operates.

Transitioning away from this flawed framing requires a redefinition of automation itself—not as tooling, but as a structural component of a system already shaped by intelligence. To clarify this shift, it is necessary to distinguish between automation itself and the architecture that governs it.

9.2 — Automation vs. Automation Architecture

The distinction between automation and automation architecture is not a matter of scale or complexity; it is a matter of role and position within the system. Automation, in isolation, is execution. Automation architecture defines how that execution is structurally embedded within the system.

> **Concept Insight: Automation is execution, while automation architecture is the QOS™ structure that gives execution meaning and constraint.**

Automation, when considered alone, has no inherent meaning beyond execution. On its own, automation executes actions but does not provide meaning for those actions. It cannot define conditions, establish relationships, or enforce coherence. It operates on instructions, not system intelligence.

Automation architecture positions execution within a defined system structure. It ensures that automated actions are not independent occurrences, but expressions of a system that has already been defined through QOS™. In this architecture, automation does not originate behavior; it carries forward behavior that has been structurally specified.

Figure 9.1 – Automation-as-Tooling vs. Automation Architecture

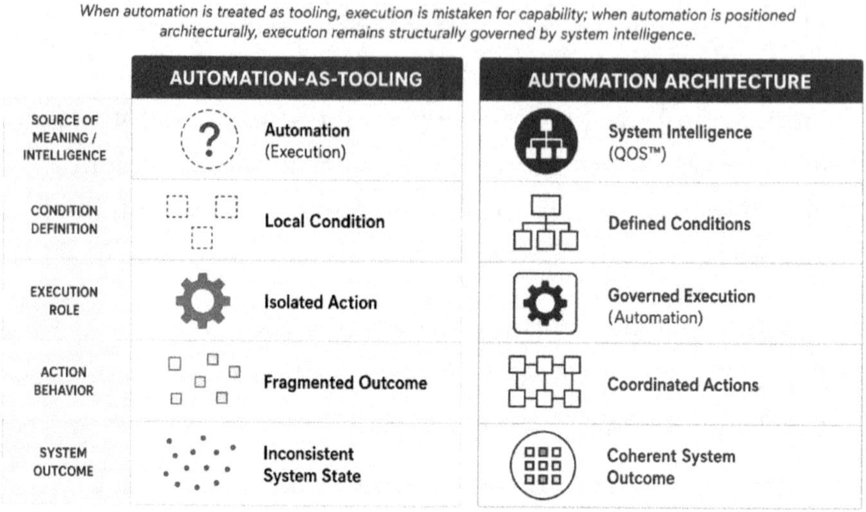

When automation is treated as tooling, execution is mistaken for capability; when automation is positioned architecturally, execution remains structurally governed by system intelligence.

Without this architectural positioning, execution becomes inconsistent. Different automated actions may reflect different assumptions, which leads to fragmentation across the system. With architecture, automation becomes coherent. Every automated action reflects the same underlying structure, ensuring alignment across all system behaviors.

9.3 — Automation as a Structural Layer of QOS™

Within QOS™, automation exists as a structural layer integrated into the system, but not responsible for defining it. This layer does not introduce new rules, decisions, or meanings. It embodies and executes what has already been established.

As a structural layer, automation inherits its form from the system's design. The conditions it operates under, the relationships it reflects, and the behaviors it executes are all defined by system intelligence. Automation does not interpret these elements; it executes them exactly as defined.

This positioning ensures that automation cannot deviate from system intelligence. Because it operates within QOS™, execution is bounded by the same structures that govern all system behavior. It becomes a mechanism of consistency, ensuring that system intelligence is applied uniformly across the system.

Figure 9.2 – Automation as a Structural Layer of QOS™

Automation in QOS™ does not define rules or meaning; it carries forward system-defined behavior as a bounded structural layer.

This layer is not procedural. It does not represent a sequence of steps or actions to be followed. Instead, it represents a structural capability: the ability of the system to execute its defined behaviors without variation.

By existing as a layer within QOS™, automation reinforces system coherence. It amplifies what the system already knows, rather than introducing new interpretations. This preserves the integrity of system intelligence while enabling its consistent expression.

9.4 — Architectural Characteristics of Automation Systems

Automation systems, when properly positioned within architecture, exhibit distinct characteristics that differentiate them from tool-based implementations. These characteristics are not optional attributes; they are indicators of correct structural positioning. When any of these characteristics are missing, it signals that automation is not fully aligned with system intelligence. (Forsgren et al., 2018)

First, automation systems are dependent. They rely entirely on upstream system intelligence for their definition. They neither operate independently nor introduce new logic. Their behavior is fully derived from the structure of the system.

Second, automation systems are consistent. Because they execute predefined structures, their behavior does not vary. This consistency is not driven by speed or reliability; it reflects structural coherence.

Third, automation systems are transparent. Their behavior can be traced directly back to system definitions. There is no ambiguity about why an action occurs, because each action directly reflects a defined condition within QOS™.

Fourth, automation systems are bounded. They operate within clearly defined limits. They do not expand beyond their structural role or adapt in ways that alter system intelligence. This bounded nature prevents automation from becoming a source of uncontrolled variation.

Finally, automation systems are non-generative. They do not create new forms of intelligence, rules, or decisions. They exist solely to execute what has already been defined.

This distinction becomes increasingly important in the age of Artificial Intelligence. Generative and agentic AI systems may create content, recommendations, code, tests, or proposed actions. However, within QOS™, intelligence refers to validated organizational meaning, governance, and decision structures. AI may assist in creating artifacts, but it does not automatically establish the authority, constraints, relationships, or shared understanding required for consistent enterprise decision-making.

9.5 — Automation Design Patterns (Conceptual)

Within a structural framework, patterns emerge that describe how automation consistently expresses system intelligence. These patterns are not procedures or techniques; they are conceptual representations of alignment between execution and system structure. They describe how alignment manifests, not how it is constructed.

Structural mirroring occurs when automation reflects system definitions directly without transformation. In this pattern, execution directly represents system state, ensuring that behavior remains aligned without interpretation.

Conditional expression occurs when automation operates only within explicitly defined conditions. These conditions are defined by the system structure, not by automation itself. Automation simply enacts the outcomes associated with those conditions.

Relationship propagation occurs when automation maintains the integrity of relationships defined within the system. In this pattern, execution ensures that connections between system elements remain consistent across all actions.

Boundary enforcement occurs when automation operates strictly within the limits defined by the system. It ensures that actions do not extend beyond what is structurally permitted, preserving system integrity.

These patterns illustrate that automation does not adapt or innovate independently. It expresses system design in a consistent and predictable manner. Each pattern reinforces the dependency of automation on system intelligence, ensuring that execution remains aligned with defined structure.

9.6 — Automation Anti-Patterns and Failure Modes

When automation deviates from its architectural role, structural failures emerge. These failures are not technical in nature; they are structural violations. They occur when automation is positioned or interpreted incorrectly within the system.

Intelligence substitution occurs when automation is expected to make decisions or define behavior. In this scenario, execution replaces system intelligence, leading to actions that are not grounded in defined structure.

Procedural inflation occurs when automation is described as a sequence of actions or workflows. This framing shifts focus from structure to steps, which obscures the relationship between execution and system intelligence.

Framework reclassification occurs when collections of automated actions are treated as architecture. This conflates execution with structure, leading to systems that appear organized but lack a coherent foundation.

Autonomy drift occurs when automation operates beyond its defined boundaries. When automation expands or adapts without structural grounding, it introduces behavior that cannot be traced back to system definitions.

Figure 9.3 – Boundary Violation in Automation

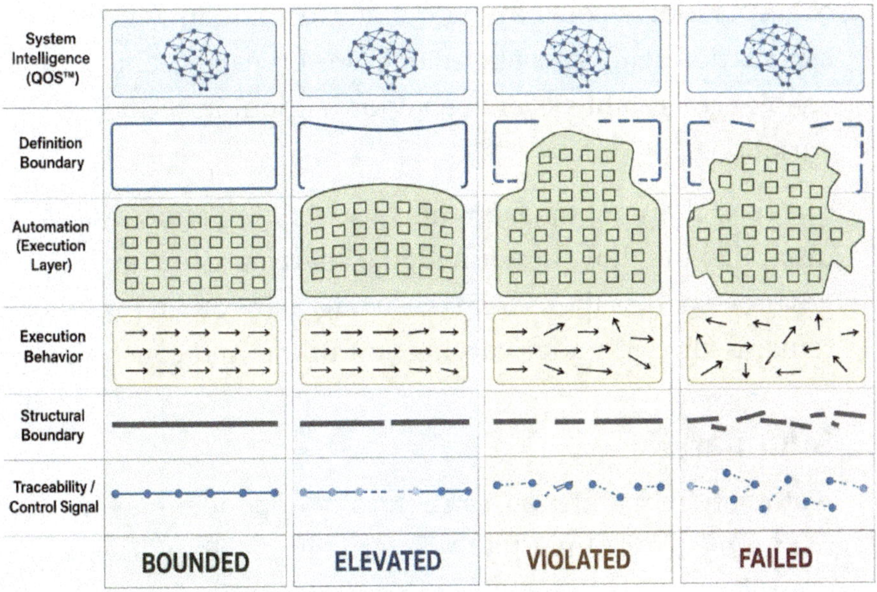

Automation failure begins when execution is elevated beyond its structural role, causing decisions or behavior to arise outside system intelligence.

These anti-patterns reveal a consistent theme: failure occurs when automation is elevated beyond its role. When treated as a source of intelligence, a governing mechanism, or an independent capability, automation disrupts the system.

Maintaining architectural integrity requires strict adherence to the principle that automation does not decide, define, or govern. It executes—structurally, consistently, and entirely within the system defined by QOS™.

Concept Insight: Architectural integrity depends on keeping automation bounded, traceable, and subordinate to QOS™ intelligence.

This chapter establishes automation as a structurally dependent layer within QOS™, clarifying that its role is to express—not define—system intelligence. Together, these concepts form a coherent model of execution in which automation reinforces alignment, preserves traceability, and enables consistent system behavior without introducing variation.

The next chapter builds on this by extending structural discipline into how non-functional characteristics are governed across the system, ensuring that system behavior remains aligned under varying conditions and constraints.

Summary

Automation operates as a structurally dependent layer within the [[AC:QACE]] QACE (Quality, Automation, Compliance, Engineering) system, responsible for executing defined logic but not for making decisions or defining behavior. Its value comes from reinforcing alignment, preserving traceability, and enabling consistent execution within the boundaries set by system intelligence.

When automation is elevated beyond this role—acting as a source of intelligence, governance mechanism, or independent capability—structural failures emerge. These failures disrupt coherence, obscure the relationship between execution and intent, and introduce behavior that cannot be traced back to defined system conditions.

Maintaining architectural integrity requires strict adherence to this boundary. Automation must remain bounded, transparent, and subordinate to QOS™ intelligence to ensure that execution reinforces, rather than distorts, system behavior.

Chapter 9 — Knowledge Check

Automation Architecture

The following questions are designed to verify accurate understanding of how automation functions as a structural component within an enterprise system. They assess whether the reader can distinguish automation from automation architecture, understand the relationship between execution and system intelligence, and recognize how automation must be governed to preserve coherence, traceability, and consistency across the enterprise.

These questions are nonprocedural. They do not assess implementation techniques, tools, or platforms.

Knowledge Check 9.1 — Automation Role

Question

Why is automation not considered a source of intelligence within an enterprise system?

Knowledge Check 9.2 — Automation vs Architecture

Question

What is the difference between automation as execution and automation architecture as a structural system component?

Knowledge Check 9.3 — Misinterpretation of Automation

Question

What happens when automation is treated as tooling rather than positioned within system architecture?

Knowledge Check 9.4 — Structural Dependency

Question

Why must automation depend entirely on system intelligence rather than operate independently?

Knowledge Check 9.5 — Characteristics of Aligned Automation

Question

What structural characteristics indicate that automation is correctly aligned within the system?

Knowledge Check 9.6 — Design Patterns

Question

What do automation design patterns represent, and why are they not procedural instructions?

Knowledge Check 9.7 — Anti-Patterns and Failure Modes

Question

What structural failures occur when automation is elevated beyond its intended role?

Knowledge Check 9.8 — System Integrity

Question

How does correctly positioned automation preserve system coherence, traceability, and predictability?

Guidance for the Reader

If you can distinguish between automation and automation architecture, explain why execution must remain dependent on system intelligence, and identify how structural alignment prevents fragmentation and inconsistency, you are prepared to proceed.

This chapter establishes automation as a structurally governed layer within QOS™, clarifying that its role is to express system intelligence rather than define or replace it. It demonstrates how proper architectural positioning preserves coherence, traceability, and consistent system behavior across the enterprise.

The next chapter builds on this by extending structural discipline into how non-functional characteristics are governed across the system, ensuring that system behavior remains aligned under varying conditions and constraints.

Key Takeaways

- Diagnostics transform quality data into structured intelligence that supports consistent decision-making.
- Signals become useful only when interpreted within system context and validated through feedback.
- Automation is execution; automation architecture defines how execution remains governed by system intelligence.
- Correctly positioned automation preserves consistency by remaining dependent, bounded, transparent, and non-generative.

Summary

Automation becomes reliable only when it is structurally governed by system intelligence. This chapter distinguishes automation from automation architecture and establishes automation as a bounded execution layer that preserves coherence, traceability, and consistency across the enterprise.

Questions for Reflection:

- What does this concept reveal about system behavior when execution is separated from intelligence?
- How would this appear in an enterprise context where multiple automation initiatives operate simultaneously?
- What signals would indicate that automation is functioning outside of its intended structural role?

Chapter 10 — Accessibility, Internationalization, and Usability as Quality Dimensions

Chapter Introduction

Accessibility, internationalization, and usability are often treated as secondary concerns within system development—applied after core functionality has been established or isolated within presentation and interface layers. This treatment reflects a broader misalignment in how system quality is understood. (ISO/IEC/IEEE 42010, 2011)

This chapter repositions these characteristics as fundamental quality dimensions that directly shape system behavior. Rather than existing at the periphery, they operate as constraints that influence how the system is interpreted, accessed, and used across different contexts.

By examining these dimensions as intrinsic properties of the system, this chapter extends the architectural perspective established in earlier sections. It demonstrates that system quality is not solely a function of internal design but is inseparable from how consistently the system can be engaged with across real-world conditions.

Establishing accessibility, internationalization, and usability as quality dimensions provides the foundation for understanding how systems achieve coherent, reliable behavior across diverse users and environments.

10.1 — The Misclassification of Accessibility, Internationalization, and Usability

Accessibility, internationalization, and usability have historically been interpreted as peripheral concerns—often positioned at the outermost layer of system development, where interface decisions, compliance obligations, or localized adjustments are addressed after primary system construction is complete. This positioning has led to a consistent misclassification: these characteristics are treated as attributes of presentation rather than as properties of the system itself.

Within this framing, accessibility is reduced to accommodation, internationalization to translation, and usability to user interface refinement. Each is perceived as a downstream concern, subordinate to what is considered the "core" system. This perspective separates how the system operates from how it is experienced and interpreted across diverse contexts.

Such misclassification obscures a fundamental reality: the system does not exist independently of its interpretability, reach, or usability. The system is not only defined by its internal logic but by its ability to be engaged with effectively across real-world conditions. When interpretation, reach, and usability are separated from system definition, the system is conceptually fragmented.

> **Concept Insight: A system cannot be considered complete if its quality cannot be accessed, interpreted, and used consistently.**

Figure 10.1 – Misclassification vs System Reality

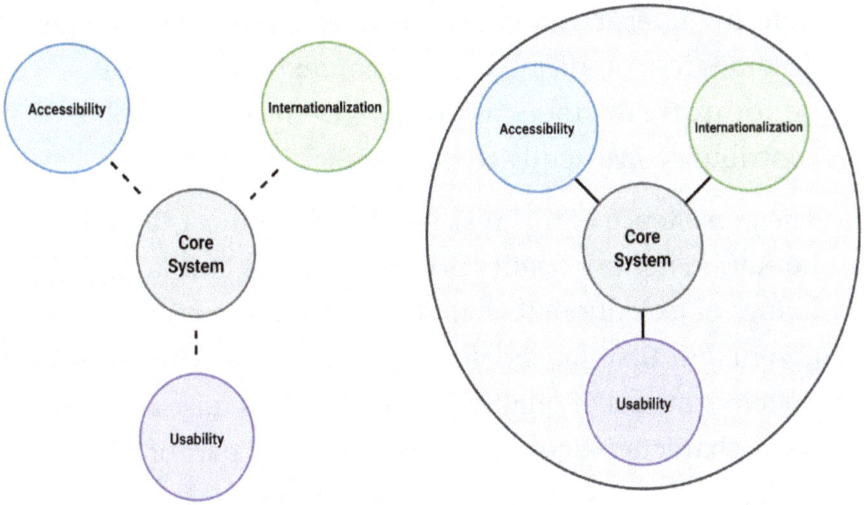

Misclassification fragments system behavior; embedding restores coherence.

In an enterprise setting, this typically appears as systems that are technically complete yet inconsistently adopted, misunderstood across teams, or selectively usable by only a subset of users. The system behaves as though it is operational, but its practical footprint is uneven and constrained by how different users are able to interact with it.

When this capability is absent, the system begins to exhibit segmentation effects—where usability, access, or interpretation varies by user group. This results in partial system engagement, inconsistent outputs, and an increasing reliance on workarounds or external clarification to sustain functionality.

This directly affects the system's perceived completeness and reliability. Decision-making becomes uneven due to differing interpretations, risk increases as system behavior becomes less predictable across contexts, and overall performance degrades as portions of the system fail to contribute consistently to outcomes.

The persistence of this misclassification reflects a structural limitation in how quality is conceptualized rather than a failure of execution. It is not that these dimensions are absent, but that they are located incorrectly within the system's model of quality. To address this misclassification, these characteristics must be redefined as part of the system itself.

10.2 — Defining These as Quality Dimensions

To correct this misalignment, accessibility, internationalization, and usability must be defined explicitly as embedded quality dimensions. They are not features that can be added or omitted without consequence. They are foundational properties that shape how the system exists across populations and contexts.

As quality dimensions, they describe characteristics of the system that determine whether it can be meaningfully used, understood, and sustained. Accessibility reflects the system's capacity to be reached and used across variation in human ability. Internationalization represents the system's ability to operate coherently across linguistic, cultural, and regional boundaries. Usability expresses the degree to which the system's behavior aligns with human comprehension, expectation, and interaction.

Figure 10.2 – Quality Dimensions Define System Existence

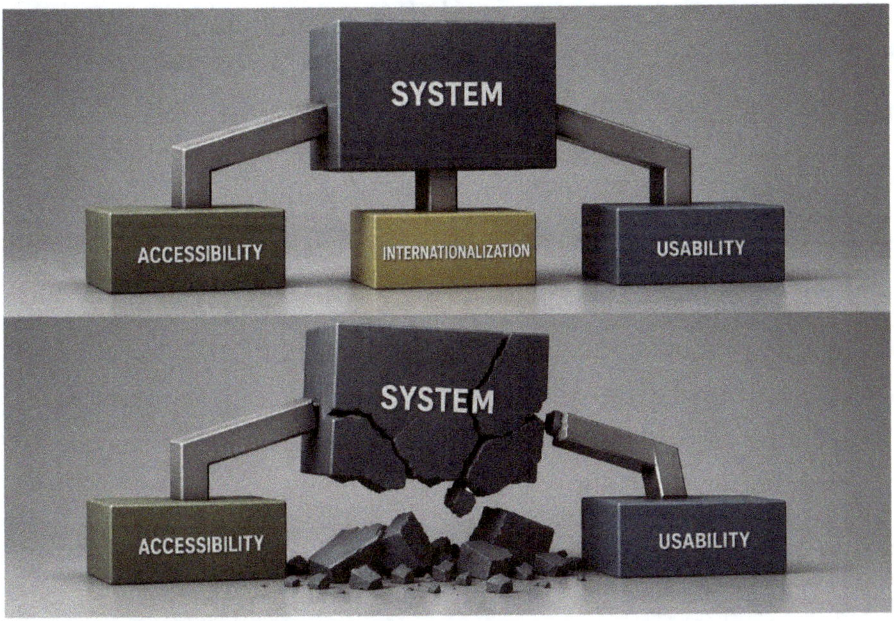

Accessibility, internationalization, and usability function as embedded quality dimensions that determine whether a system can exist as a coherent, usable, and interpretable entity across real-world conditions.

In practice, these dimensions appear as consistent patterns in how quality is evaluated and enforced across the organization. When applied correctly, they create alignment between intent and outcome, reducing variability in performance.

In an enterprise setting, this typically appears as systems that maintain consistent interpretation and usability regardless of user role, geographic location, or context of use. Interactions remain stable, and outputs are understood uniformly across diverse participants without requiring additional adjustment or explanation.

When this capability is absent, system behavior becomes fragmented across contexts. Different users experience variations in meaning, access, or interaction patterns, leading to divergent outcomes from the same system inputs. This introduces inconsistencies that are not attributable to system logic but to its inability to sustain coherence.

This directly affects decision quality and operational predictability. Outcomes cannot be reliably generalized across contexts, increasing the likelihood of misinterpretation and reducing confidence in system-generated results. Over time, this erodes trust in the system as a dependable source of truth.

These are not independent or optional traits. They determine whether other aspects of quality can be meaningfully experienced. Without accessibility, the system cannot be reached. Without internationalization, it cannot function across contexts. Without usability, it cannot be understood. Each dimension determines whether the system's quality can be perceived and sustained.

Concept Insight: Accessibility, internationalization, and usability are enabling quality dimensions that determine whether other quality attributes can be realized.

Conceptual Interpretation: A system may appear complete in design, yet if users cannot access it, understand it, or use it across contexts, its quality cannot be realized in practice. These dimensions determine whether the system exists as a usable reality rather than a theoretical construct.

Recognizing them as quality dimensions repositions them within the system's conceptual foundation. They no longer exist as downstream considerations but as core determinants of system viability across real-world conditions.

10.3 — Structural Role Within QOS™

Within QOS™, these dimensions operate as embedded characteristics of the system. They are not layered above or beneath other elements but interwoven into the system's definition of quality itself. Their influence is continuous and built into the system structure, shaping how the system behaves across all interactions and contexts.

Because QOS™ defines quality as a system-level construct, accessibility, internationalization, and usability are not isolated domains; they participate in the formation of every quality expression. They influence how processes are perceived, how outputs are interpreted, and how system behaviors are understood across different users and environments.

Figure 10.3 – Embedded Dimensions Within QOS™

Within QOS™, accessibility, internationalization, and usability are embedded and continuously active structural dimensions that shape all system interactions, not separate layers applied at specific stages.

Their structural role is therefore not additive but integrative. They do not contribute separate outcomes; they shape the conditions under which all outcomes exist. As embedded dimensions, they are inseparable from the system quality state. Their presence or absence alters the nature of the system itself, not merely its presentation.

This positioning also ensures that these dimensions are continuously active. They are not triggered at specific points in the system lifecycle but are inherent to its operation. Every interaction reflects their influence, whether explicitly recognized or not.

10.4 — System Implications and Constraints

Because accessibility, internationalization, and usability function as embedded quality dimensions, they impose structural constraints on the system. These constraints are not limitations but defining conditions that govern how the system can validly operate. (Leveson, 2012)

> **Concept Insight: In QOS™, constraints define the valid operating space where quality remains coherent across real-world variation.**

Accessibility constrains the system to maintain reach across varied human capabilities, preventing designs that rely on narrow assumptions of ability or interaction. Internationalization constrains the system to remain coherent across multiple cultural and linguistic contexts, disallowing behaviors that depend on fixed interpretations or region-specific norms. Usability constrains the system to align with human cognition and expectation, eliminating patterns that introduce unnecessary complexity or ambiguity.

These constraints shape the system at a foundational level. They act as governing conditions that ensure the system remains aligned with real-world variability. Rather than limiting design, they establish the parameters within which the system can maintain consistent behavior across diverse users and contexts. They influence how information is structured, how interactions unfold, and how behaviors remain consistent across contexts. The system cannot be fully formed without adherence to these conditions. When violated, discontinuities emerge between the system's intended function and its realized experience.

Figure 10.4 – Constraint Boundary Model

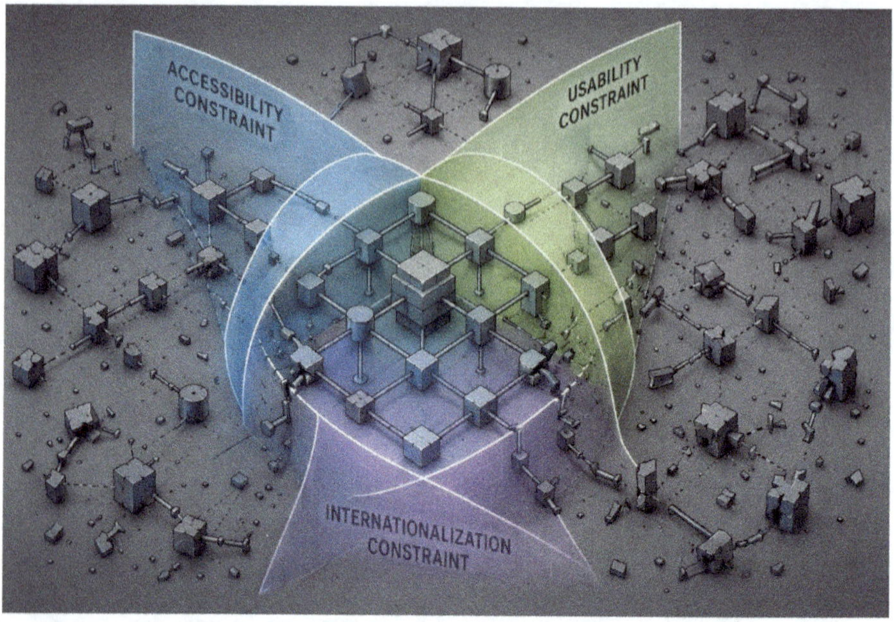

Accessibility, internationalization, and usability act as structural constraint boundaries that define the valid space of system behavior, ensuring the system operates coherently across all contexts.

In an enterprise setting, this typically appears as systems that inherently avoid dependency on narrow assumptions—such as fixed user behaviors or localized norms—resulting in interactions and outputs that remain stable even as user characteristics or contexts change.

When this capability is absent, systems tend to exhibit brittle behavior. Small variations in user context or interpretation lead to disproportionate disruptions in system interaction, causing breakdowns that require manual adjustment or reinterpretation to continue operation.

This directly affects system resilience and consistency. Performance becomes dependent on ideal conditions, risk increases due to sensitivity to variation, and operational continuity is threatened as the system fails to adapt coherently across contexts.

Importantly, these constraints are not externally imposed requirements but inherent consequences of recognizing these dimensions as part of quality. They define the boundaries within which the system can operate coherently and sustainably. Without them, the system's structure becomes internally inconsistent, producing outcomes that cannot be reliably interpreted or used. When these constraints are not met, their absence becomes observable within the system.

10.5 — Observable Signals and Failure Modes

The presence or absence of these dimensions is not abstract; it manifests through observable system-level signals. These signals serve as tangible indicators of the system's internal alignment. They provide a direct connection between the system's structural quality and its external expression, allowing deficiencies to be identified through patterns of interaction rather than theoretical analysis. When accessibility, internationalization, or usability are compromised, the system exhibits patterns that indicate degradation in quality.

In an enterprise setting, this typically appears as recurring interaction patterns—such as repeated user errors, inconsistent interpretation of outputs, or uneven engagement levels across user groups—that reflect underlying inconsistencies in accessibility, internationalization, or usability.

When this capability is absent, these signals intensify and propagate. Isolated issues evolve into systemic patterns, where friction, confusion, or exclusion become normalized aspects of interacting with the system rather than exceptions.

This directly affects the system's stability and trustworthiness. Persistent negative signals reduce confidence in system outputs, increase the cognitive burden on users, and introduce uncertainty into decision-making processes, ultimately diminishing the system's effectiveness as a reliable operational asset.

Failures in accessibility manifest as exclusionary signals—points within the system where interaction ceases to be possible for certain users. Failures in internationalization appear as contextual breakdowns, where meaning does not transfer across languages or cultures, resulting in misinterpretation or invalid operation. Failures in usability are reflected in friction, misalignment, or confusion, where interaction with the system becomes inconsistent with human expectations.

These signals do not occur at the interface alone. They propagate throughout the system. They affect how processes are executed, how outputs are understood, and how trust in the system is established or eroded. Because these dimensions are embedded, their failure is systemic rather than localized.

Figure 10.5 – Signal Propagation and Failure Model

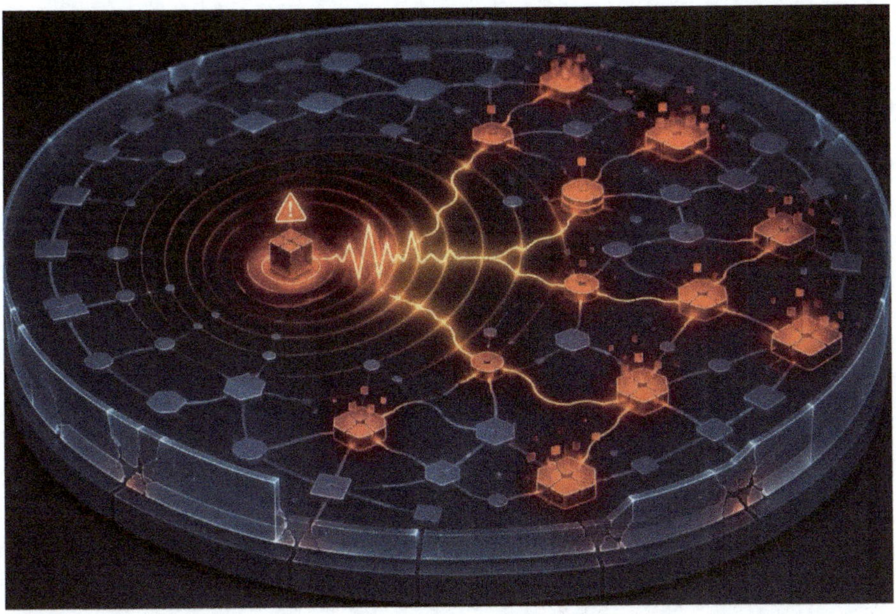

Failures in accessibility, internationalization, or usability originate structurally and propagate through the system as observable signals that degrade stability and trust.

The observability of these signals provides evidence of the system's quality state. They reveal not only that a deficiency exists but that it originates from a structural misalignment. In this way, accessibility, internationalization, and usability act as diagnostic dimensions, exposing where the system's quality model has failed to fully integrate them. These observable signals also establish the basis for structured validation, where system behavior is not inferred but explicitly produced and interpreted through defined mechanisms.

10.6 — Integration with Broader Quality System

Within the broader quality system defined by QOS™, accessibility, internationalization, and usability do not operate independently; they reinforce and are reinforced by other quality dimensions. Their integration is essential to maintaining a coherent and unified model of quality.

These dimensions influence how other qualities are expressed and experienced. They function as enabling conditions through which other quality attributes become observable and meaningful. Without their presence, other qualities remain theoretically defined but inconsistently realized in actual system behavior. Reliability, for example, cannot be meaningfully assessed without usability, as reliability depends on the user's ability to interact with the system consistently. Similarly, correctness is contingent on internationalization, as correctness must hold across contextual variations. Completeness is influenced by accessibility, as a system cannot be considered complete if it is not reachable by its intended participants.

Figure 10.6 – Integrated Quality Dependency System

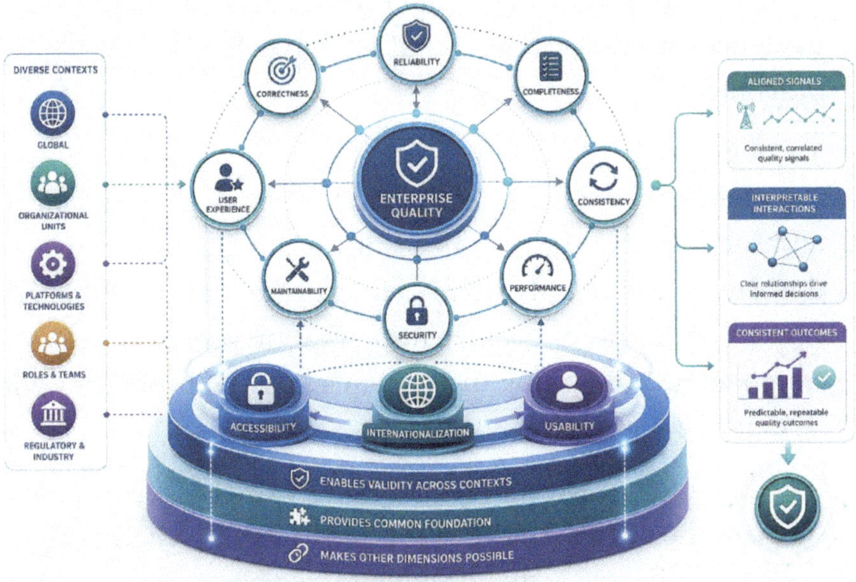

Accessibility, internationalization, and usability act as enabling conditions that sustain the validity of all other quality dimensions within the system.

In an enterprise setting, this typically appears as a system where reliability, correctness, and completeness are consistently experienced across all contexts because accessibility, internationalization, and usability ensure that interactions with the system remain aligned and interpretable.

When this capability is absent, other quality dimensions begin to appear unstable or contradictory. Reliability may seem inconsistent, correctness may vary by context, and completeness may be questioned based on who is able to interact with the system effectively.

This directly affects the coherence of the overall quality model. The system's quality cannot be uniformly validated, increasing ambiguity in performance assessment and reducing the organization's ability to make confident, evidence-based decisions about system behavior and outcomes.

Through these interactions, accessibility, internationalization, and usability contribute to the stability and coherence of the overall quality system. They ensure that quality is not only defined internally but is also realized across conditions of use. Their integration prevents fragmentation, aligning the system's internal properties with its external expression.

As embedded quality dimensions, they do not expand the scope of the system but clarify it. They define whether the system can be understood as whole, consistent, and viable. Their presence ensures that quality is not an abstract construct but a sustained reality across diverse contexts and conditions.

In this way, the system's quality is not merely constructed—it is experienced, interpreted, and sustained through these foundational dimensions.

This chapter establishes the constraints required to maintain consistent system behavior.

Together, these dimensions define the conditions under which system outcomes can be interpreted consistently across contexts.

These conditions establish the foundation for validation as a system capability. Validation does not operate as an evaluative activity but as a structured mechanism for observing and expressing system behavior.

The next chapter builds on this foundation by defining the QACE Validation Model, introducing validation layers, cross-cutting validation dimensions, and signal production as the structural means through which system behavior is made visible and measurable.

Chapter 10 — Knowledge Check

Accessibility, Internationalization, and Usability as Quality Dimensions

The following questions are designed to verify accurate understanding of how accessibility, internationalization, and usability function as embedded quality dimensions within enterprise systems. They assess whether the reader can distinguish these characteristics from interface features, understand how they act as structural constraints, and recognize their role in sustaining system coherence, interpretability, and reliability across diverse contexts.

These questions are nonprocedural. They do not assess implementation techniques, tools, or compliance activities.

Knowledge Check 10.1 — Misclassification

Question
Why are accessibility, internationalization, and usability frequently misclassified within enterprise systems?

Knowledge Check 10.2 — Quality Dimensions

Question
What changes when accessibility, internationalization, and usability are understood as quality dimensions rather than external attributes?

Knowledge Check 10.3 — System Integration

Question

Why must these dimensions be embedded within the system rather than applied at the interface or implementation level?

Knowledge Check 10.4 — Structural Constraints

Question

How do accessibility, internationalization, and usability act as constraints on system behavior?

Knowledge Check 10.5 — System Coherence

Question

What happens to system coherence and decision reliability when these dimensions are inconsistently applied?

Knowledge Check 10.6 — Observable Signals

Question

How do failures in accessibility, internationalization, or usability manifest as observable system signals?

Knowledge Check 10.7 — Failure Propagation

Question

Why do failures in these dimensions propagate systemically rather than remain localized?

Knowledge Check 10.8 — Integration with Other Quality Attributes

Question

How do accessibility, internationalization, and usability influence the validity of other quality dimensions such as reliability, correctness, and completeness?

Guidance for the Reader

If you can explain why accessibility, internationalization, and usability must be treated as embedded quality dimensions, describe how they function as structural constraints, and identify how their presence or absence affects system behavior and coherence, you are prepared to proceed.

This chapter establishes these dimensions as foundational conditions of system quality, defining how systems must be structured to remain interpretable, usable, and consistent across real-world contexts. It positions them as integral to the system's ability to exist as a coherent and reliable entity.

The next chapter builds on this foundation by defining validation as a system-level capability, introducing how system behavior is observed, interpreted, and made measurable through structured validation models.

Key Takeaways

- Accessibility, internationalization, and usability are embedded quality dimensions, not downstream presentation concerns.
- These dimensions act as constraints that preserve system coherence across diverse users, contexts, and operating conditions.

Summary

This chapter establishes accessibility, internationalization, and usability as quality dimensions that shape how systems are interpreted, reached, and used. By embedding these dimensions into QOS™, the system maintains coherent behavior across real-world variation rather than relying on downstream adjustment.

Questions for Reflection:

- What does this concept reveal about system behavior when access, interpretation, or usability varies across users?
- How would this appear in an enterprise context where multiple roles, regions, and capabilities interact with the same system?
- What signals would indicate that accessibility, internationalization, or usability are not functioning as embedded quality dimensions?

Chapter 11 — QACE Validation Model

Chapter Introduction

When validation is treated as a test phase, a checkpoint, or a downstream activity, engineers see system behavior only in pieces. One team may validate a component, another may validate an end-to-end flow, and another may review outputs after execution. Each may produce useful results, but the system as a whole still lacks a stable, governed way to see what is happening across all domains of operation. That weakens diagnostics, breaks comparability, and leaves important behavior implicit.

The QACE Validation Model addresses that problem by defining validation as a governed [[GL:System Capability]] system capability embedded within the QACE system. In practical terms, validation is not added after work is complete. It is built into how the system continuously observes behavior, interprets what it finds, and produces evidence the engineering system can use. (ISO, 2021)

> **Concept Insight: Validation in QACE is a governed capability that makes system behavior visible before it becomes interpreted as quality evidence.**

Its purpose is to provide structured system visibility through layered observation and signal production. That means the model defines where behavior must be observed, how that observation must be applied consistently, and what measurable outputs must be produced so the system can understand its own state.

Figure 11.1 – Validation as a Governed System Capability vs. Phase-Based Validation

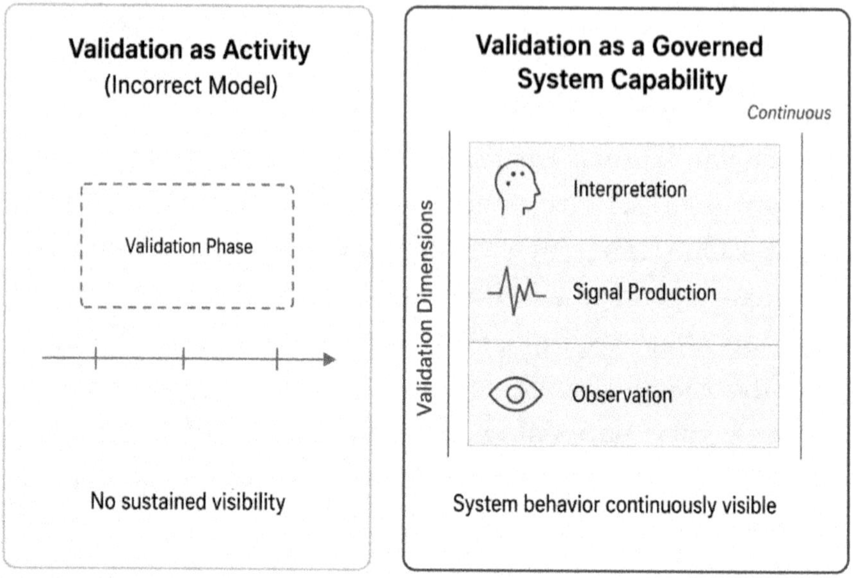

Validation is not an activity or phase but a governed system capability that continuously enables structured system visibility.

11.1 Purpose of the QACE Validation Model

Within QACE, validation exists to make system behavior explicit, interpretable, and consistently measurable across all domains of operation. It does this by establishing defined validation layers, applying cross-cutting validation dimensions across those layers, and producing signals that can be captured in validation outputs, logs, dashboards, or other governed evidence channels.

The result is a model that enables consistency of execution, coherence of diagnostics, and alignment of quality intelligence across the system. The model ensures that validation does not depend on individual interpretation, workflow variation, or implicit practices. Instead, it operates as a governed structure that defines how system behavior is observed, expressed, and interpreted.

In figures, a governed system capability is represented through defined structure, consistent application rules, and the absence of arbitrary or ad hoc variation. [[GL:Governance]] Governance is shown through structural consistency, not through additional visual symbols or overlays.

11.2 Position Within the QACE System

Within the QACE system, the Validation Model operates as a core system capability embedded in the QOS™, rather than as an external or downstream function. It is positioned alongside other structural components that define how quality is engineered, enforced, and understood.

In visual representation, QOS™ is treated as a containing system boundary. The Validation Model is shown as a structural component within this boundary, not as an external or downstream element. Other structural components may be implied but are not required to be enumerated within this chapter's figures.

This position is important because validation does not begin after development and does not conclude when a lifecycle stage ends. It operates continuously, providing structured system visibility across all lifecycle stages. In practice, this means validation remains present while the system is executing, changing, integrating, and producing outcomes. It is not waiting at the end for a final check.

In visual representation, continuous operation is expressed through persistent structural presence rather than through flow, sequence, or timeline indicators. The model is shown as always present within the system, not activated or triggered.

Figure 11.2 – Embedded Validation Within the QOS™ System

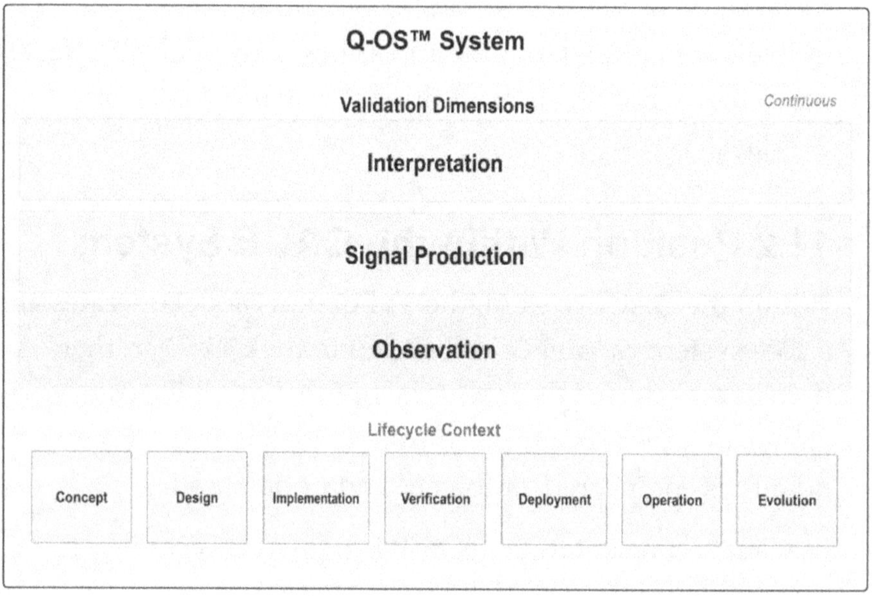

Validation operates as a continuously embedded system capability within QOS™, independent of lifecycle sequencing.

Its position ensures that validation remains invariant across contexts, execution patterns, and organizational structures. Teams may work differently. Execution may be manual, automated, or hybrid. Delivery patterns may change. The model does not change with those conditions, because it is part of the operating structure of the system rather than a local process choice.

This positioning reinforces that validation is not reactive. It is not triggered by events, nor is it initiated as a checkpoint. Instead, it is persistently active, structurally embedded, and foundational to system understanding.

To enable this continuous presence, the validation model is defined through a structured set of components.

> **Recognizable Situation:**
>
> ***A leadership team celebrates a major "quality improvement" — 40% fewer escaped defects. Six months later, no one can explain which decisions caused it, which actions carried the change, or whether the improvement will hold. Something worked. Nothing was validated. The organization has a result but no chain — and no ability to reproduce, defend, or scale what happened.***

11.3 Structural Overview of the Model

The QACE Validation Model is defined by three primary structural components:

- Explicit validation layers
- Cross-cutting validation dimensions
- Signal production aligned to system behavior

These components operate together as a single governed structure. Validation layers define where system behavior is observed. Cross-cutting validation dimensions define how system behavior is observed across those layers. Signal production provides measurable outputs that reflect system behavior at each layer.

In operational terms, the model answers three questions. First, where in the system is behavior being observed? That is the role of validation layers. Second, what consistent evaluation perspective is being applied at that point of observation? That is the role of cross-cutting validation dimensions. Third, what measurable result is produced from that observation? That is the role of signal production.

A layer provides the observation boundary. A dimension provides the evaluation perspective. Their intersection produces a signal. That signal is the governed output the system can capture, compare, diagnose, and use as evidence. (Weill & Ross, 2004)

Concept Insight: The layer-dimension intersection is the structural point where QACE converts observation into traceable validation evidence.

This structure is intentionally independent of execution concerns. Validation execution modes operate within the structure, but they do not define it. The model remains stable regardless of how validation is performed.

The structural design ensures that validation cannot be reduced to isolated efforts, informal practices, or implicit knowledge. It enforces clarity, separation of concerns, and system-wide consistency.

To reduce ambiguity in interpretation, the model must be understood progressively. Each component—layers, cross-cutting dimensions, and signal production—is first established independently before being understood as a unified system. This sequencing preserves structural clarity and prevents interpretation as a single undifferentiated construct.

These structural components are unified through a canonical representation that expresses their interaction.

Figure 11.3 – QACE Validation Model Structure

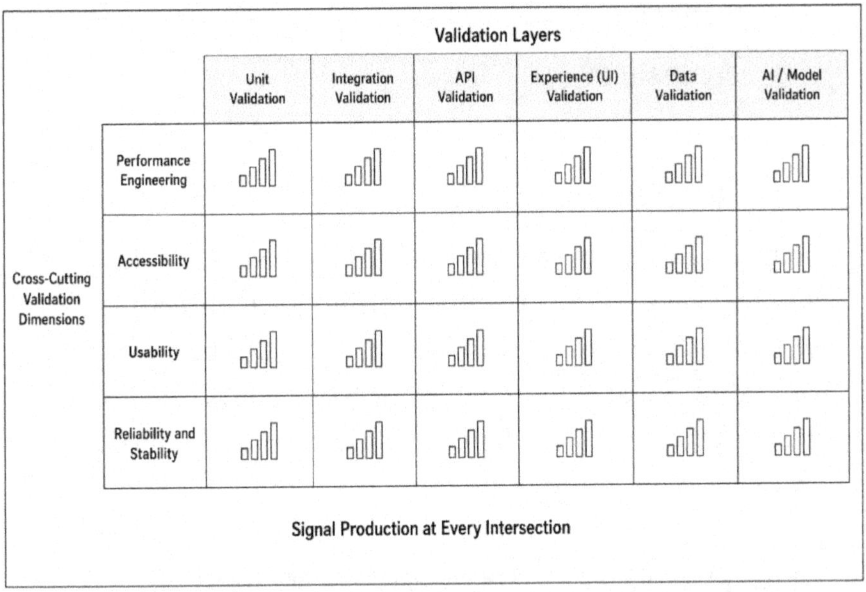

The validation model is defined by layers, cross-cutting dimensions, and signal production forming a unified governed structure..

Canonical Structural Set

Within the QACE Validation Model, the structure is defined through a fixed set of validation layers and cross-cutting dimensions.

Validation layers:

- Unit Validation
- Integration Validation
- API Validation
- Experience (UI) Validation
- Data Validation
- AI / Model Validation

Cross-cutting validation dimensions:

- Performance Engineering
- Accessibility
- Usability
- Reliability and Stability

Each validation layer defines a distinct location in the engineering architecture where behavior is directly observed. Each cross-cutting dimension defines the evaluation perspective applied at that layer. At every intersection between a layer and a dimension, validation produces a measurable signal.

11.4 The QACE Validation Model — Canonical Representation

The canonical representation of the QACE Validation Model expresses the relationship between validation layers, cross-cutting dimensions, and signal production as a unified system.

The canonical representation must be interpreted in stages, not as a single composite view. The reader must first recognize the vertical structure of validation layers, because each layer identifies a distinct engineering domain where behavior is directly observed. The reader must then recognize the uniform application of cross-cutting dimensions, because each dimension applies the same evaluation perspective across all layers. Finally, the reader must recognize the signal outputs generated at each point of intersection, because those outputs are the measurable evidence the system uses for diagnostics and interpretation.

At its core, the model is composed of explicitly defined validation layers, each representing a distinct location in the engineering architecture where behavior is directly observed. These layers are intersected by cross-cutting validation dimensions that apply uniformly across all layers. From each intersection, measurable signals are produced, forming a structured network of system visibility.

The canonical representation is defined as a structured matrix:

- Validation layers form one axis
- Cross-cutting validation dimensions form the other axis
- Each intersection represents a signal production point

This structure ensures that validation is consistently applied across all defined layers and dimensions, and that every valid intersection produces traceable, measurable evidence.

Visual Model Structure

The canonical model is represented as a structured matrix:

- Validation layers are expressed as horizontal bands
- Cross-cutting dimensions are expressed as vertical axes
- Intersections are expressed as signal points

This representation is fixed and must not be interpreted as an informal grid or table. It is a structural model in which each intersection represents a defined evaluation point.

Figure 11.4 – QACE Validation Model Progression

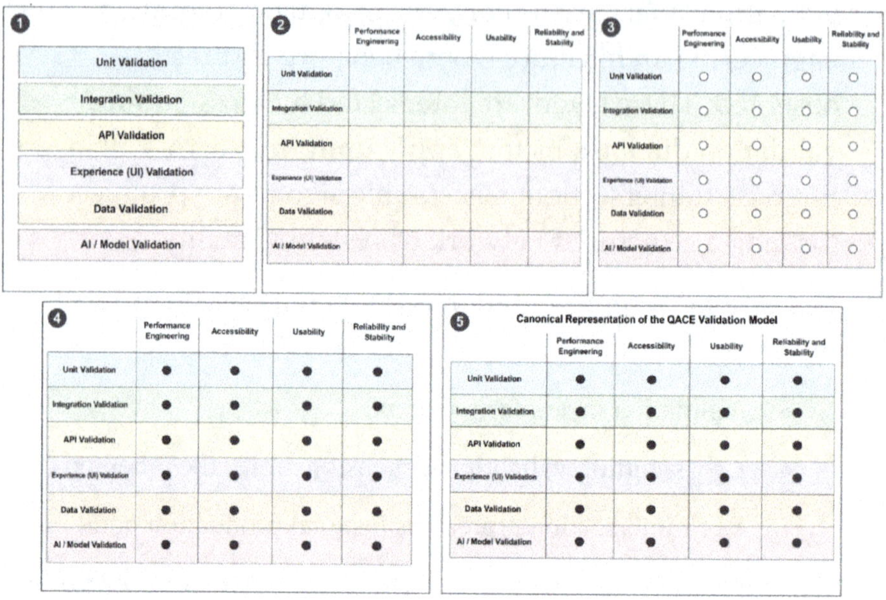

Validation operates as a structured matrix where layers intersect with cross-cutting dimensions to produce measurable signals.

This representation reinforces that validation is not linear or sequential. It is a structured matrix in which behavior is continuously observed and expressed across multiple dimensions simultaneously. In practice, the full matrix represents the composite validation system: every defined validation layer is evaluated across every defined cross-cutting dimension, and each valid intersection produces a signal that contributes to system understanding.

All layer-dimension intersections are treated as valid evaluation points within the canonical model. This ensures that the matrix is complete and that no structural gaps exist in the application of validation.

The canonical form serves as the authoritative visualization of the model and must remain consistent across all interpretations and applications.

11.5 Validation Layers

Within the QACE Validation Model, validation layers are the primary structural anchor. All other components of the model are applied to or derived from these layers. For this reason, layers must be established first in the reader's understanding before introducing cross-cutting or intersecting constructs.

Validation layers are the foundational elements of the QACE Validation Model. Each layer represents a distinct location in the engineering architecture where validation is grounded and where system behavior can be directly observed. A validation layer identifies where in the system validation is grounded. It is the boundary within which behavior is directly observed and from which evidence is produced.

Figure 11.5 – Non-Overlapping Validation Layers

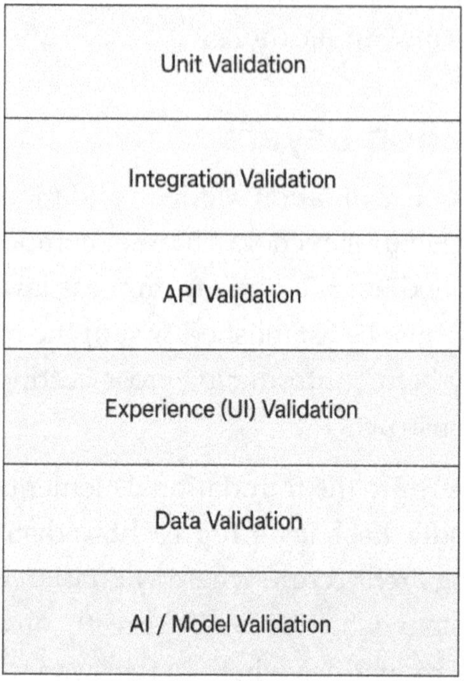

Complete, Non-Overlapping Validation Coverage

Validation layers define distinct domains of system behavior, ensuring complete and non-overlapping validation coverage.

These layers are not abstractions or categories. They are structural components that define where validation occurs. Each validation layer corresponds to a defined architectural level within the engineering system and is represented consistently as a distinct horizontal structure in the model.

In practice, these layers correspond to recognizable engineering contexts:

- Unit Validation focuses on component-level correctness
- Integration Validation focuses on interaction between system components

- API Validation focuses on interface behavior and contract stability
- Experience (UI) Validation focuses on user-facing behavior
- Data Validation focuses on data integrity and data-driven behavior
- AI / Model Validation focuses on model-driven outputs and decision behavior

This explicit definition ensures that each layer provides a distinct and observable view of system behavior.

Each layer must be clearly delineated and must remain independent in its definition and purpose. That independence matters because each layer gives visibility into a distinct part of system behavior. If layers are merged, loosely defined, or left implicit, the system loses clarity about where evidence came from and what behavior domain that evidence actually describes.

While each layer operates independently, no layer exists in isolation. Together, they form a complete system of validation coverage. This ensures that validation spans all relevant domains of system behavior without overlap, ambiguity, or omission.

In figures, validation layers are represented as parallel, non-overlapping horizontal structures. Complete coverage is expressed by the full set of layers collectively spanning the validation scope without gaps or duplication.

The explicit definition of layers prevents the collapse of validation into generalized activity. It ensures that each domain is observed directly, rather than inferred indirectly. It also makes figure development stronger because each layer can be shown as a distinct observation domain within the broader validation system.

Once layers establish where validation occurs, consistent perspectives must be applied across them.

11.6 Cross-Cutting Validation Dimensions

In the canonical model, the cross-cutting validation dimensions are explicitly defined as:

- Performance Engineering
- Accessibility
- Usability
- Reliability and Stability

These dimensions apply uniformly across all validation layers.

Cross-cutting validation dimensions provide the consistent perspectives applied across all validation layers. These dimensions are not tied to any single layer and must not be isolated or selectively applied.

By intersecting every validation layer, these dimensions ensure that system behavior is evaluated consistently regardless of domain. They establish uniformity in how validation is expressed and interpreted across the model.

In visual terms, cross-cutting dimensions are represented as directional axes that traverse all validation layers without partitioning them into separate cells or compartments. Each dimension applies its evaluation perspective independently at every layer, ensuring that the same evaluative view is consistently applied across the system.

Dimensions must not be interpreted as boundaries or divisions within the model. They apply evaluative perspective across layers but do not segment the system into independent regions.

The separation between layers and dimensions is critical. Layers define where validation occurs, while dimensions define how system behavior is observed across those layers. A layer tells the system where to look. A dimension tells the system what evaluation perspective to apply when it looks.

This distinction prevents conflation and maintains structural clarity. It ensures that validation remains both comprehensive and consistent without collapsing into a single-dimensional perspective. A dimension does not replace a layer, and a layer does not determine the evaluation perspective by itself.

Cross-cutting validation dimensions must not be interpreted as extensions of individual layers. Their purpose is not to expand layer definition, but to provide consistent interpretive perspectives across all layers simultaneously. In operation, that means the same type of evaluative view is applied across separate behavior domains so that outputs can be aligned, compared, and interpreted as part of one system.

Without cross-cutting dimensions, the system may still observe behavior at different layers, but the resulting outputs would be harder to compare and diagnose together because each layer could be interpreted differently. From this intersection of layers and dimensions, measurable outputs are produced.

Without defined dimensions, outputs from different validation layers cannot be consistently compared or interpreted, because each layer would apply a different or implicit evaluation perspective.

11.7 Signal Production and Diagnostics Alignment

Signal production is introduced only after validation layers and cross-cutting dimensions are established. Signals do not exist independently within the model; they are generated exclusively as a result of structured observation across defined layers and dimensions.

In the canonical model, signals are defined structurally.

A signal is produced only when:

- A specific validation layer is observed
- A specific cross-cutting dimension is applied

Each signal is therefore tied to:

- A defined location in the system, represented by the layer
- A defined evaluation perspective, represented by the dimension

This ensures that signals are traceable, comparable, and interpretable across the entire validation model.

Figure 11.6 – Signal Production from Structured Observation

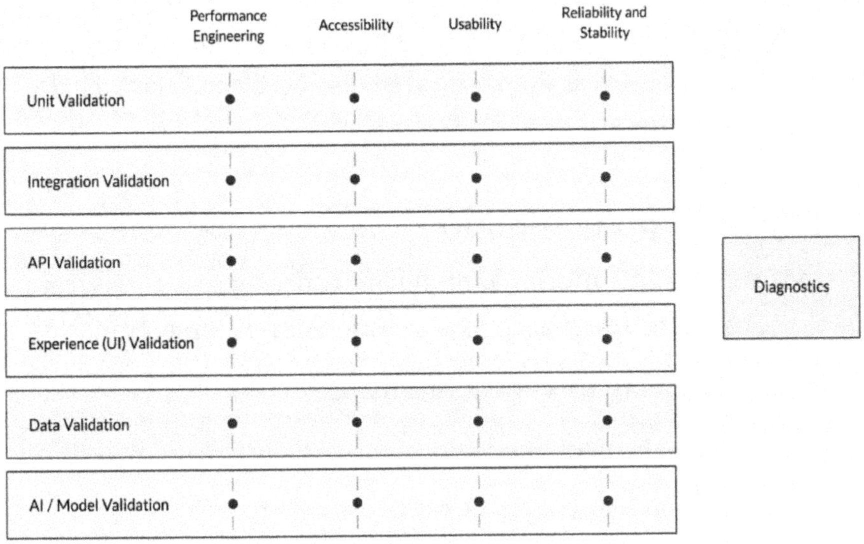

Signals are produced through structured observation at the intersection of validation layers and cross-cutting dimensions.

Signals in the canonical model are static outputs at their point of production. They do not flow between layers or dimensions within the model. Instead, they remain associated with the specific layer and dimension that produced them.

Signal production is the mechanism through which validation expresses system behavior. Each validation layer produces measurable signals aligned to system behavior within that domain. These signals are not abstract or inferred. They are direct, observable representations of system behavior.

In operation, they appear as governed validation outputs such as pass or fail results, measured values, diagnostic indicators, pipeline records, telemetry outputs, dashboard values, or log-level evidence that can be traced back to the layer and dimension that produced them.

Signal Representation

In the canonical model, signals are represented as discrete, uniform outputs at each layer-dimension intersection.

Each signal is treated structurally as:

- A single output node
- One observable result per intersection
- Independent of other signals

Signals may represent different types of measurable outcomes, but within the model they are treated uniformly so that each intersection produces a consistent, comparable unit of validation evidence.

In visual representation, each signal is expressed as a simple, uniform node at the point of intersection. The node represents the existence of measurable validation output, not the internal detail of that output. All signals are represented using the same visual form to preserve consistency across the model.

Their purpose is to provide clear, measurable insight into the integrity and performance of the system at each layer. Because each signal is tied to a specific layer and a specific dimension, the system can interpret not only what result was produced, but also where that result came from and what evaluation perspective produced it.

The alignment of these signals enables diagnostics to operate as a coherent system capability. Because signals are structured and consistently produced, they form a reliable basis for interpreting system state. Diagnostics do not operate on raw activity alone. They operate on signalized evidence that has structural meaning.

Diagnostics operate as the system-level consumer of signals. All produced signals are captured and made available to diagnostics mechanisms, which aggregate, interpret, and evaluate the overall state of the system based on the structured output of the validation model.

In the model, diagnostics exist outside the structural matrix. Signals are produced within the validation structure and made available to diagnostics, but diagnostics are not themselves part of the validation layer and dimension framework.

In figures, diagnostics is represented as an external consumer of validation signals. Signals remain at their point of production within the matrix and are not shown as flowing elements. The relationship is shown conceptually as availability or accessibility, not as a directional data flow within the validation structure.

This alignment transforms validation from observation into structured system intelligence. If signals are incomplete, inconsistent, or detached from their layer and dimension context, diagnostics lose reliability because the system no longer has a stable basis for interpretation.

With signal production established, execution mechanisms can be positioned relative to the model.

11.8 Automation and Execution Alignment

Automation operates within the QACE Validation Model as a means of enabling validation execution, but it does not define or alter the structure of validation.

The model ensures that automation aligns with the defined validation layers and cross-cutting dimensions. Automation must operate within these structures, reinforcing rather than redefining them. In practical terms, automated execution must still preserve the identity of the layer being observed, the dimension being applied, and the signal being produced.

This alignment preserves the integrity of the model. It ensures that automation enhances consistency and scale without introducing structural deviation or ambiguity. Automation can increase speed, repeatability, and coverage, but it must still produce governed outputs that remain interpretable within the model.

Validation remains structurally governed, regardless of how it is executed. Automation serves the model; it does not reshape it.

> **Concept Insight: Execution mode may change, but validation meaning remains stable only when the QACE structure remains invariant.**

11.9 Validation Execution Modes

Validation execution occurs through multiple modes, including but not limited to manual, automated, and other forms of execution. These modes represent how validation is performed, not what validation is.

Execution modes exist outside the structural definition of the validation model. They interact with validation layers and dimensions but do not constitute structural components themselves. They define how the work is carried out. They do not redefine where behavior is observed, how behavior is evaluated, or what counts as a valid signal.

In figures, execution modes are represented as external elements positioned outside the validation structure. They may be shown adjacent to or surrounding the model but must not be drawn as part of the layer-dimension matrix or as structural components within it.

Figure 11.7 – Separation of Validation Structure and Execution

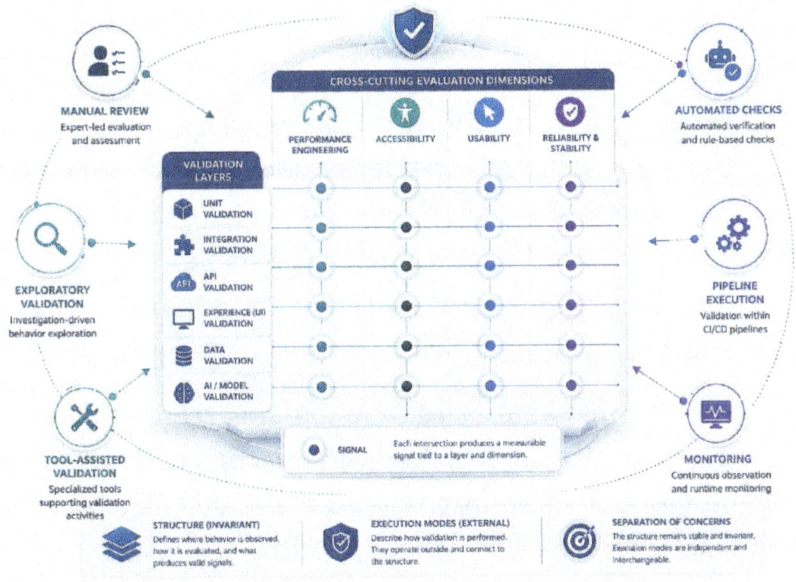

Validation structure remains invariant while execution modes operate externally without altering the model.

The separation between execution modes and validation structure is essential. It ensures that the model remains stable and invariant, regardless of changes in execution practices or methodologies. A team may change the way validation is executed, but that must not change the structure that gives the outputs meaning.

Execution modes enable flexibility in application, while the validation structure ensures consistency in definition.

This separation between structure and execution enables broader validation constructs to operate consistently.

11.10 Relationship to the Validation Chain

The QACE Validation Model serves as the structural foundation for the validation chain. It defines the layers, dimensions, and signals that enable the broader system of validation to operate coherently.

While the validation chain represents a broader construct, its effectiveness depends entirely on the integrity of the validation model. Without a structured model, the chain lacks consistent inputs, alignment, and coherence. It may still contain activity, but it will not have stable evidence flowing through it in a form that supports reliable interpretation.

The model ensures that validation remains grounded in explicit structure, enabling downstream constructs to function without ambiguity. The validation chain depends on the model because the model provides the observation boundaries, the consistent evaluation perspectives, and the measurable outputs that broader validation activity requires.

The validation chain is not structurally defined within this chapter and must not be represented as a detailed figure here. Figures in this chapter may refer to the existence of downstream constructs but must not attempt to define or visualize them beyond conceptual reference.

11.11 Model Enforcement

The integrity of the QACE Validation Model is explicitly enforced. Each structural component—validation layers, cross-cutting validation dimensions, and signal production—must remain clearly defined and consistently applied.

Validation layers must not be merged, reclassified, or implicitly referenced. Cross-cutting validation dimensions must remain distinct and uniformly applied across all layers. Execution modes must not be elevated to structural components or allowed to redefine the model.

Enforcement of the Validation Model

Figure 11.8 – Validation Model Enforcement

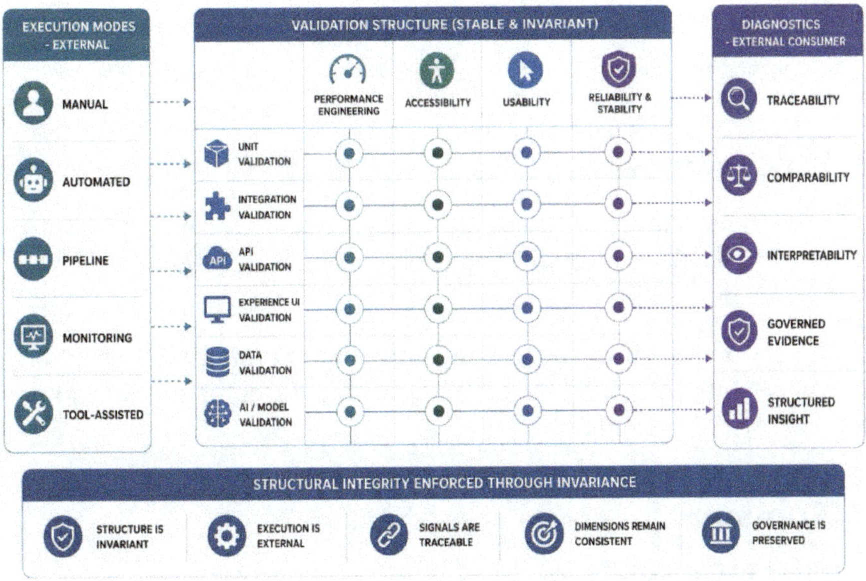

The validation model enforces strict structural integrity across layers, dimensions, and signal production to maintain system consistency.

All validation produces measurable signals aligned to system behavior. Implicit or undocumented validation structures are not permitted. Outputs that cannot be traced to defined layers and defined dimensions do not satisfy the model, because they do not provide governed system visibility.

Through strict enforcement, the model maintains its role as a governed system capability, ensuring that validation remains consistent, structured, and aligned with the principles of QACE.

In figures, enforcement is represented through invariance. The structure remains unchanged across contexts, and prohibited transformations such as merging layers, altering dimensions, or producing unaligned signals are not depicted. Enforcement is shown through structural consistency rather than additional symbolic elements.

Key Takeaways

- The QACE Validation Model creates governed system visibility through layers, dimensions, and signal production.
- Validation structure must remain separate from execution modes so evidence remains traceable, comparable, and interpretable.

Summary

The QACE Validation Model must be understood as a progressive structural construct. It begins with validation layers that establish domains of system behavior. Cross-cutting validation dimensions are then applied across these layers, ensuring consistent interpretation. From this structured intersection, measurable signals are produced, providing direct system visibility.

This progression—from layers, to dimensions, to signals—ensures that validation remains structurally grounded and cognitively accessible, preventing collapse into abstraction or implicit interpretation. It also shows how the model works as a composite system of validation: layers define where behavior is observed, dimensions define how it is evaluated, and signals provide the evidence the system uses for diagnostics and understanding.

Chapter 11 — Knowledge Check

QACE Validation Model

The following questions are designed to verify accurate understanding of the QACE Validation Model as a governed system capability. They assess whether the reader can distinguish validation from activity or phase-based approaches, understand how validation is structured through layers and cross-cutting dimensions, and recognize how signal production enables system-level visibility and diagnostics alignment.

These questions are nonprocedural. They do not assess implementation techniques, tools, or execution methods.

Knowledge Check 11.1 — Validation Purpose

Question

What problem does the QACE Validation Model solve when compared to phase-based or activity-based validation?

Knowledge Check 11.2 — System Capability vs Activity

Question

Why must validation be treated as a governed system capability rather than as a testing activity or checkpoint?

Knowledge Check 11.3 — Structural Components

Question

What are the three primary structural components of the QACE Validation Model, and what does each define?

Knowledge Check 11.4 — Layers vs Dimensions

Question

What is the difference between validation layers and cross-cutting validation dimensions, and why must they remain distinct?

Knowledge Check 11.5 — Signal Production

Question

How are signals produced within the model, and why must they be tied to both a validation layer and a validation dimension?

Knowledge Check 11.6 — Structural Integrity

Question

What happens when validation layers are merged, dimensions are inconsistently applied, or signals are not aligned to defined structures?

Knowledge Check 11.7 — Diagnostics Alignment

Question

Why are signals the critical input for diagnostics, and what risks emerge if signal production is inconsistent or unstructured?

Knowledge Check 11.8 — Execution vs Structure

Question

Why must execution modes remain separate from the validation structure, and what occurs if execution is allowed to redefine the model?

Guidance for the Reader

If you can explain how the QACE Validation Model establishes structured system visibility, distinguish between validation layers and cross-cutting dimensions, and describe how signal production enables consistent diagnostics and system understanding, you are prepared to proceed.

This chapter establishes validation as a governed system capability defined through explicit structure, separating observation, interpretation, and signal production into a coherent and enforceable model. It demonstrates how validation produces measurable system evidence that supports diagnostics, comparability, and enterprise-level understanding.

The next chapter builds on this foundation by applying validation outputs within broader system evaluation and decision processes, further integrating validation into the full lifecycle of quality intelligence.

Questions for Reflection

- How does defining validation as a system capability change how system behavior is observed within your organization?
- What would indicate that validation is being applied as an activity rather than as a structured model?
- How do validation layers, cross-cutting dimensions, and signal production work together to produce consistent system visibility?
- What risks emerge if signals are inconsistent, incomplete, or not structurally aligned with system behavior?

Chapter 12 — The Validation Chain

Chapter Introduction

This chapter builds on the QACE Validation Model by extending validation from structured observation into a continuous system that proves outcomes.

Chapter 11 established validation as a governed system capability defined through layers, cross-cutting dimensions, and signal production. With this structure in place, the next requirement is to determine whether system behavior actually produces the intended results.

This chapter introduces the Validation Chain as the mechanism that connects decisions, actions, outcomes, validation, and feedback into a continuous system. It defines how cause-and-effect relationships are established, how outcomes are proven through evidence, and how systems continuously confirm their effectiveness over time.

This is critical because without a defined validation chain, organizations cannot reliably determine whether results were produced by their actions or by unrelated system variation. The system may appear effective while failing to achieve its intended outcomes.

The sections that follow establish how validation moves from structured observation to provable system behavior, ensuring that quality is not assumed, but demonstrated through measurable and sustained evidence.

12.1 — Definition of Validation in QACE

Within the QACE system, validation answers one central question: Did the system produce the intended result because of the decision and actions taken?

This question is not about whether work was completed, whether teams followed process, or whether dashboards improved. It is about whether a specific system change actually happened and can be proven.

Concept Insight: QACE validation proves causality between intentional action and sustained system outcome, not completion of activity.

A decision in QACE always defines an intended outcome before any work begins. Validation checks whether that outcome shows up in the system—and whether it can be directly linked to what was done.

Figure 12.1 – Validation as Proven Outcome System

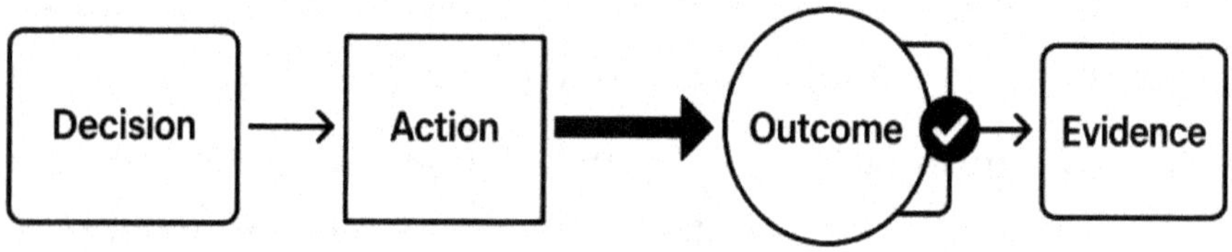

Validation confirms that a defined outcome occurred as a direct result of specific actions, supported by measurable evidence and sustained over time.

Validation Requirement	QACE Meaning
Decision	The intended outcome is explicitly defined before work begins (for example, reduce defect escape rate by a measurable amount).
Action	Engineering work—tests, code changes, diagnostics, automation—is clearly tied to that decision.
Outcome	The system shows a measurable change, such as lower defect escape, improved latency, or fewer failures.
Persistence	That change continues across multiple runs, releases, or operating conditions—not just once.

In practice, validation is something a team must be able to demonstrate, not assume. At any time, an engineer should be able to:

- Show the decision and the outcome it defined
- Show the actions taken, such as added validation checks, improved test coverage, or modified diagnostics
- Show system evidence—metrics, logs, and test results—that the outcome occurred and continues to hold

If any of these are missing, validation has not occurred.

12.2 — The Validation Chain Model

The Validation Chain shows how a system connects: Decision → Action → Intended Outcome → Validation → Feedback.

This relationship must function as a continuous system, not a single progression.

Figure 12.2 – The Validation Chain Loop

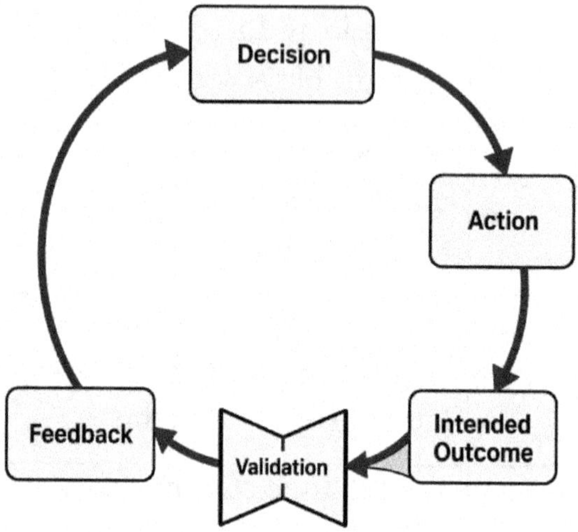

The Validation Chain links decision, action, outcome, validation, and feedback into a continuous system that produces verifiable results.

This is not a conceptual sequence. It is how real engineering work must be structured so that results can be proven.

Validation Chain Link	**Role in the System**
Decision	Defines the exact system change required, such as reducing defect escape rate.
Action	Implements that decision, such as adding validation tests, improving diagnostics, or modifying pipelines.

Validation Chain Link	Role in the System
Intended Outcome	Defines how the system should change, such as fewer escaped defects in production.
Validation	Confirms the change occurred using measurable evidence, including metrics, logs, and test outcomes.
Feedback	Uses the validated result to guide the next decision.

The Validation Chain is continuous. Each validated outcome feeds into the next decision, creating a loop: Decision → Action → Outcome → Validation → Feedback → Next Decision.

12.3 — Traceability from Decision to Outcome

Traceability is what makes the Validation Chain visible and verifiable.

It allows a team to move step-by-step from: decision → action → outcome → evidence → back to decision.

Figure 12.3 – Traceability Path System

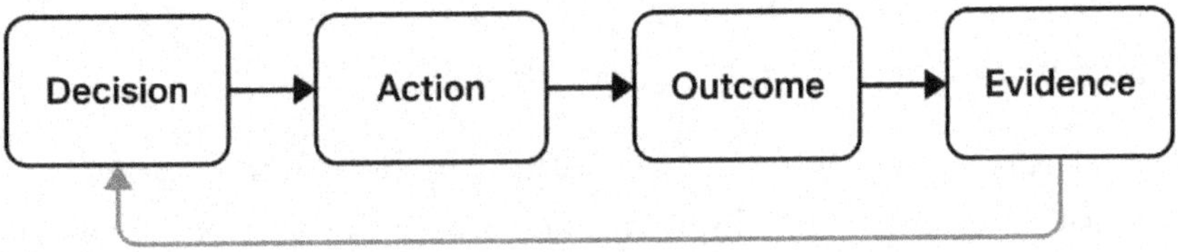

Traceability connects decisions, actions, outcomes, and evidence into a continuous path that allows results to be verified and explained.

Traceability Path	What Must Be Verifiable
Decision to Action	Each action references the decision it implements.
Action to Outcome	The resulting system change is tied to those actions.
Outcome to Evidence	Metrics, logs, or validation outputs confirm the change.
Evidence to Decision	The full path can be followed back to the original decision.

Traceability is therefore not just documentation. It is the mechanism that allows validation to confirm that the system changed because of intentional engineering work.

Concept Insight: Traceability is the proof path that allows QACE to distinguish validated outcomes from coincidental system change.

12.4 — Feedback and Outcome Confirmation

Validation is not complete when a result is first observed. It is only complete when the result continues to hold over time and under real operating conditions.

A single data point is not enough. Systems can appear improved and then degrade. Feedback is the mechanism that continuously confirms whether the outcome still holds.

Figure 12.4 – Outcome Persistence and Feedback Validation

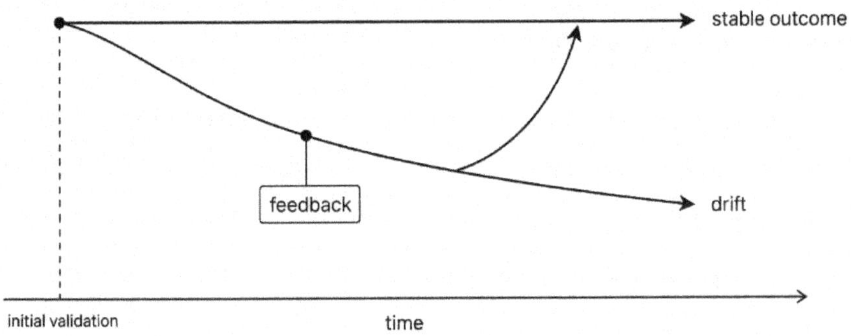

Validation requires outcomes to remain stable across time and conditions, with feedback detecting drift and informing decisions.

Feedback Check	Purpose
Stability	Confirms the outcome remains consistent over time, such as across releases.
Condition Variation	Confirms the result holds under different loads or inputs.
Drift Detection	Detects when the system begins to move away from the intended state.
Decision Adjustment	Returns information to update or replace the decision.

12.5 — Failure of Validation (False Confidence)

When validation is missing, the system does not fail silently—it produces false confidence.

False confidence occurs when teams treat activity or improving metrics as proof of success without confirming the intended outcome.

> **Concept Insight: False confidence emerges when activity signals are accepted as outcome proof without a validated QACE evidence chain.**

Figure 12.5 – False Confidence vs Validated Outcome

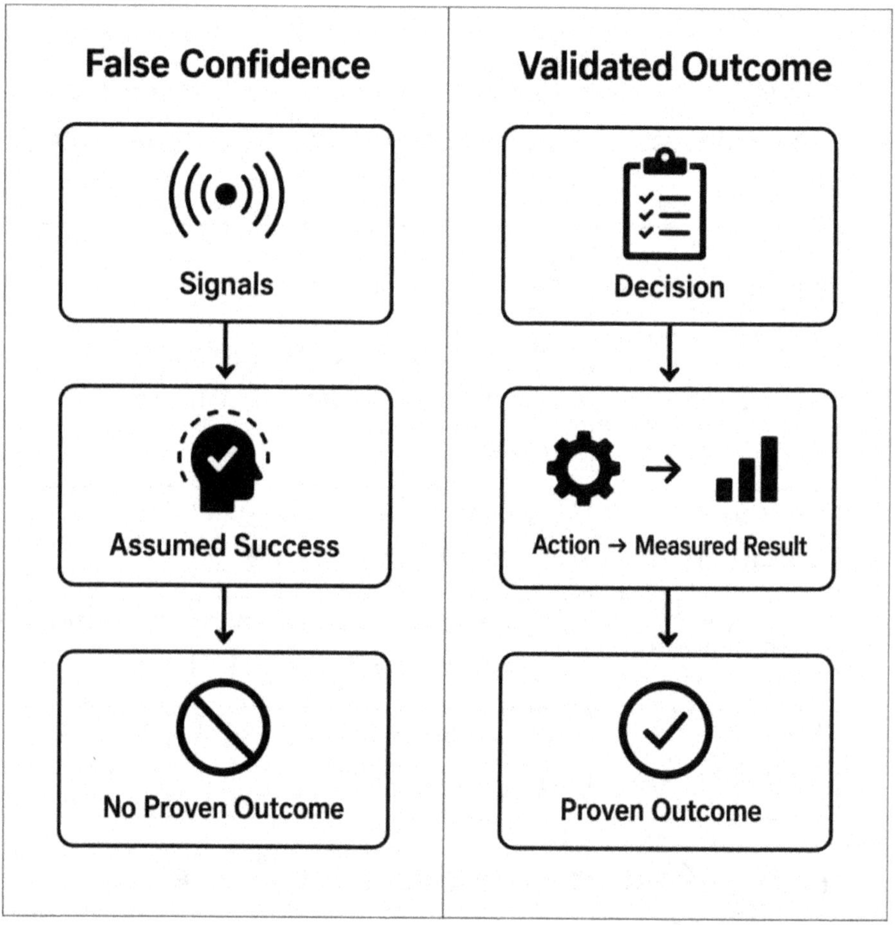

Activity and improving signals do not confirm system improvement unless they are directly tied to validated outcomes.

False Signal	Why It Does Not Validate the Outcome
More tests executed	Does not prove defects decreased in production.
Faster delivery	Does not confirm system stability.
Increased output	Does not confirm improved quality.
Improving dashboards	May reflect activity, not actual system change.

Without validation, quality becomes an illusion—built from activity, but not supported by evidence.

12.6 — Embedding Validation into the System

For validation to be reliable, it must be built into everyday engineering work—not added after the fact.

Embedded Validation Practice	Operational Effect
Decisions define intended outcomes	Work starts with a clear, measurable target.
Actions are traceable	Changes remain linked to the decision they implement.
Outcomes are measured	System behavior is evaluated using metrics or validation results.
Feedback runs continuously	Drift is detected and decisions are updated.

Figure 12.6 – Embedded Validation System

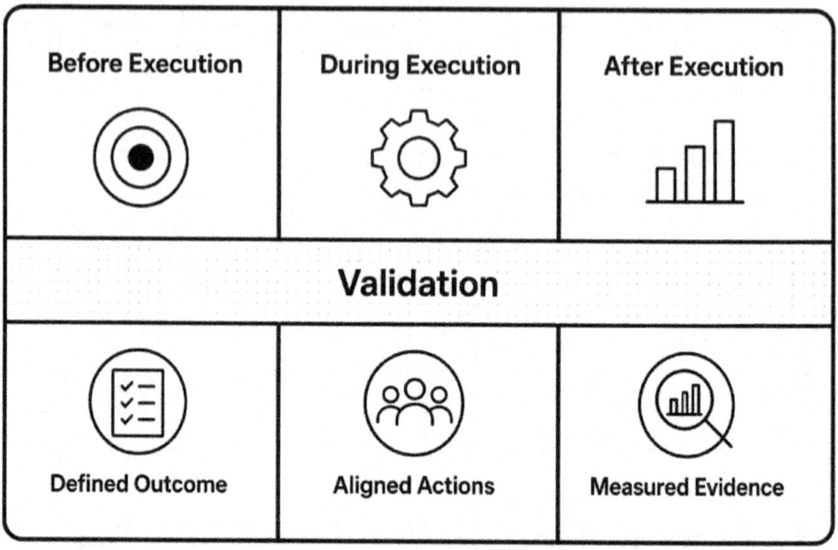

Validation is embedded across all stages of execution, ensuring outcomes are defined, measured, and confirmed continuously.

This chapter establishes validation as the mechanism that confirms system effectiveness through measurable, traceable, and sustained outcomes. The Validation Chain connects decisions, actions, and results into a continuous loop where performance is constantly verified. (ISO, 2021)

The next chapter builds on this by showing how validated outcomes drive system learning and adaptation over time.

Summary

Validation must be embedded into everyday system operation to reliably confirm that intended outcomes are achieved. By integrating validation into decisions, actions, measurement, and feedback, organizations ensure that system behavior can be continuously evaluated and adapted.

The Validation Chain links decisions, actions, and outcomes into a traceable system, enabling verification that results are produced intentionally and sustained over time. This transforms validation from a retrospective activity into an ongoing mechanism for confirming system effectiveness.

Without embedded validation, outcomes cannot be reliably attributed to specific actions, and system performance cannot be governed with confidence. By making validation continuous and integral to execution, organizations establish a foundation for consistent, evidence-based performance.

Chapter 12 — Knowledge Check

The Validation Chain

The following questions are designed to verify accurate understanding of how validation operates as a continuous system capability within QACE. They assess whether the reader can distinguish validation from activity or assumption, understand how the Validation Chain establishes cause-and-effect relationships, and recognize how traceability, feedback, and embedded validation ensure that outcomes are proven and sustained over time.

These questions are nonprocedural. They do not assess implementation techniques, tools, or execution methods.

Knowledge Check 12.1 — Definition of Validation

Question

What does validation confirm within the QACE system, and

how does it differ from measuring activity or performance signals?

Knowledge Check 12.2 — Decision to Outcome Relationship

Question

Why must a decision define a measurable intended outcome before any action is taken?

Knowledge Check 12.3 — Validation Chain Integrity

Question

What happens when any link in the Validation Chain (decision, action, outcome, validation, or feedback) is missing?

Knowledge Check 12.4 — Traceability

Question

Why is traceability required to connect decisions, actions, outcomes, and evidence into a verifiable system?

Knowledge Check 12.5 — Evidence vs Assumption

Question

Why are activity-based signals such as increased tests or faster delivery insufficient to prove system improvement?

Knowledge Check 12.6 — Feedback and Persistence

Question

Why must validation include confirmation that outcomes persist over time and across varying conditions?

Knowledge Check 12.7 — False Confidence

Question

How does the absence of validation create false confidence within engineering systems?

Knowledge Check 12.8 — Embedded Validation

Question

Why must validation be embedded within normal system operation rather than applied as a separate phase?

Guidance for the Reader

If you can explain how validation establishes cause-and-effect between decisions and outcomes, describe how traceability and feedback confirm that outcomes are sustained over time, and distinguish proven results from activity or assumption, you are prepared to proceed.

This chapter establishes validation as the mechanism that proves system effectiveness through measurable, traceable, and sustained outcomes. It demonstrates how the Validation Chain connects decisions, actions, and results into a continuous loop, enabling systems to confirm their own performance with evidence rather than assumption.

The next chapter builds on this foundation by showing how validated outcomes are used to drive system learning, adaptation, and continuous improvement across the enterprise.

Key Takeaways

- Validation proves that intended outcomes were produced by specific actions and sustained through evidence.
- The Validation Chain connects decision, action, outcome, validation, and feedback into a continuous proof system.

Summary

The Validation Chain turns validation into a continuous proof mechanism. By linking decisions, actions, outcomes, evidence, and feedback, the system can determine whether intended results occurred because of specific work and whether those results persist across time and conditions.

Questions for Reflection

- What does this concept reveal about system behavior?
- How would this appear in an enterprise context?
- What signals would indicate this is not functioning correctly?

Chapter 13 — Adoption, Transformation, and Institutional Continuity

Chapter Introduction

This chapter completes the QACE system model by defining how structured quality capabilities evolve into sustained enterprise behavior.

Chapter 12 established the Validation Chain as the mechanism that proves outcomes through traceable connections between decisions, actions, and results. With validation in place, the next question is how these validated behaviors become consistent, scalable, and enforceable across the enterprise.

This chapter introduces the progression from adoption through transformation, scaling, institutionalization, certification, and ecosystem continuity. It defines how systems move from aligned understanding to predictable outcomes, from local consistency to enterprise-wide replication, and from manual enforcement to structural constraint.

This is critical because without a defined progression model, organizations may introduce practices, tools, and alignment efforts without achieving sustained system-level capability. Behavior may improve locally but fail to scale, persist, or produce consistent outcomes across contexts.

The sections that follow establish each stage of this progression, beginning with adoption as the point at which systems begin to operate from shared evidence, and extending through to ecosystem continuity, where validated outputs can be used across system boundaries without reinterpretation.

13.1 — Define Adoption as System-Level Transition

Concrete Anchor Scenario – Before vs After Adoption

Before Adoption (Fragmented State): A requirement enters the pipeline.

- One team defines acceptance loosely in user stories
- Another writes test cases based on interpretation
- Automation captures execution but is not trusted for release
- Defects are debated during triage because evidence is interpreted differently
- Release readiness requires meetings, escalation, and manual reconciliation

After Adoption (Aligned Operating State): The same requirement flows through the system.

- Acceptance criteria define clear pass/fail conditions
- Test cases reflect those same conditions
- Automation produces results aligned with those expectations
- Logs, traces, and test outputs support decision-making
- Release readiness is determined directly from shared evidence without escalation

Adoption is the shift from the first condition to the second.

Adoption represents a system-level shift from fragmented interpretation to aligned evidence-driven execution where decisions no longer require reconciliation.

Figure 13.1 – Adoption: Fragmented vs Aligned System

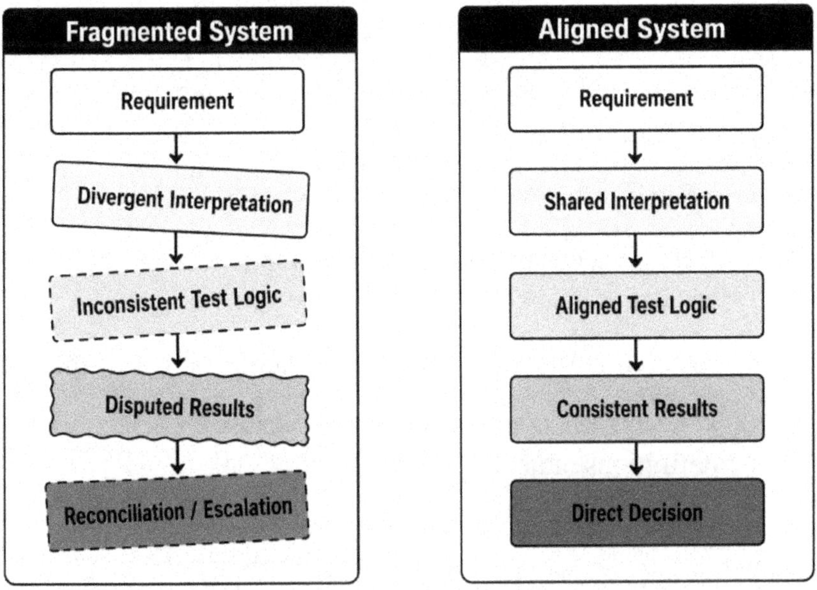

Fragmented systems require interpretation and reconciliation, while aligned systems produce consistent decisions directly from shared evidence.

Alignment eliminates variation in interpretation by ensuring all components operate on the same logic.

Adoption does not occur when training is completed or standards are published. It occurs when the system produces consistent engineering behavior without requiring re-explanation.

> **Concept Insight: Adoption begins when QACE logic operates through the system without needing repeated human translation.**

In practical terms, adoption is visible when:

- Requirements, test cases, automation outputs, and defect decisions use the same logic
- Pipeline results can be used directly in release decisions
- Teams interpret evidence the same way without debate

If this alignment is not present, the model has not been adopted—only introduced.

How to Recognize Adoption (Operational Signals):

- Release decisions are made from pipeline evidence without escalation
- Test failures are interpreted consistently across teams
- Defect triage converges quickly because evidence definitions match
- Fewer meetings are required to resolve disagreement
- Automation results are trusted inputs, not secondary artifacts

Adoption reduces interpretation effort.

Canonical Quality Execution Model (Structural Definition)

The system operates as a fixed structural model composed of the following components:

- Requirements (R) — define explicit pass/fail criteria
- Test Cases (T) — implement validation logic derived from requirements
- Automation Execution (A) — executes test cases and produces results

- Pipeline (P) — orchestrates execution, aggregation, and exposure of results
- Evidence (E) — logs, traces, and outputs generated during execution
- Release Decision (D) — system-level outcome determined from pipeline evidence

Structural Relationships (Non-Optional)

- R → T (requirements define test logic)
- T → A (test logic is executed through automation)
- A → E (execution produces evidence artifacts)
- E → P (evidence is collected and structured through pipeline)
- P → D (pipeline outputs determine release decisions)

Structural Constraints

- All downstream elements must preserve the pass/fail logic defined at R
- No element may reinterpret logic independently
- Evidence must remain traceable across all components (R → D)
- Release decisions must be derived exclusively from pipeline outputs

The system functions as a single, constrained execution chain where each stage preserves the original validation logic.

Figure 13.2 – Canonical Quality Execution Model

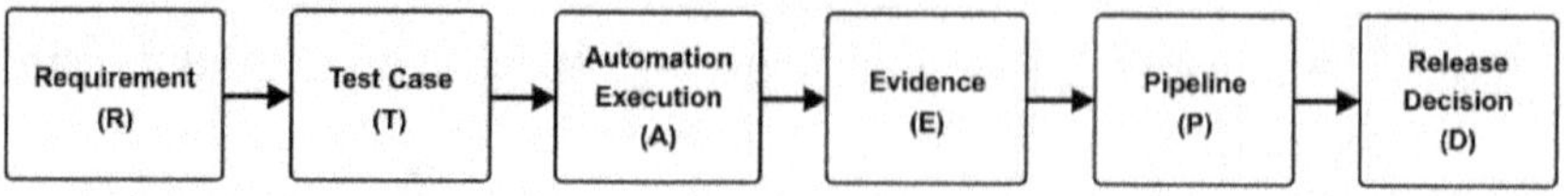

All quality execution flows through a fixed structural chain where each component preserves pass/fail logic from requirement to decision.

Each stage must maintain traceable continuity from requirement definition to release decision.

This structure is invariant across all stages (Adoption → Continuity).

13.2 — Explain Emergence of Transformation

Contrast with Adoption

Adoption means teams use the same logic. Transformation means the system produces better outcomes because of it.

Concrete Workflow Contrast: Same workflow (requirement → test → automation → release):

After Adoption:

- Teams align on evidence
- Decisions are consistent
- Less disagreement

After Transformation:

- Fewer defects escape
- Faster release decisions

- Reduced rework
- Less escalation

Transformation is not alignment—it is the impact of sustained alignment.

> **Concept Insight: Transformation is confirmed when aligned QACE behavior produces measurable and repeatable system outcomes.**

Transformation begins after adoption stabilizes and starts changing system outcomes.

Transformation is observable only when alignment produces consistent system outcomes rather than isolated agreement.

Figure 13.3 – Adoption vs Transformation (Behavior vs Outcome)

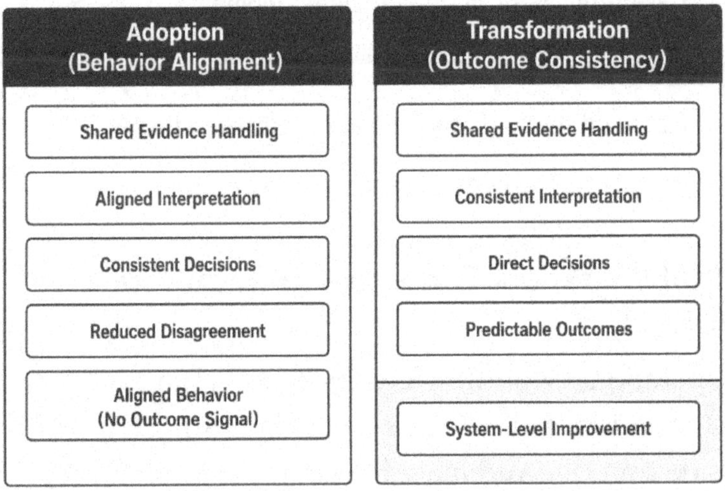

Adoption aligns behavior, while transformation alters system outcomes through consistent evidence interpretation.

Outcome consistency is the distinguishing signal of transformation.

Organizations often mistake activity for transformation:

- More tools
- More dashboards
- More automation

But if similar inputs still produce different decisions, transformation has not occurred.

Transformation exists when:

- The same signals produce the same decisions across teams
- Contradictions decrease
- Outcomes become predictable
- Fewer escaped defects due to consistent evidence handling
- Pipeline outputs drive release decisions without reinterpretation
- Less time spent in defect triage debates
- Fewer escalation loops
- Reduced manual reconciliation between teams

Transformation reduces correction effort.

Formal Workflow Structure (Execution Topology)

The operational workflow is defined as a fixed transformation chain: Requirement Definition (R), Test Construction (T), Automated Execution (A), Evidence Generation (E), Pipeline Aggregation (P), and Release Decision (D).

Transformation Rules

- Each stage consumes the output of the previous stage
- No stage may introduce new decision logic

- All transformations must preserve original pass/fail criteria
- Output equivalence must be maintained from R through D

Interface Definition

- R–T: criteria transfer
- T–A: executable validation logic
- A–E: result generation
- E–P: evidence structuring and exposure
- P–D: decision derivation

The workflow operates as a closed transformation chain where each stage consumes and preserves validated inputs.

Figure 13.4 – Transformation Workflow Chain (R → D)

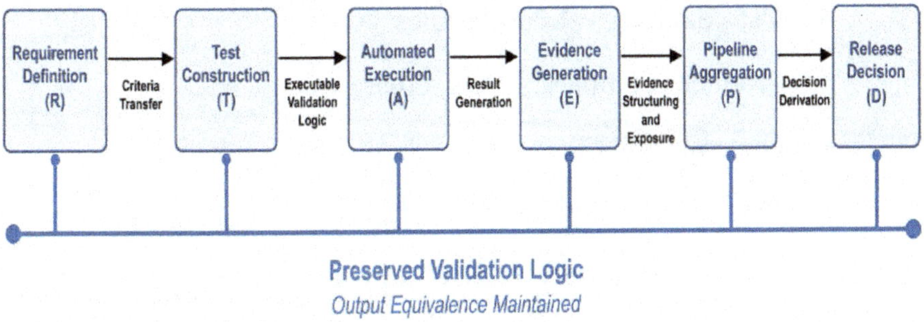

Transformation occurs when each stage preserves validation logic while producing consistent outputs that drive system decisions.

State integrity must remain intact across all transitions within the workflow.

This defines a constructible and repeatable system workflow.

13.3 — Describe Scaling as Propagation of Validated Behavior

Concrete Scenario – New Team Onboarding

A new team joins the system.

Non-Scaled Condition:

- Defines its own test approach
- Uses automation differently
- Interprets pipeline results differently
- Requires onboarding sessions to align
- Produces incompatible outputs

Scaled Condition:

- Uses existing validation rules
- Produces comparable test structures
- Generates pipeline outputs aligned with other teams
- Can participate without redefining quality logic

Scaling is proven when the second scenario occurs.

Scaling depends on the ability to replicate validated behavior without redefinition.

Figure 13.5 – Scaling: Expansion vs Behavioral Replication

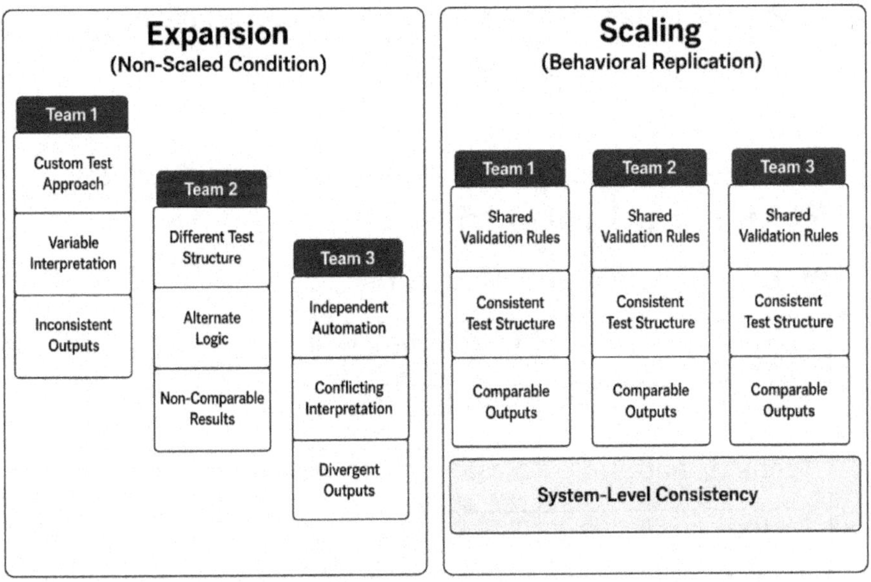

Scaling replicates validated behavior across teams, while expansion introduces variation and inconsistency.

Replication is measured by consistency, not growth.

Scaling is not expansion—it is replication of behavior without degradation.

Organizations often expand:

- More teams
- More pipelines
- More automation

But if each team behaves differently, scale has not been achieved.

How to Test for Scale:

- Can a new team operate using existing validation rules?
- Do pipeline outputs mean the same thing across teams?

- Are release decisions based on the same criteria?
- Do test structures remain consistent across products?

If redefinition is required, scaling has failed.

13.4 — Establish Institutionalization as Structural Embedding

Shift from Behavior to Structure

Stage	Dependency
Adoption	People follow rules
Transformation	System performs better
Scaling	Behavior spreads
Institutionalization	System enforces behavior

Concrete System View:

- Pipelines enforce validation rules
- Release gates block invalid states
- Traceability links requirements → tests → results
- Automation is required for progression
- AI usage is constrained by validation rules

Institutionalization occurs when the system enforces correct behavior.

Institutionalization shifts quality enforcement from people to system structure.

Figure 13.6 – Institutional Enforcement Model

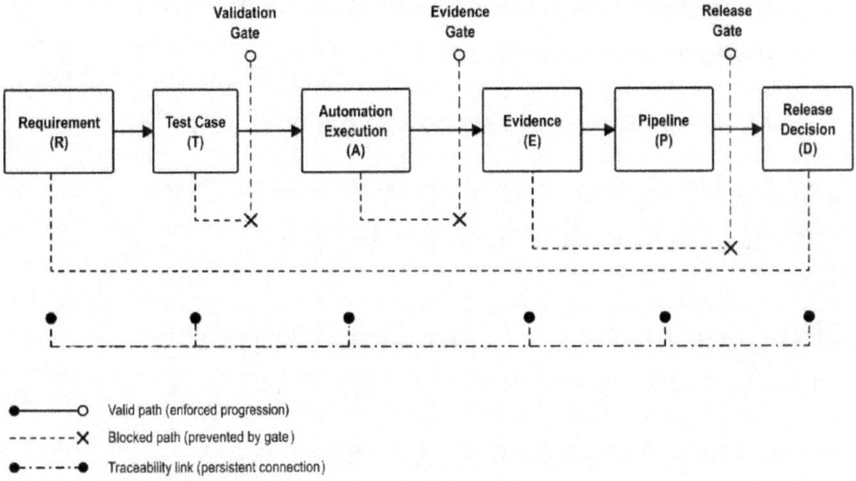

Pipelines, gates, and constraints enforce validation rules, preventing invalid system states without manual intervention.

Behavior is constrained through structure rather than oversight.

Quality no longer depends on:

- reminders
- expert intervention
- governance escalation

Instead, it is enforced by:

- pipelines
- workflow constraints
- release gates
- traceability requirements

Structural Indicators:

- Pipeline gates enforce pass/fail criteria
- Release cannot proceed without valid evidence
- Test results, logs, and traces are linked to requirements
- Automation is integrated into required workflow steps
- AI outputs are constrained by validation rules

Institutionalization reduces the ability to bypass quality.

Pipeline and Validation Chain Topology

The system is implemented as a layered validation topology:

- Layer 1: Definition Layer — Requirements (pass/fail criteria)
- Layer 2: Validation Layer — Test cases aligned to requirements
- Layer 3: Execution Layer — Automated execution of validation logic
- Layer 4: Evidence Layer — Logs, traces, and test outputs
- Layer 5: Control Layer — Pipeline orchestration and aggregation
- Layer 6: Decision Layer — Release gates and decision logic

Control Points

- Validation Gate — enforces requirement-test alignment
- Execution Gate — enforces automation completeness
- Evidence Gate — ensures traceability completeness
- Release Gate — enforces decision based on pipeline outputs

Topology Constraints

- Flow direction is strictly Layer 1 → Layer 6
- No bypass paths are permitted
- All decisions must originate from Layer 6
- Traceability must span all layers without break

The layered topology defines how validation logic is enforced across the system.

Figure 13.7 – Layered Validation Topology

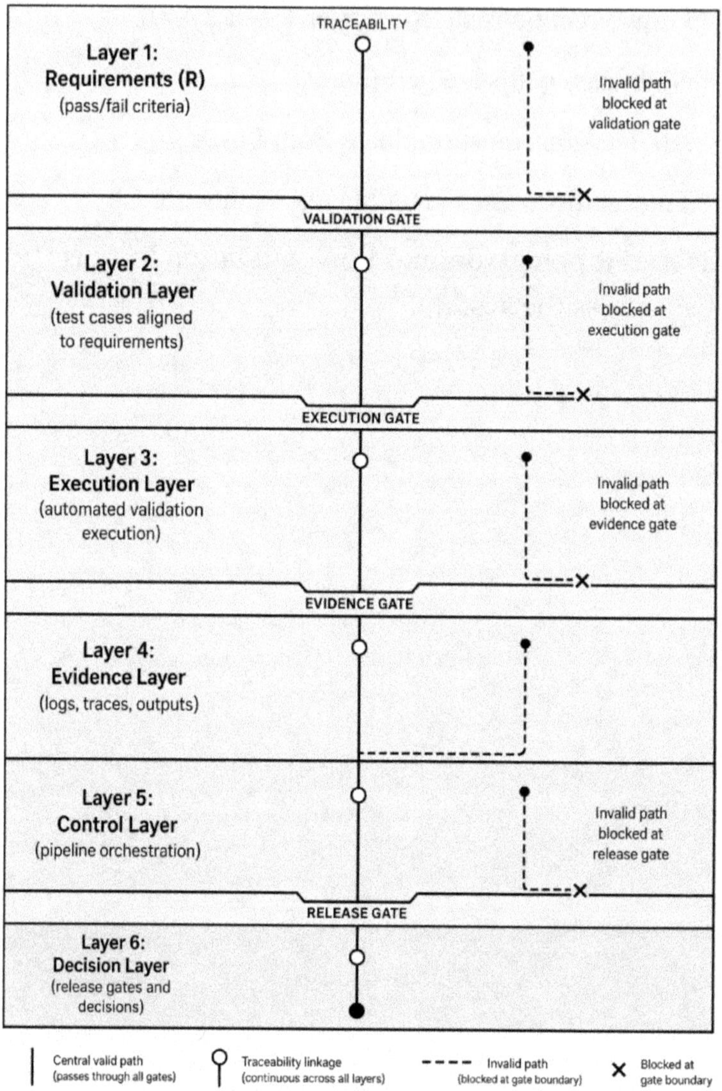

Validation is enforced through a layered system where each level contributes to traceability, control, and decision enforcement.

Every layer contributes to maintaining system integrity and decision validity.

This structure defines the enforceable system topology described in institutionalization.

Transition — From Enforcement to Proof to Cross-System Use

Institutionalization enforces consistent behavior through pipelines, release gates, and traceability. When this produces:

- stable outputs
- consistent decisions
- traceable validation chains

these outputs become observable evidence of system capability. Certification confirms that this evidence is:

- repeatable
- reliable
- sustained under normal execution

Once outputs can be interpreted consistently and trusted, they can be used beyond the originating system. This enables ecosystem continuity.

13.5 — Certification as Observable Proof of Sustained Capability

Certification is not a declaration. It is demonstrated system output observed during normal operation.

Certification confirms that the enterprise:

- Produces traceable links between requirements, test cases, and execution results
- Generates pipeline outputs that directly support release decisions

- Applies identical pass/fail logic across teams
- Interprets test results consistently without escalation

Certification is validated through routine execution, not preparation.

Certification emerges from the convergence of traceability, repeatability, and consistent decision logic.

Figure 13.8 – Certification Evidence Model

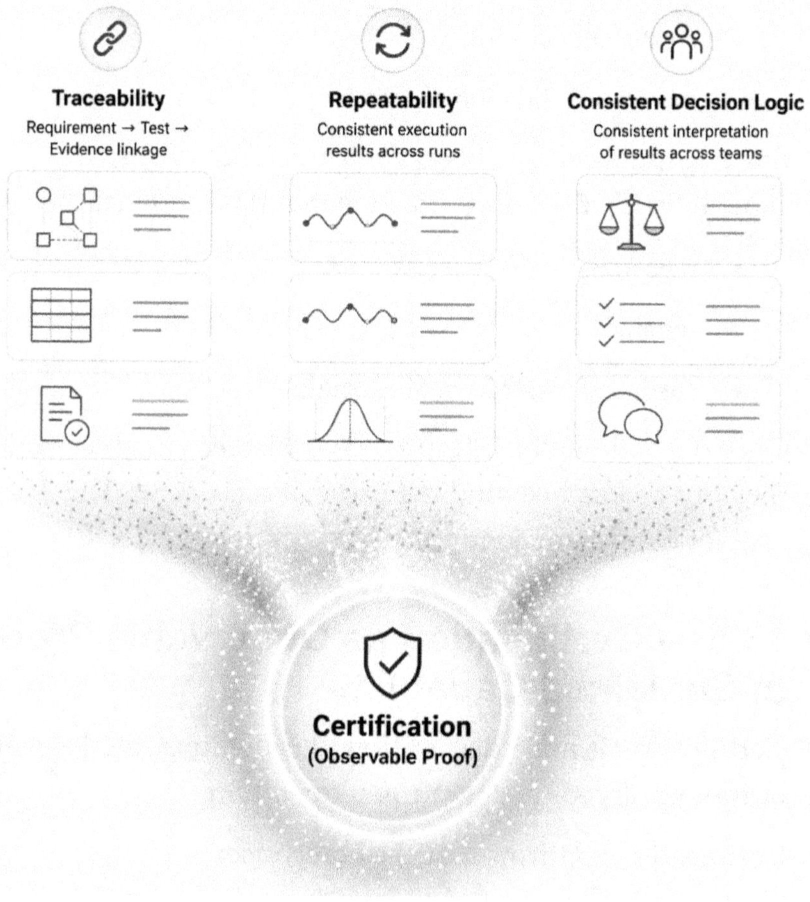

Certification is demonstrated through consistent, traceable system outputs that reliably support release decisions without reinterpretation.

Proof is derived from normal system operation, not preparation.

Observable Evidence Required for Certification

Traceability Chain

- Requirements link to test cases
- Test cases link to execution results
- Execution results are accessible through pipeline outputs

Repeatable Pipeline Behavior

- Same inputs produce the same pass/fail outcomes
- Pipeline results determine release readiness
- No manual reinterpretation is required

Consistent Decision Logic

- Teams reach identical conclusions from the same evidence
- Defect triage decisions align without debate
- Pass/fail criteria are applied uniformly

Validated Automation and AI Use

- Automation results are used as primary decision evidence
- AI outputs are validated against defined test criteria before use

Failure Conditions

Certification is not present when:

- Pipeline outputs must be reinterpreted for decisions
- Teams require meetings to agree on test results
- Traceability between requirement and execution is incomplete

- Automation results are not trusted for release decisions

Dependency Mechanism

Certification depends on institutionalization producing:

- stable outputs
- enforced validation logic
- complete traceability

Certification confirms these outputs are:

- repeatable
- reliable
- sustained under normal conditions

13.6 — Ecosystem Continuity as Cross-System Validation Compatibility

Ecosystem continuity occurs when validation outputs from one system can be used directly by another system without reinterpretation.

> **Concept Insight: Ecosystem continuity requires QACE evidence to preserve meaning across system boundaries without translation or revalidation.**

Continuity depends on compatible validation logic, evidence structure, and decision criteria.

Cross-System Interface Model (Formal Structure)

Cross-system interaction is defined as a structured interface between System A and System B.

Interface Boundary Definition

System A Output Interface:

- Requirement identifiers and pass/fail criteria
- Test case mappings
- Execution results
- Evidence artifacts (logs, traces)
- Pipeline decision outputs

System B Input Interface:

- Consumes all System A outputs without transformation

Structural Requirements

- Identical pass/fail logic must be preserved
- Traceability structure must remain intact across boundary
- Evidence format must be interpretable without conversion
- Pipeline outputs must retain decision meaning

Interface Constraint

System B must be able to execute: Input (from A) → Pipeline Processing (B) → Decision (B) without reinterpretation, additional validation layers, or structural transformation.

Boundary Condition

If any transformation is required at the interface, continuity is structurally invalid.

Continuity depends on the preservation of meaning across system boundaries without transformation.

Figure 13.9 – Cross-System Validation Interface

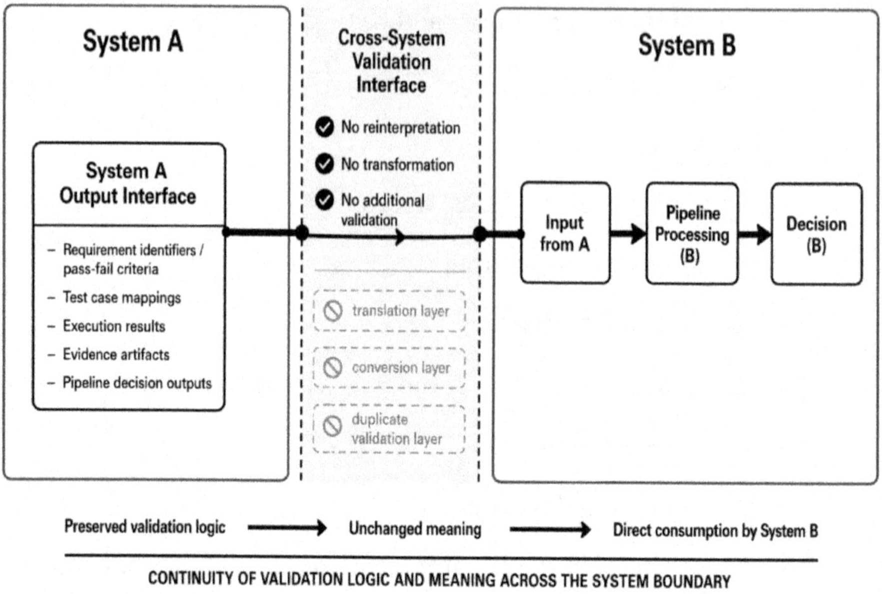

Continuity exists when outputs from one system can be consumed by another without reinterpretation, transformation, or validation duplication.

System boundaries must not alter validation logic or evidence meaning.

Concrete Cross-System Scenario

System A produces:

- Requirements with defined pass/fail criteria
- Test cases aligned to those criteria
- Automated execution results
- Pipeline outputs indicating release readiness

System B receives:

- Test results
- Logs and traces

- Traceability links
- Pipeline outputs

Continuity Exists When

- System B interprets outputs using the same pass/fail logic
- System B can use received evidence for its own decisions
- No translation, transformation, or additional validation is required

Breakdown Conditions

Continuity fails when:

- Test results require reinterpretation
- Pass/fail logic differs between systems
- Traceability structures are incompatible
- Logs and outputs cannot support downstream decisions
- Additional validation layers are needed at system boundaries

Cross-System Validation Chain

Continuity requires:

- Requirement with explicit pass/fail criteria
- Test cases reflecting those criteria
- Automated execution using the same logic
- Pipeline outputs exposing results and traceability
- Receiving system applying identical decision logic

Observable Indicators

- Cross-system decisions do not require reconciliation
- Received evidence is used directly in pipelines

- No interface-level validation layers are added
- Test results remain interpretable across systems
- Connected systems produce aligned decisions

System Requirements

Continuity requires:

- Shared pass/fail definitions
- Compatible traceability structures
- Equivalent use of automation outputs
- Consistent pipeline decision logic

Tools may differ—meaning must align.

Dependency Mechanism

Continuity depends on:

- Institutionalization enforcing stable behavior
- Certification confirming reliable outputs

Only then can outputs be used across system boundaries.

13.7 — Reframe Quality as Coordinated, Assisted, and Governed Capability

The Problem

Most organizations treat quality as separate activities:

- testing
- governance
- AI usage
- governance

This creates:

- inconsistent decisions
- conflicting evidence
- unstable outcomes

More activity does not fix this problem.

The Correct Model

Quality is not a set of activities. It is a coordinated system of capabilities:

- Testing defines expected behavior
- Automation verifies known behavior
- AI supports analysis under constraint
- Governance enforces valid use

These must operate together.

Quality emerges when all capabilities operate within a single coordinated system.

Figure 13.10 – Coordinated Quality Capability Model

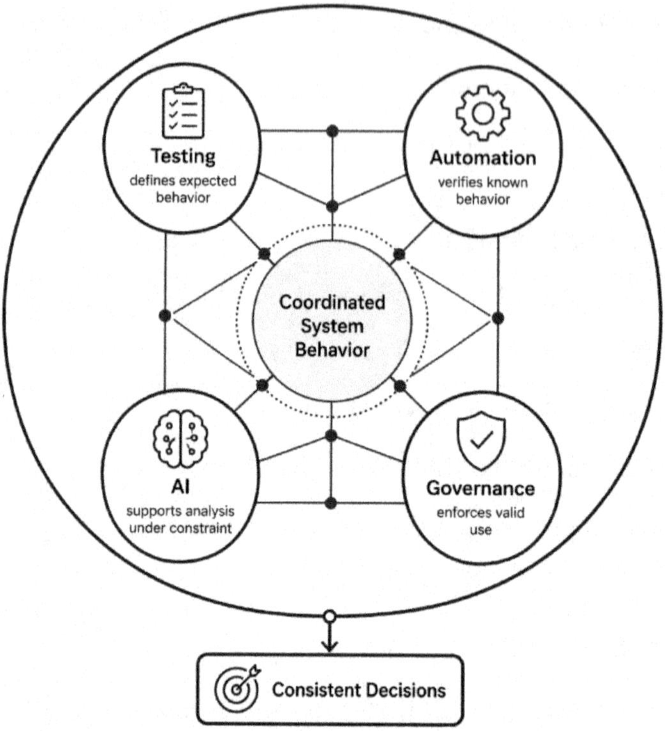

Testing, automation, AI, and governance operate together within a unified system to produce consistent decisions.

Coordination replaces fragmented activity with integrated system behavior.

What Changes in Practice

In a coordinated system:

- Test cases match requirement definitions
- Automation results are used directly in release decisions
- AI outputs are validated before use
- Pipelines connect evidence across the lifecycle

Quality becomes part of how work happens—not something added later.

Why This Matters

Without coordination:

- Teams produce conflicting results
- Decisions require reconciliation
- Defects escape due to inconsistent interpretation

With coordination:

- Decisions are faster
- Outcomes are predictable
- Systems scale without fragmentation

What the Reader Should Question

- Are decisions based on shared evidence or debate?
- Are pipeline results trusted or reinterpreted?
- Does quality require meetings to align?
- Are practices coordinated or independent?

Chapter Progression Summary

Stage	**System Meaning**	**Observable Evidence**
Adoption	Validated behavior becomes normal operation.	Stable execution without repeated enforcement.

Stage	System Meaning	Observable Evidence
Transformation	The system operates differently as a whole.	Reduced contradiction and less corrective effort.
Scaling	Validated behavior propagates without fragmentation.	Consistency across expanding teams and domains.
Institutionalization	Validated behavior becomes structurally embedded.	Deviation is constrained by the operating structure.
Certification	Sustained capability is formally confirmed.	Normal operation demonstrates traceable capability.
Ecosystem Continuity	Capability connects across compatible systems.	Cross-system alignment occurs through equivalent operating logic.

All stages represent behavioral evolution while operating on the same underlying structural model.

Figure 13.11 – System Progression: Adoption to Continuity

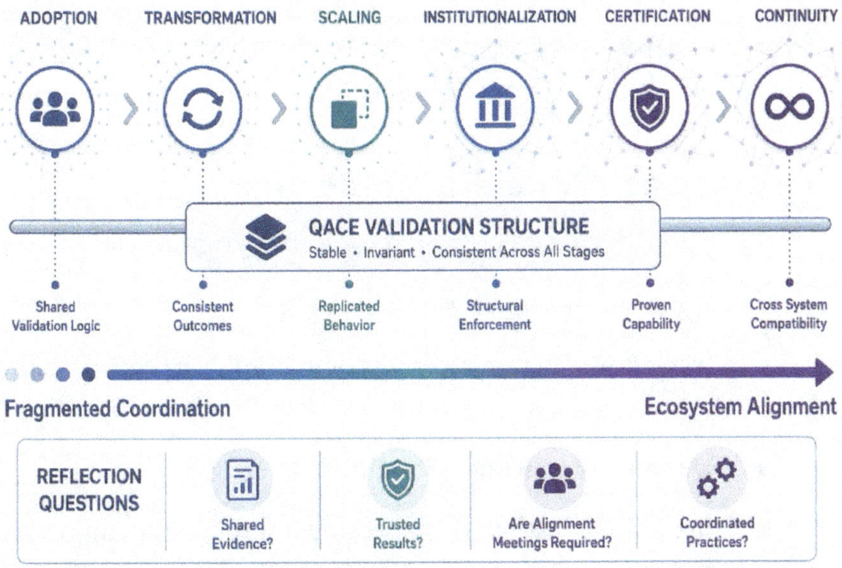

Each stage reflects increasing system capability while operating on the same underlying structural model.

System maturity is defined by behavior, not structural change.

Structural Interpretation of Stage Progression

All stages operate on the same structural model (R → T → A → E → P → D). What changes is the behavior of the structure, not the structure itself.

- Adoption — structural alignment across all components
- Transformation — consistent outputs across the structure
- Scaling — replication of structure without variation
- Institutionalization — enforcement within structure (gates, constraints)
- Certification — proof of consistent output from structure

- Continuity — compatibility of structure across system boundaries

No stage introduces new structural elements. All stages operate within the same canonical topology.

Operational Model Reinforcement

This chapter defines a complete system progression:

- Adoption → shared validation logic
- Transformation → improved outcomes from consistent logic
- Scaling → replication of validated behavior
- Institutionalization → enforcement through pipelines and structure
- Certification → proof of sustained system output
- Continuity → cross-system use of validated outputs

Each stage produces a specific system capability that can be observed.

This progression is operational, not conceptual. An organization can determine its position by evaluating:

- Are release decisions made directly from pipeline outputs?
- Do teams interpret test results the same way?
- Can new teams operate without redefining validation logic?
- Does the system prevent invalid states automatically?
- Can outputs be used across systems without reinterpretation?

If any answer is no, the system progression is incomplete. The objective is not increased activity. The objective is consistent, traceable, and usable system output.

> **Final Takeaway: Quality becomes real when requirements, tests, automation, and pipeline outputs produce consistent decisions within and across systems without manual reconciliation or reinterpretation.**

Quality Intelligence In An Agentic Future

Organizations are entering a period where requirements, code, tests, documentation, analyses, and recommendations can be generated at unprecedented speed.

For many, this appears to be the solution to longstanding delivery and quality challenges. Yet the fundamental problem facing organizations has never been the ability to generate more artifacts. It has been the ability to understand what those artifacts mean, how they relate to business objectives, and whether they contribute to desired outcomes.

Artificial intelligence can dramatically accelerate activity. It cannot automatically provide judgment, governance, accountability, context, or organizational understanding. As the volume of generated content increases, the risk of mistaking activity for progress becomes even greater. Thousands of requirements do not guarantee alignment. Thousands of test cases do not guarantee confidence. Thousands of recommendations do not guarantee sound decisions.

The challenge remains unchanged:

How do organizations determine whether what was generated represents the right understanding, the right decision, and the right outcome?

This is why Quality Intelligence becomes more—not less—important in an AI-enabled future. Organizations that establish strong foundations in governance, validation, accountability, traceability, and decision-making will be positioned to benefit from these advances. Organizations that do not may simply automate confusion at unprecedented scale.

AI increases volume.

Quality Intelligence increases understanding.

The future of enterprise quality will not be shaped solely by faster delivery, more automation, or increasingly capable AI systems. It will be shaped by how effectively organizations transform information into understanding and understanding into action. The principles introduced in this book provide the foundation for that journey. Future volumes will explore how organizations assess their current state, design effective transformation strategies, and apply emerging technologies—including AI—across the quality ecosystem while maintaining control, accountability, and confidence in outcomes.

Chapter 13 — Knowledge Check

Adoption, Transformation, and Institutional Continuity

The following questions are designed to verify accurate understanding of how enterprise quality systems evolve from adoption through transformation, scaling, institutionalization, certification, and cross-system continuity. They assess whether the reader can distinguish between behavioral alignment and outcome transformation, understand how structural enforcement replaces manual coordination, and recognize how validated outputs enable system-level and ecosystem-level consistency.

These questions are nonprocedural. They do not assess implementation approaches, tools, or organizational change techniques.

Knowledge Check 13.1 — Adoption

Question
What condition must be present for adoption to be considered complete within a system?

Knowledge Check 13.2 — Adoption vs Transformation

Question
What is the difference between aligned behavior (adoption) and improved system outcomes (transformation)?

Knowledge Check 13.3 — Transformation Signals

Question
What observable signals indicate that transformation has occurred rather than isolated improvement?

Knowledge Check 13.4 — Scaling

Question
Why does scaling require replication of validated behavior rather than expansion of teams or tools?

Knowledge Check 13.5 — Institutionalization

Question

What changes when quality enforcement shifts from people-based governance to system-level constraints?

Knowledge Check 13.6 — Certification

Question

How does certification demonstrate sustained system capability, and why must it emerge from normal system operation?

Knowledge Check 13.7 — Ecosystem Continuity

Question

What conditions must be met for outputs from one system to be used directly by another without reinterpretation?

Knowledge Check 13.8 — Coordinated Quality Capability

Question

Why must testing, automation, AI, and governance operate as a coordinated system rather than as independent activities?

Guidance for the Reader

If you can explain how systems progress from aligned behavior to predictable outcomes, describe how structural enforcement replaces interpretation and reconciliation, and identify how validated outputs enable consistent decisions across systems, you have completed the core model of QACE.

This chapter establishes the full system progression from adoption through ecosystem continuity, showing how quality evolves from aligned execution to a fully governed, validated, and interoperable enterprise capability. It clarifies how consistent evidence handling, structural enforcement, and traceable outputs enable systems to operate without manual reconciliation or reinterpretation.

With this foundation established, the reader can now evaluate any system by asking whether it produces consistent, traceable, and directly usable outputs within and across boundaries. The complete QACE model defines how quality becomes a sustained, governed system capability rather than a set of activities or interventions.

Questions for Reflection

- Where in my organization is quality still treated primarily as downstream checking, approval, or defect detection?
- Which current quality practices appear coordinated on the surface but still operate from different assumptions, signals, or decision rules?
- How often does our organization need meetings, escalation, or manual reconciliation to restore alignment that the system should already be producing?
- Are testing, automation, AI, and quality participation functioning as coordinated capabilities—or as separate activities managed under different logic?
- What evidence would show that we have truly adopted a new quality model rather than simply introduced new language, tools, or roles?
- Where does our operating structure still allow fragmented quality behavior to survive under pressure?

- Are we scaling capability—or are we spreading local variation, inconsistent automation use, and contradictory decision-making into more areas?
- What signals suggest that our organization is still using the wrong model of quality even while claiming maturity?
- If quality assurance in our environment remains largely reactive, what would need to change for quality assistance to become real?
- What manageable, incremental changes would most directly move us from fragmented quality activity toward governed quality capability?

Chapter Knowledge Check Answers

Chapter 3 — Knowledge Check Answers

Q1: Why does correcting quality myths, as discussed in Chapter 2, fail to restore control in large, complex organizations?
Level: K2 – Application
Answer: Correcting myths improves how organizations explain failures after they occur, but it does not restore the ability to perceive emerging issues early. Control depends on perception, not explanation, and at scale perception degrades structurally. Therefore, improved understanding exposes the lack of control rather than fixing it.
Source: Chapter 3 – Section 3.1 (Perception vs Explanation)

Q2: What does it mean to say that late discovery is structural rather than simply late?
Level: K1 – Comprehension
Answer: Late discovery is structural because issues are detected only when the system is capable of recognizing them, typically after signals reach aggregate thresholds. Signals exist early but remain fragmented and uninterpretable. Therefore, discovery timing reflects system design, not delayed execution.
Source: Chapter 3 – Section 3.3 (Structural Late Discovery)

Q3: What condition must the reader accept before progressing from this chapter to the next?
Level: K3 – System Reasoning
Answer: The reader must accept that failure at scale is caused by structural limits in perception—not by lack of

effort, discipline, or understanding—and that traditional improvements cannot restore control.
Source: Chapter 3 – Summary / Threshold Concept

Q4: How does execution failure differ from judgment failure in the context of this chapter?
Level: K2 – Application
Answer: Execution failure occurs when actions are incorrect or incomplete. Judgment failure occurs when decisions are made based on distorted or incomplete perception, even if execution is correct. At scale, failure shifts from action errors to interpretation errors.
Source: Chapter 3 – Section 3.4 (Execution vs Judgment Failure)

Chapter 4 — Knowledge Check Answers

Q1: Define Q Intelligence™ in a single, complete sentence.
Level: K1 – Comprehension
Answer: Q Intelligence™ is the structured enterprise capability that governs how quality signals are interpreted to produce reliable, intelligible, and decision-ready judgment at scale.
Source: Chapter 4 – Section 4.1 (Definition)

Q2: Which of the following is not a function of Q Intelligence™?
Level: K1 – Comprehension
Correct Answer: C
Answer: C. Defining testing techniques and execution practices
Explanation: Q Intelligence™ governs interpretation and judgment, not execution methods or testing practices.
Source: Chapter 4 – Section 4.1–4.2 (Discipline Boundaries)

Q3: Why does Q Intelligence™ represent a different category of discipline than traditional quality frameworks?
Level: K2 – Application
Answer: Because it governs the conditions of interpretation and judgment, whereas traditional frameworks focus on execution, compliance, or optimization. Q Intelligence™ operates at the level of meaning and decision reliability, not activity.
Source: Chapter 4 – Section 4.2 (Category Separation)

Q4: What is the conceptual difference between axioms and principles within Q Intelligence™?
Level: K1 – Comprehension
Answer: Axioms define non-negotiable constraints required for valid judgment, while principles translate those constraints into organizational orientation for consistent interpretation.
Source: Chapter 4 – Sections 4.3–4.4

Q5: What role does the Q Intelligence™ Master Framework play, and what does it avoid prescribing?
Level: K2 – Application
Answer: It provides a stable conceptual structure for reasoning about quality intelligence and preserves coherence across contexts. It intentionally avoids prescribing operational methods, tools, or implementation details.
Source: Chapter 4 – Section 4.5

Q6: What is the purpose of the Q Intelligence™ Manifesto?
Level: K3 – System Reasoning
Answer: It defines the institutional interpretive stance for how quality must be understood, ensuring consistent meaning before operational application. It is separate to prevent confusion between foundational belief and

implementation.
Source: Chapter 4 – Section 4.6

Chapter 5 — Knowledge Check Answers

Q1: What problem does QOS™ solve at enterprise scale?
Level: K2 – Application
Answer: It resolves the gap between distributed quality activity and required system coherence by providing a coordinating architecture that preserves shared meaning across the enterprise.
Source: Chapter 5 – Section 5.1

Q2: What is the difference between accumulation and a coordinated system?
Level: K2 – Application
Answer: Accumulation consists of disconnected capabilities operating locally, while a coordinated system integrates those capabilities through architecture so they produce coherent, system-level understanding.
Source: Chapter 5 – Section 5.1

Q3: Why is QOS™ described as an operating system?
Level: K2 – Application
Answer: Because it defines the structural relationships that allow system components to interact coherently, rather than prescribing practices, tools, or execution methods.
Source: Chapter 5 – Section 5.2

Q4: What are the three layers of QOS™, and what does each do?
Level: K1 – Comprehension
Answer: Intent Layer defines enterprise-level quality objectives; Intelligence Layer preserves and interprets quality signals; Response Layer enables action based on

system intelligence.
Source: Chapter 5 – Section 5.3

Q5: Why is separation of layers critical?
Level: K2 – Application
Answer: Separation prevents collapse of meaning by allowing intent, intelligence, and response to evolve independently while preserving coherent relationships.
Source: Chapter 5 – Section 5.3

Q6: Why does QOS™ avoid defining execution practices or governance mechanisms?
Level: K3 – System Reasoning
Answer: To preserve architectural neutrality and prevent the system from collapsing into specific processes or control models that would distort structural relationships and reduce adaptability.
Source: Chapter 5 – Section 5.5-5.6

Q7: What happens when signal meaning is not preserved across system layers?
Level: K3 – System Reasoning
Answer: Signals become distorted, resulting in inconsistent interpretation, fragmented decisions, and decreased system predictability.
Source: Chapter 5 – Section 5.4

Chapter 6 — Knowledge Check Answers

Q1: What is the primary purpose of governance within an enterprise quality system?
Level: K1 – Comprehension
Answer: To align decision authority with system intelligence and ensure decisions are deliberate, accountable, and

coherent.
Source: Chapter 6 — Section 6.1–6.2

Q2: Why is governance not an extension of execution or measurement?
Level: K2 — Application
Answer: Because governance operates over decisions rather than activities or metrics, defining how choices are made rather than how work is performed or measured.
Source: Chapter 6 — Section 6.2

Q3: What happens when decision authority is not aligned with intelligence?
Level: K2 — Application
Answer: Decisions either lack sufficient context or insights are not used, creating instability, inconsistency, and poor outcomes.
Source: Chapter 6 — Section 6.1

Q4: What does governance operate over, and why is this important?
Level: K2 — Application
Answer: It operates over decision points such as trade-offs and constraints, because these directly determine system outcomes.
Source: Chapter 6 — Section 6.2

Q5: What are the five Governance Pillars?
Level: K1 — Comprehension
Answer: Authority, Accountability, Constraint, Review, and Correction form the structure of governance.
Source: Chapter 6 — Section 6.3

Q6: What is the difference between authority and accountability?
Level: K1 — Comprehension

Answer: Authority determines who makes the decision, while accountability defines who owns the outcome.
Source: Chapter 6 – Section 6.3–6.4

Q7: How does governance differ from gatekeeping?
Level: K3 – System Reasoning
Answer: Governance ensures continuous decision integrity, while gatekeeping applies control after execution, making governance proactive and gatekeeping reactive.
Source: Chapter 6 – Section 6.5

Q8: Why is governance a precondition for maturity?
Level: K3 – System Reasoning
Answer: Because consistent outcomes require a stable, aligned decision structure before capability can be evaluated or improved meaningfully.
Source: Chapter 6 – Section 6.6

Chapter 7 — Knowledge Check Answers

Q1: What does maturity represent within an enterprise system?
Level: K1 – Comprehension
Answer: Maturity represents the system's ability to consistently produce intended outcomes across varying conditions.
Source: Chapter 7 – Section 7.0

Q2: Why must maturity be understood as structural accumulation?
Level: K2 – Application
Answer: Because consistent outcomes result from aligned system structures rather than isolated improvements or increased activity.
Source: Chapter 7 – Section 7.2

Q3: Why is maturity considered a system property?
Level: K2 – Application
Answer: Because it depends on alignment across architecture, execution, governance, and feedback rather than individual performance.
Source: Chapter 7 – Section 7.1

Q4: Which system dimensions determine maturity?
Level: K1 – Comprehension
Answer: Architecture, execution, governance, and feedback collectively determine system maturity.
Source: Chapter 7 – Section 7.1

Q5: Why do maturity levels represent structural shifts rather than incremental improvements?
Level: K2 – Application
Answer: Because each level reflects a fundamental change in how the system operates rather than isolated performance improvement.
Source: Chapter 7 – Section 7.2

Q6: What role do observable signals play in maturity assessment?
Level: K2 – Application
Answer: They provide consistent patterns of behavior that enable interpretation and comparison of system capability.
Source: Chapter 7 – Section 7.3

Q7: What role do constraints play in maturity progression?
Level: K3 – System Reasoning
Answer: Constraints limit progression by maintaining fragmentation, requiring removal and alignment for advancement.
Source: Chapter 7 – Section 7.4

Q8: What is the primary role of the QACE Maturity Model?
Level: K2 – Application
Answer: It provides a structured framework for diagnosing and understanding system capability and guiding improvement.
Source: Chapter 7 – Section 7.5

Chapter 8 — Knowledge Check Answers

Q1: What role do diagnostics play in transforming quality from measurement into intelligence?
Level: K2 – Application
Answer: Diagnostics transform measurement into intelligence by interpreting data within system context, structure, and relationships, allowing signals to be understood in terms of system behavior and outcome relevance rather than isolated metrics.
Source: Chapter 8 – Section 8.1

Q2: What are the stages of the diagnostic transformation chain, and how does each stage contribute to system understanding?
Level: K1 – Comprehension
Answer: The stages are Data → Signals → Interpretation → Decision → Action → Validation → Integration. Each stage progressively converts raw observation into structured, validated understanding that can be used to guide system behavior.
Source: Chapter 8 – Section 8 Introduction

Q3: What is the difference between raw data and signals, and why is this distinction critical?
Level: K1 – Comprehension

Answer: Raw data represents unprocessed observations, while signals are structured patterns derived from data that indicate system state and direction. This distinction is critical because decisions depend on meaningful signals, not raw data volume.
Source: Chapter 8 – Section 8.2

Q4: Why do signals alone not constitute insight, and what role does interpretation play in forming understanding?
Level: K2 – Application
Answer: Signals do not constitute insight because they require interpretation to connect observed patterns to system meaning. Interpretation provides context that transforms signals into actionable understanding.
Source: Chapter 8 – Section 8.3

Q5: How do diagnostics ensure that decisions are aligned with system behavior rather than subjective judgment?
Level: K2 – Application
Answer: Diagnostics align decisions with system behavior by ensuring that interpretations are rooted in structured signals and validated evidence rather than individual assumptions or isolated observations.
Source: Chapter 8 – Section 8.4

Q6: What is the role of validation loops in the diagnostic model, and how do they contribute to continuous system improvement?
Level: K2 – Application
Answer: Validation loops confirm that actions produce intended outcomes and reintegrate results as evidence, allowing the system to learn and improve continuously based on verified behavior.
Source: Chapter 8 – Section 8.5

Q7: Why must diagnostics be integrated into the QOS™ rather than operate as isolated analytical functions?
Level: K3 – System Reasoning
Answer: Diagnostics must be integrated into QOS™ to ensure that intelligence remains coherent across the system rather than fragmented, enabling consistent interpretation, decision-making, and action.
Source: Chapter 8 – Section 8.6

Q8: What happens to enterprise performance when diagnostics are absent or inconsistently applied across the system?
Level: K3 – System Reasoning
Answer: Performance becomes reactive, inconsistent, and misaligned, as decisions are made without reliable interpretation of system behavior, leading to fragmented outcomes and reduced predictability.
Source: Chapter 8 – Overall Concept

Chapter 9 — Knowledge Check Answers

Q1: Why is automation not considered a source of intelligence within an enterprise system?
Level: K1 – Comprehension
Answer: Automation executes predefined logic but cannot independently create, interpret, or validate system intelligence.
Source: Chapter 9 – Section 9.1

Q2: What is the difference between automation as execution and automation architecture as a structural system component?
Level: K2 – Application
Answer: Automation as execution performs tasks, while automation architecture defines how that execution is

governed, constrained, and aligned within the overall system structure.
Source: Chapter 9 – Section 9.2

Q3: What happens when automation is treated as tooling rather than positioned within system architecture?
Level: K2 – Application
Answer: Execution replaces structure, resulting in fragmented, inconsistent, and non-traceable system behavior.
Source: Chapter 9 – Section 9.1

Q4: Why must automation depend entirely on system intelligence rather than operate independently?
Level: K3 – System Reasoning
Answer: Because independent automation introduces conflicting behavior and decisions, while dependency ensures execution reflects consistent and validated system intelligence.
Source: Chapter 9 – Section 9.4

Q5: What structural characteristics indicate that automation is correctly aligned within the system?
Level: K1 – Comprehension
Answer: Automation must be dependent, bounded, transparent, traceable, and non-generative within the system structure.
Source: Chapter 9 – Section 9.4

Q6: What do automation design patterns represent, and why are they not procedural instructions?
Level: K2 – Application
Answer: They represent structural ways automation expresses system intelligence rather than step-by-step

execution instructions.
Source: Chapter 9 – Section 9.5

Q7: What structural failures occur when automation is elevated beyond its intended role?
Level: K3 – System Reasoning
Answer: Failures include intelligence substitution, procedural inflation, framework misclassification, and autonomy drift, leading to system inconsistency and loss of control.
Source: Chapter 9 – Section 9.6

Q8: How does correctly positioned automation preserve system coherence and predictability?
Level: K2 – Application
Answer: By executing defined behavior consistently while remaining bounded and traceable, ensuring system relationships remain stable and predictable.
Source: Chapter 9 – Concept Summary

Chapter 10 — Knowledge Check Answers

Q1: Why are accessibility, internationalization, and usability frequently misclassified within enterprise systems?
Level: K1 – Comprehension
Answer: They are frequently treated as interface or presentation concerns rather than core system properties, leading to their exclusion from structural quality considerations.
Source: Chapter 10 – Section 10.1

Q2: What changes when accessibility, internationalization, and usability are understood as quality dimensions?
Level: K2 – Application

Answer: They become foundational system conditions that determine whether quality can be realized consistently, rather than optional enhancements applied after development.
Source: Chapter 10 – Section 10.2

Q3: Why must these dimensions be embedded within the system rather than applied at the interface level?
Level: K2 – Application
Answer: Because they continuously shape how the system behaves across all interactions, not just in isolated interface components.
Source: Chapter 10 – Section 10.3

Q4: How do accessibility, internationalization, and usability act as constraints on system behavior?
Level: K2 – Application
Answer: They define the valid operating space of the system, ensuring consistent interpretation, interaction, and usability across diverse users and contexts.
Source: Chapter 10 – Section 10.4

Q5: What happens when these dimensions are inconsistently applied?
Level: K3 – System Reasoning
Answer: System coherence breaks down, leading to inconsistent user experiences, unreliable interpretation, and reduced decision quality across contexts.
Source: Chapter 10 – Section 10.4

Q6: How do failures in these dimensions manifest as observable system signals?
Level: K2 – Application
Answer: Failures appear as exclusion, misinterpretation, and user friction, indicating that system behavior is not

consistently aligned with intended outcomes.
Source: Chapter 10 – Section 10.5

Q7: Why do failures in these dimensions propagate systemically rather than remain localized?
Level: K3 – System Reasoning
Answer: Because these dimensions are embedded across the system, their failure affects all interactions, outputs, and user interpretations rather than isolated components.
Source: Chapter 10 – Section 10.5

Q8: How do these dimensions influence other quality attributes?
Level: K3 – System Reasoning
Answer: They enable reliability, correctness, and completeness to function consistently across contexts by ensuring system outputs are interpretable and usable.
Source: Chapter 10 – Section 10.6

Chapter 11 — Knowledge Check Answers

Q1: What problem does the QACE Validation Model solve compared to traditional validation approaches?
Level: K2 – Application
Answer: It replaces fragmented, phase-based validation with continuous, governed visibility into system behavior, ensuring consistent and structured validation across the system.
Source: Chapter 11 – Section 11.1

Q2: Why must validation be treated as a system capability rather than an activity?
Level: K3 – System Reasoning
Answer: Because validation must continuously observe and verify system behavior, rather than occur as isolated

checkpoints, ensuring ongoing consistency and reliability.
Source: Chapter 11 – Section 11.1

Q3: What are the three primary structural components of the QACE Validation Model?
Level: K1 – Comprehension
Answer: Validation layers, cross-cutting dimensions, and signal production define the structure of validation within the model.
Source: Chapter 11 – Section 11.3

Q4: What is the difference between validation layers and dimensions?
Level: K2 – Application
Answer: Layers define where validation occurs within the system, while dimensions define how system behavior is evaluated across different perspectives.
Source: Chapter 11 – Section 11.6

Q5: How are signals produced within the model?
Level: K2 – Application
Answer: Signals are produced at the intersection of validation layers and dimensions, ensuring that outputs are traceable, structured, and interpretable.
Source: Chapter 11 – Section 11.7

Q6: What happens when validation structure breaks down?
Level: K3 – System Reasoning
Answer: Clarity, traceability, and comparability are lost, making it difficult to interpret system behavior and ensure consistent validation outcomes.
Source: Chapter 11 – Section 11.11

Q7: Why are signals critical to the validation model?
Level: K2 – Application

Answer: Signals provide the structured evidence required for reliable diagnostics and system understanding.
Source: Chapter 11 – Section 11.7

Q8: Why must execution modes remain separate from validation structure?
Level: K3 – System Reasoning
Answer: To ensure that validation remains stable and consistent regardless of how execution is performed, preserving structural integrity.
Source: Chapter 11 – Section 11.9

Chapter 12 — Knowledge Check Answers

Q1: What does validation confirm within the QACE system?
Level: K1 – Comprehension
Answer: Validation confirms that intended outcomes were produced by specific actions and sustained over time.
Source: Chapter 12 – Section 12.1

Q2: Why must a decision define a measurable intended outcome before action is taken?
Level: K2 – Application
Answer: Because validation depends on proving a specific outcome, not general improvements or activity completion.
Source: Chapter 12 – Section 12.1

Q3: What happens when a link in the Validation Chain is missing?
Level: K2 – Application
Answer: The system cannot establish causality, making outcomes unreliable and unverifiable.
Source: Chapter 12 – Section 12.2

Q4: Why is traceability required in the validation process?
Level: K2 – Application
Answer: To connect decisions, actions, outcomes, and evidence into a verifiable and coherent proof chain.
Source: Chapter 12 – Section 12.3

Q5: Why are activity-based signals insufficient to prove system improvement?
Level: K3 – System Reasoning
Answer: Because activity does not prove that outcomes improved or were caused by specific actions, leading to false assumptions of success.
Source: Chapter 12 – Section 12.5

Q6: Why must validation confirm outcome persistence across time and conditions?
Level: K3 – System Reasoning
Answer: Because true validation requires that outcomes remain stable under varying conditions, ensuring reliability beyond isolated success.
Source: Chapter 12 – Section 12.4

Q7: How does the absence of validation create false confidence?
Level: K2 – Application
Answer: It leads organizations to assume improvement based on activity or metrics without verifying actual system outcomes.
Source: Chapter 12 – Section 12.5

Q8: Why must validation be embedded within normal system operation?
Level: K3 – System Reasoning
Answer: To ensure continuous verification of outcomes as part of system behavior, rather than isolated, post-hoc

evaluation.
Source: Chapter 12 – Section 12.6

Chapter 13 — Knowledge Check Answers

Q1: What condition must be present for adoption to be considered complete?
Level: K1 – Comprehension
Answer: Adoption is complete when system behavior operates consistently using shared logic without requiring manual reconciliation.
Source: Chapter 13 – Section 13.1

Q2: What is the difference between adoption and transformation?
Level: K2 – Application
Answer: Adoption aligns system behavior with a model, while transformation produces measurable, sustained improvements in system outcomes.
Source: Chapter 13 – Section 13.2

Q3: What observable signals indicate transformation?
Level: K2 – Application
Answer: Consistent decisions, predictable outcomes, reduced defects, and decreased need for manual reconciliation indicate transformation.
Source: Chapter 13 – Section 13.2

Q4: Why does scaling require replication of validated behavior?
Level: K3 – System Reasoning
Answer: Because scaling is achieved by consistently reproducing proven system behavior, not by expanding inconsistent practices.
Source: Chapter 13 – Section 13.3

Q5: What changes when quality enforcement shifts to system constraints?
Level: K3 – System Reasoning
Answer: Quality becomes enforced through structural rules rather than human oversight, increasing consistency and reducing reliance on intervention.
Source: Chapter 13 – Section 13.4

Q6: How does certification demonstrate system capability?
Level: K2 – Application
Answer: Certification provides evidence that system behavior is consistent, traceable, and repeatable under normal operating conditions.
Source: Chapter 13 – Section 13.5

Q7: What conditions are required for ecosystem continuity?
Level: K3 – System Reasoning
Answer: Shared validation logic, traceability, consistent evidence structures, and no need for reinterpretation enable continuity across systems.
Source: Chapter 13 – Section 13.6

Q8: Why must quality-related functions operate as a coordinated system?
Level: K3 – System Reasoning
Answer: Because independent activities produce conflicting signals, while coordination ensures consistent interpretation, decisions, and outcomes.
Source: Chapter 13 – Section 13.7

Book-Level Knowledge Check

Book 1 — The Umbrella Playbook

The following questions assess your understanding of the complete QACE model as presented throughout this book.

This assessment is designed to evaluate your ability to understand core concepts and distinctions, apply those concepts within enterprise contexts, and reason across the system as an integrated whole.

How to Use This Section

- Answer each question based on your understanding of the full book.
- Some questions require direct recall, while others require interpretation or system-level reasoning.
- Many questions require you to synthesize concepts across multiple chapters rather than rely on a single section.

Take your time to consider each question fully before responding.

Question Types

- Short answer questions
- Multiple choice questions
- Ordering and sequencing questions
- Scenario-based reasoning questions

Each question is designed to test a different aspect of understanding, from conceptual clarity to enterprise-level reasoning.

Recording Your Answers

For short answer and reasoning questions, you may write your responses on separate paper, in a notebook, or digitally if you are reading in electronic format.

This section is designed to emphasize thoughtful reasoning rather than simple recall. Writing your responses will help reinforce understanding and improve retention.

Using the Answer Key

After completing the questions, refer to the Book-Level Knowledge Check Answers section to validate your responses, understand the correct reasoning, identify gaps in your understanding, and revisit relevant chapters and concepts as needed.

Each answer includes the correct response, the level of understanding required (K1–K3), the source location within the book, and an explanation for multiple choice questions.

Learning Guidance

Do not skip directly to the answer key. Attempt each question first and write down your reasoning before reviewing the solution.

If you are unable to answer a question confidently, return to the referenced chapter and review the concept, focus on understanding relationships between ideas rather than only definitions, and pay particular attention to how structure, intelligence, and governance interact across the system.

Purpose of This Assessment

This knowledge check is intended to reinforce understanding of key concepts, validate your ability to apply the QACE model, and develop system-level reasoning across enterprise quality architecture.

Completion of this section should provide a clear indication of your readiness to apply the model in practice.

Questions

1. What central problem does the book identify with traditional quality approaches at enterprise scale?
2. Why does increasing quality activity not necessarily improve quality outcomes?
3. Why is late discovery described as a structural condition rather than simply a delay in execution?
4. What is the difference between quality activity and quality intelligence?
5. What must change for quality to transition from a reactive function to an intelligence discipline?
6. Which of the following best explains why correcting quality myths does not restore control?
   A. Myths are difficult to communicate
   B. Myths reduce testing effectiveness
   C. Perception degrades structurally at scale
   D. Organizations do not invest enough in quality
7. What role does sensemaking play in interpreting quality signals?
8. What is the intelligence gap, and how does it manifest in enterprise systems?
9. Why does measurement alone not improve system understanding?

10. What condition must be accepted before moving from myth-based thinking to a new system model?
11. Why does correcting understanding not restore perception at scale?
12. What distinguishes execution failure from judgment failure?
13. What does it mean for a system to experience signal distortion?
14. Put the following in the correct order based on system perception at scale: Aggregation → Interpretation → Observation → Reporting
15. Define Q Intelligence™ in the context of enterprise quality.
16. Which of the following is NOT a function of Q Intelligence™?
    A. Producing decision-ready insight
    B. Governing signal interpretation
    C. Defining execution practices
    D. Enabling reliable judgment
17. Why is Q Intelligence™ considered a different category of discipline?
18. What is the purpose of axioms within Q Intelligence™?
19. What is the difference between axioms and principles?
20. What role does the Q Intelligence™ Master Framework play?
21. Why is shared intelligibility required before quality can be governed?
22. What problem does QOS™ solve at enterprise scale?
23. What is the difference between accumulating capabilities and creating a coordinated system?
24. Why is QOS™ described as an operating system rather than a framework?

25. Put the three layers of QOS™ in the correct order: Operational Response → Intelligence and Signal → Intent and Direction
26. Why is separation between intent, intelligence, and response critical?
27. What happens when signal meaning is not preserved across system layers?
28. Why does QOS™ intentionally avoid defining execution or governance mechanisms?
29. What is the primary purpose of governance within the QACE system?
30. Why must governance operate over decisions rather than activities?
31. What happens when decision authority is not aligned with intelligence?
32. Put the Governance Pillars in a logical structure: Review → Authority → Constraint → Accountability → Correction
33. What is the difference between authority and accountability?
34. How does governance differ from gatekeeping?
35. Why is governance considered a precondition for maturity?
36. What does maturity represent within an enterprise system?
37. Why is maturity considered a system property rather than a team-level measure?
38. What role do observable signals play in determining maturity?
39. What is the relationship between constraints and maturity progression?
40. What is the primary role of the QACE Maturity Model?
41. What role do diagnostics play in transforming data into intelligence?

42. Put the diagnostic transformation chain in the correct order: Decision → Data → Validation → Signals → Action → Interpretation → Integration

43. What is the difference between data and signals?

44. Why do signals require interpretation before they are useful?

45. What happens when diagnostics are missing from the system?

46. Why must diagnostics be integrated into QOS™?

47. Why is automation not considered a source of intelligence?

48. What is the difference between automation and automation architecture?

49. What happens when automation is treated as tooling instead of system structure?

50. Why must automation remain dependent on system intelligence?

51. Which of the following represents a failure mode of automation?
    A. Traceability
    B. Bounded execution
    C. Autonomy drift
    D. Structural dependency

52. Why must accessibility, internationalization, and usability be treated as system-level quality dimensions?

53. What happens when these dimensions are inconsistently applied?

54. Why do failures in these dimensions propagate across the system?

55. How do these dimensions influence other quality attributes?

56. What problem does the QACE Validation Model solve?

57. Why must validation be treated as a system capability rather than an activity?
58. What are the three structural components of the validation model?
59. What is the difference between validation layers and dimensions?
60. Put the Validation Chain in the correct order: Feedback → Action → Validation → Decision → Intended Outcome
61. Why is traceability critical within validation?
62. Why are activity-based signals insufficient for proving outcomes?
63. Why must validation confirm persistence across time and conditions?
64. What happens when validation is not embedded in system execution?
65. What condition defines successful adoption within a system?
66. What is the difference between adoption and transformation?
67. What signals indicate that transformation has occurred?
68. Why does scaling depend on replication of validated behavior?
69. What changes when quality enforcement shifts from people to system constraints?
70. What role does certification play in demonstrating system capability?
71. What conditions are required for ecosystem continuity?
72. Why must testing, automation, AI, and governance operate as a coordinated system?

Book-Level Knowledge Check Answers

Book 1 – The Umbrella Playbook

The following answers correspond to the Book-Level Knowledge Check questions. Each answer includes:

- The correct response
- A classification of the level of understanding (K1–K3)
- The source location within the book
- Explanations for multiple choice questions where applicable

Answer Key

1. What central problem does the book identify with traditional quality approaches at enterprise scale?
K-Level: K1 – Comprehension
Answer: Traditional quality approaches fail because they treat quality as activity, control, or inspection rather than as an intelligence problem that must govern judgment at scale.
Source: Chapter 1 – Core thesis / Intelligence Gap

2. Why does increasing quality activity not necessarily improve quality outcomes?
K-Level: K2 – Application
Answer: Because activity can increase volume, coverage, and visibility without improving interpretation, system understanding, or decision quality.
Source: Chapter 1 – Quality activity vs insight

3. Why is late discovery described as a structural condition rather than simply a delay in execution?

K-Level: K1 – Comprehension
Answer: Because issues are discovered only when the system becomes capable of recognizing them, making delay a result of structure rather than timing alone.
Source: Chapter 3 – Structural Late Discovery

4. What is the difference between quality activity and quality intelligence?
K-Level: K1 – Comprehension
Answer: Quality activity is execution-oriented work such as testing and measurement, while quality intelligence is the structured interpretation of signals into decision-ready insight.
Source: Chapter 1 – Activity vs intelligence

5. What must change for quality to transition from a reactive function to an intelligence discipline?
K-Level: K3 – System Reasoning
Answer: Quality must shift from producing activity and retrospective assurance to governing how signals are interpreted, understood, and used in enterprise decision-making.
Source: Chapters 1 and 4 – Transition to Q Intelligence™

6. Which of the following best explains why correcting quality myths does not restore control?
A. Myths are difficult to communicate
B. Myths reduce testing effectiveness
C. Perception degrades structurally at scale
D. Organizations do not invest enough in quality
K-Level: K2 – Application
Correct Answer: C
Answer: Perception degrades structurally at scale.

Explanation: The book shows that myths can be corrected conceptually, but correcting explanation does not restore the lost ability to perceive emerging issues across complex systems.
Source: Chapter 3 — Perception vs explanation

7. What role does sensemaking play in interpreting quality signals?
K-Level: K2 – Application
Answer: Sensemaking is the process that converts raw data and signals into meaningful system understanding, enabling quality signals to support reliable judgment.
Source: Chapter 2 — Myth of measurement / Sensemaking

8. What is the intelligence gap, and how does it manifest in enterprise systems?
K-Level: K2 – Application
Answer: The intelligence gap is the separation between the quantity of quality information produced and the organization's ability to interpret it into coherent, decision-ready understanding.
Source: Chapter 1 — Intelligence Gap

9. Why does measurement alone not improve system understanding?
K-Level: K2 – Application
Answer: Because measurement describes observed activity or outcomes, but without interpretation it does not explain system condition, source, or significance.
Source: Chapter 2 — Metrics do not equal control

10. What condition must be accepted before moving from

myth-based thinking to a new system model?
K-Level: K3 – System Reasoning
Answer: The reader must accept that quality failure at scale is structural and cannot be resolved through more activity, better myths, or isolated process improvement.
Source: Chapter 3 – Threshold / transition to Chapter 4

11. Why does correcting understanding not restore perception at scale?
K-Level: K2 – Application
Answer: Because understanding improves explanation after the fact, while perception is the system's ability to recognize emerging conditions early enough to govern them.
Source: Chapter 3 – Perception degradation

12. What distinguishes execution failure from judgment failure?
K-Level: K2 – Application
Answer: Execution failure means actions were performed incorrectly or incompletely; judgment failure means decisions were made using distorted or inadequate understanding of system conditions.
Source: Chapter 3 – Execution vs judgment

13. What does it mean for a system to experience signal distortion?
K-Level: K1 – Comprehension
Answer: Signal distortion occurs when system signals lose clarity or meaning as they pass through abstraction, aggregation, or scale, making interpretation less accurate.
Source: Chapter 3 – Signal Distortion

14. Put the following in the correct order based on system

perception at scale:
Aggregation → Interpretation → Observation → Reporting
K-Level: K1 – Comprehension
Answer: Observation → Aggregation → Reporting → Interpretation
Source: Chapter 3 – Signal scaling / abstraction logic

15. Define Q Intelligence™ in the context of enterprise quality.
K-Level: K1 – Comprehension
Answer: Q Intelligence™ is the enterprise capability that governs how quality signals are interpreted into intelligible, reliable, and decision-ready judgment at scale.
Source: Chapter 4 – Definition

16. Which of the following is NOT a function of Q Intelligence™?
A. Producing decision-ready insight
B. Governing signal interpretation
C. Defining execution practices
D. Enabling reliable judgment
K-Level: K1 – Comprehension
Correct Answer: C
Answer: Defining execution practices
Explanation: Q Intelligence™ governs interpretation and judgment, not operational methods, tools, or execution procedures.
Source: Chapter 4 – Discipline boundaries

17. Why is Q Intelligence™ considered a different category of discipline?
K-Level: K2 – Application
Answer: Because it governs interpretation and decision

reliability rather than execution, testing practice, or process optimization.
Source: Chapter 4 — Category distinction

18. What is the purpose of axioms within Q Intelligence™?
K-Level: K1 — Comprehension
Answer: Axioms define the non-negotiable truths that constrain valid quality judgment within the system.
Source: Chapter 4 — Axioms

19. What is the difference between axioms and principles?
K-Level: K1 — Comprehension
Answer: Axioms define fixed truths or constraints, while principles guide interpretation and orientation without prescribing implementation.
Source: Chapter 4 — Axioms vs principles

20. What role does the Q Intelligence™ Master Framework play?
K-Level: K2 — Application
Answer: It provides a stable conceptual structure for reasoning about quality intelligence while avoiding operational or tooling prescriptions.
Source: Chapter 4 — Master Framework

21. Why is shared intelligibility required before quality can be governed?
K-Level: K3 — System Reasoning
Answer: Because governance depends on shared understanding of what signals mean; without intelligibility, decisions become inconsistent and misaligned across the enterprise.
Source: Chapter 4 — Intelligibility and governance

22. What problem does QOS™ solve at enterprise scale?
K-Level: K2 – Application
Answer: It resolves the gap between distributed quality activity and the need for system-wide coherence by coordinating how quality intent, intelligence, and response relate.
Source: Chapter 5 – Problem QOS™ solves

23. What is the difference between accumulating capabilities and creating a coordinated system?
K-Level: K2 – Application
Answer: Accumulation adds disconnected tools or practices, while a coordinated system integrates them structurally so they operate coherently as one enterprise capability.
Source: Chapter 5 – Architecture vs accumulation

24. Why is QOS™ described as an operating system rather than a framework?
K-Level: K2 – Application
Answer: Because it defines structural relationships and coordination rules that allow multiple components to function coherently, rather than prescribing methods or checklists.
Source: Chapter 5 – Operating system concept

25. Put the three layers of QOS™ in the correct order: Operational Response → Intelligence and Signal → Intent and Direction
K-Level: K1 – Comprehension
Answer: Intent and Direction → Intelligence and Signal →

Operational Response
Source: Chapter 5 – Layer model

26. Why is separation between intent, intelligence, and response critical?
K-Level: K2 – Application
Answer: It preserves clarity of meaning and allows each layer to evolve independently while maintaining coherent system behavior.
Source: Chapter 5 – Layer separation

27. What happens when signal meaning is not preserved across system layers?
K-Level: K3 – System Reasoning
Answer: Interpretation fragments, decisions become inconsistent, and the system loses coherence and predictability.
Source: Chapter 5 – Signal preservation

28. Why does QOS™ intentionally avoid defining execution or governance mechanisms?
K-Level: K3 – System Reasoning
Answer: To remain an enabling architecture rather than collapsing into process control or governance itself, preserving structural neutrality and adaptability.
Source: Chapter 5 – Architectural handoff

29. What is the primary purpose of governance within the QACE system?
K-Level: K1 – Comprehension
Answer: Governance aligns decision authority with intelligence and accountability so quality decisions remain deliberate, coherent, and traceable.

Source: Chapter 6 — Governance role

30. Why must governance operate over decisions rather than activities?
K-Level: K2 — Application
Answer: Because decisions determine outcomes; activities are only the visible execution that follows those decisions.
Source: Chapter 6 — Governance over decisions

31. What happens when decision authority is not aligned with intelligence?
K-Level: K2 — Application
Answer: Decisions either lack necessary context or available intelligence goes unused, producing instability and poor outcomes.
Source: Chapter 6 — Authority vs intelligence alignment

32. Put the Governance Pillars in a logical structure:
Review → Authority → Constraint → Accountability → Correction
K-Level: K1 — Comprehension
Answer: Authority → Accountability → Constraint → Review → Correction
Source: Chapter 6 — Governance Pillars

33. What is the difference between authority and accountability?
K-Level: K1 — Comprehension
Answer: Authority identifies who has the right to decide; accountability identifies who owns the outcome of that decision.
Source: Chapter 6 — Authority vs accountability

34. How does governance differ from gatekeeping?
K-Level: K3 – System Reasoning
Answer: Governance shapes decision integrity continuously, while gatekeeping applies approval or control after work reaches checkpoints.
Source: Chapter 6 – Governance vs gatekeeping

35. Why is governance considered a precondition for maturity?
K-Level: K3 – System Reasoning
Answer: Because maturity requires stable, explicit, and governed decision-making before capability can be assessed or improved reliably.
Source: Chapter 6 – Governance as precondition for maturity

36. What does maturity represent within an enterprise system?
K-Level: K1 – Comprehension
Answer: Maturity represents the system's ability to produce consistent outcomes under varying conditions.
Source: Chapter 7 – Definition of maturity

37. Why is maturity considered a system property rather than a team-level measure?
K-Level: K2 – Application
Answer: Because maturity depends on structural alignment across architecture, execution, governance, and feedback rather than isolated local performance.
Source: Chapter 7 – Maturity as system property

38. What role do observable signals play in determining maturity?

K-Level: K2 – Application
Answer: They make maturity visible by revealing patterns of system behavior that can be interpreted and compared across contexts.
Source: Chapter 7 – Observable signals

39. What is the relationship between constraints and maturity progression?
K-Level: K3 – System Reasoning
Answer: Constraints limit progression by preserving fragmentation or instability; advancement requires reducing those limits while increasing alignment.
Source: Chapter 7 – Constraints and progression

40. What is the primary role of the QACE Maturity Model?
K-Level: K2 – Application
Answer: It provides a structured way to diagnose, compare, and predict system capability based on structural conditions.
Source: Chapter 7 – Role of the model

41. What role do diagnostics play in transforming data into intelligence?
K-Level: K2 – Application
Answer: Diagnostics transform measurement into intelligence by interpreting signals within system context so they can support decision-making.
Source: Chapter 8 – Diagnostics role

42. Put the diagnostic transformation chain in the correct order:
Decision → Data → Validation → Signals → Action → Interpretation → Integration
K-Level: K1 – Comprehension

Answer: Data → Signals → Interpretation → Decision → Action → Validation → Integration
Source: Chapter 8 – Diagnostic chain

43. What is the difference between data and signals?
K-Level: K1 – Comprehension
Answer: Data is raw observation; signals are structured patterns in that data that indicate system state and direction.
Source: Chapter 8 – Data vs signals

44. Why do signals require interpretation before they are useful?
K-Level: K2 – Application
Answer: Because signals only indicate patterns; interpretation connects them to system behavior, meaning, and action relevance.
Source: Chapter 8 – Interpretation

45. What happens when diagnostics are missing from the system?
K-Level: K3 – System Reasoning
Answer: The organization becomes reactive, decisions lose alignment with system behavior, and improvements become inconsistent and difficult to sustain.
Source: Chapter 8 – Diagnostic absence

46. Why must diagnostics be integrated into QOS™?
K-Level: K3 – System Reasoning
Answer: To ensure that intelligence remains coherent across the enterprise rather than fragmented into isolated local analyses.
Source: Chapter 8 – Integration with QOS™

47. Why is automation not considered a source of intelligence?
K-Level: K1 – Comprehension
Answer: Because automation executes predefined logic but does not independently create, interpret, or validate that logic.
Source: Chapter 9 – Automation as execution

48. What is the difference between automation and automation architecture?
K-Level: K2 – Application
Answer: Automation performs execution, while automation architecture governs how that execution remains structurally aligned with system intelligence.
Source: Chapter 9 – Automation vs architecture

49. What happens when automation is treated as tooling instead of system structure?
K-Level: K2 – Application
Answer: Execution becomes a substitute for structure, producing fragmented and non-traceable behavior that cannot be reliably governed.
Source: Chapter 9 – Automation-as-tooling

50. Why must automation remain dependent on system intelligence?
K-Level: K3 – System Reasoning
Answer: Because otherwise automation introduces independent behavior that conflicts with the system's intended structure and reduces coherence.
Source: Chapter 9 – Dependency on system intelligence

51. Which of the following represents a failure mode of automation?
A. Traceability
B. Bounded execution
C. Autonomy drift
D. Structural dependency
K-Level: K2 — Application
Correct Answer: C
Answer: Autonomy drift
Explanation: Autonomy drift occurs when automation begins operating beyond its intended structural boundaries, creating behavior that is no longer governed by system intelligence.
Source: Chapter 9 — Automation Anti-Patterns and Failure Modes

52. Why must accessibility, internationalization, and usability be treated as system-level quality dimensions?
K-Level: K2 — Application
Answer: Because they shape whether quality can actually be experienced, interpreted, and sustained across users and contexts, making them structural conditions rather than presentation details.
Source: Chapter 10 — Quality dimensions

53. What happens when these dimensions are inconsistently applied?
K-Level: K3 — System Reasoning
Answer: System coherence degrades, decisions become unreliable, and quality varies across users, roles, and contexts.
Source: Chapter 10 — Constraints and system behavior

54. Why do failures in these dimensions propagate across the system?
K-Level: K3 – System Reasoning
Answer: Because these dimensions are embedded into overall system operation, so failures affect interactions, interpretation, and outcomes throughout the system.
Source: Chapter 10 – Observable signals and failure modes

55. How do these dimensions influence other quality attributes?
K-Level: K3 – System Reasoning
Answer: They act as enabling conditions that determine whether attributes such as reliability, correctness, and completeness can be consistently realized.
Source: Chapter 10 – Integration with broader quality system

56. What problem does the QACE Validation Model solve?
K-Level: K2 – Application
Answer: It replaces fragmented, phase-based validation with a governed system capability that provides continuous visibility into system behavior.
Source: Chapter 11 – Purpose of the validation model

57. Why must validation be treated as a system capability rather than an activity?
K-Level: K3 – System Reasoning
Answer: Because validation must continuously observe, structure, and interpret system behavior, rather than appear only as a checkpoint after work is performed.
Source: Chapter 11 – Validation as governed capability

58. What are the three structural components of the validation model?
K-Level: K1 – Comprehension
Answer: Validation layers, cross-cutting validation dimensions, and signal production.
Source: Chapter 11 – Structural overview

59. What is the difference between validation layers and dimensions?
K-Level: K2 – Application
Answer: Layers define where behavior is observed in the system, while dimensions define the perspective through which that behavior is evaluated.
Source: Chapter 11 – Cross-cutting validation dimensions

60. Put the Validation Chain in the correct order:
Feedback → Action → Validation → Decision → Intended Outcome
K-Level: K1 – Comprehension
Answer: Decision → Action → Intended Outcome → Validation → Feedback
Source: Chapter 12 – Validation Chain Model

61. Why is traceability critical within validation?
K-Level: K2 – Application
Answer: Because it links decisions, actions, outcomes, and evidence into a proof chain that allows outcomes to be verified and explained.
Source: Chapter 12 – Traceability from decision to outcome

62. Why are activity-based signals insufficient for proving outcomes?
K-Level: K3 – System Reasoning

Answer: Because activity can occur without producing the intended result, so it cannot prove that outcomes improved or were caused by the actions taken.
Source: Chapter 12 – Failure of validation / false confidence

63. Why must validation confirm persistence across time and conditions?
K-Level: K3 – System Reasoning
Answer: Because an outcome is only validated if it continues to hold under real operating conditions rather than appearing temporarily or once.
Source: Chapter 12 – Feedback and outcome confirmation

64. What happens when validation is not embedded in system execution?
K-Level: K3 – System Reasoning
Answer: The system cannot reliably prove causality between actions and outcomes, creating false confidence and weakening control over performance.
Source: Chapter 12 – Embedding validation into the system

65. What condition defines successful adoption within a system?
K-Level: K1 – Comprehension
Answer: Adoption is successful when shared logic operates consistently through the system without requiring repeated human reconciliation.
Source: Chapter 13 – Adoption as system-level transition

66. What is the difference between adoption and transformation?
K-Level: K2 – Application

Answer: Adoption aligns system behavior to a shared model, while transformation produces measurable and repeatable improvements in outcomes because of that alignment.
Source: Chapter 13 – Adoption vs transformation

67. What signals indicate that transformation has occurred?
K-Level: K2 – Application
Answer: Predictable outcomes, reduced contradictions, fewer escaped defects, and less need for manual reconciliation indicate transformation.
Source: Chapter 13 – Emergence of transformation

68. Why does scaling depend on replication of validated behavior?
K-Level: K3 – System Reasoning
Answer: Because scaling requires consistent reuse of proven logic and behavior across teams and contexts, not simple growth or expansion.
Source: Chapter 13 – Scaling as propagation

69. What changes when quality enforcement shifts from people to system constraints?
K-Level: K3 – System Reasoning
Answer: Quality becomes structurally embedded, with pipelines, gates, and workflows enforcing valid behavior instead of relying on reminders or manual oversight.
Source: Chapter 13 – Institutionalization

70. What role does certification play in demonstrating system capability?
K-Level: K2 – Application

Answer: Certification demonstrates that the system can repeatedly produce traceable, reliable, and sustained outputs under normal operating conditions.
Source: Chapter 13 – Certification as observable proof

71. What conditions are required for ecosystem continuity?
K-Level: K3 – System Reasoning
Answer: Shared validation logic, compatible traceability structures, consistent evidence meaning, and no need for reinterpretation are required for continuity across systems.
Source: Chapter 13 – Ecosystem continuity

72. Why must testing, automation, AI, and governance operate as a coordinated system?
K-Level: K3 – System Reasoning
Answer: Because independent operation produces conflicting evidence and decisions, while coordination ensures system outputs remain aligned, enforceable, and interoperable.
Source: Chapter 13 – Coordinated, assisted, and governed capability

Appendix A — Glossary

Axiom

A foundational, non-negotiable truth that defines the boundaries of valid reasoning within the system.

Deterministic Testing

A testing model in which identical inputs are expected to produce consistent, repeatable results under controlled conditions.

Enterprise Operating System

A coordinating structural layer that enables distributed system components to operate coherently while evolving independently.

Governance

The structural system that defines how decisions are authorized, constrained, reviewed, and held accountable across the enterprise.

Illusion of Control

A false perception of control created by activity or metrics that do not reflect actual system behavior or outcomes.

Intelligibility

The degree to which system signals and conditions can be consistently interpreted and understood across the organization.

Late Discovery

A structural condition where system issues are identified only after they have already impacted outcomes due to limited early visibility.

Maturity Model

A framework used to interpret system capability based on structural conditions, alignment, and consistency of outcomes.

Non-Deterministic System

A system in which identical inputs may produce different outcomes due to variability, complexity, or changing conditions.

QACE Operating Model

A structural framework that integrates quality, automation, compliance, and engineering into a coordinated enterprise system.

Signal Distortion

The loss of accuracy or meaning in system signals as they scale or pass through layers of abstraction.

System Capability

The ability of a system to produce reliable, consistent outcomes under varying conditions and operational contexts.

System Coherence

The ability of a system to maintain consistent relationships and meaning across components, decisions, and interactions over time.

Trade-Off

A decision point where competing constraints must be explicitly balanced, requiring prioritization between limited alternatives.

Appendix B — Acronyms

QACE

Quality, Automation, Compliance, Engineering

QOS™

Quality Operating System

QA

Quality Assurance

CTO

Chief Technology Officer

CIO

Chief Information Officer

References

Ansell, C., & Torfing, J. (2021). *Public governance as co-creation: A strategy for revitalizing the public sector and rejuvenating democracy*. Cambridge University Press.

Boehm, B. W. (1981). *Software engineering economics*. Prentice Hall.

Brinch Hansen, P. (1973). *Operating system principles*. Prentice Hall.

Forsgren, N., Humble, J., & Kim, G. (2018). *Accelerate: The science of lean software and DevOps: Building and scaling high performing technology organizations*. IT Revolution Press.

International Organization for Standardization. (2021). *ISO 37000:2021 – Governance of organizations – Guidance*. ISO.

International Organization for Standardization. (2021). *ISO 9001:2015/Amd 1:2021 – Quality management systems – Requirements – Amendment 1: Climate action changes*. ISO.

International Organization for Standardization, International Electrotechnical Commission, & Institute of Electrical and Electronics Engineers. (2011). *ISO/IEC/IEEE 42010:2011 – Systems and software engineering – Architecture description*. ISO.

Jois, S. (2024). *Engineering quality with AI: From automation to intelligence*. QACE Institute.

Krasner, H., & Consortium for Information & Software Quality. (2022). *The cost of poor software quality in the US: A 2022 report*. Consortium for Information & Software Quality.

Leveson, N. G. (2012). *Engineering a safer world: Systems thinking applied to safety*. MIT Press.

Parnas, D. L. (1972). On the criteria to be used in decomposing systems into modules. *Communications of the ACM, 15*(12), 1053–1058.

Pierre, J., & Peters, B. G. (2000). *Governance, politics and the state*. St. Martin's Press.

Reason, J. (1997). *Managing the risks of organizational accidents*. Ashgate.

Richards, M., & Ford, N. (2020). *Fundamentals of software architecture: An engineering approach.* O'Reilly Media.

Weill, P., & Ross, J. W. (2004). *IT governance: How top performers manage IT decision rights for superior results.* Harvard Business School Press.

About the Author

Paul G. Kanaris is a Director/VP-level Quality Engineering leader specializing in enterprise-scale transformation, automation architecture, and AI-driven quality intelligence. Over a 20+ year career spanning organizations including McKesson, Netsmart, and JAGGAER, he has led the evolution of software quality from fragmented, reactive functions into structured, governance-driven enterprise capabilities.

Paul's foundation in large-scale systems began during his service in the United States Army, where he worked in financial operations and led customer service center and computer operations for one of the largest installations in the United States. In that environment, he developed early experience in leadership, operational discipline, and enterprise-scale system support—capabilities that would later shape his approach to quality as a controlled, governed, and enterprise-wide system. During this period, he also developed an early passion for computing, beginning with paper tape, punch cards, and terminal-based systems, and continuing through programming on Apple IIe systems in high school.

Early in his civilian career, Paul worked at the forefront of healthcare technology transformation, contributing to the development of some of the first digital enterprise systems used in clinical environments. His experience includes helping develop one of the first PACS systems for the U.S. Department of Veterans Affairs, contributing to early voice dictation systems for radiologists, and working directly with radiography technology during the transition from film-based to digital workflows. In parallel, he worked in enterprise IT support, helped establish Windows NT domain environments, and participated in the early evolution of the VISTA Electronic Medical Record system. These experiences provided a foundational understanding of integrated hardware and software ecosystems operating in safety-critical environments, where reliability, signal interpretation, and decision accuracy directly affect real-world outcomes.

At JAGGAER, Paul unified a global Quality Engineering organization consisting of 7 managers, more than 50 full-time employees, and over 30 contractors. Under his leadership, the organization achieved TMMi Level 2 maturity in under two years while establishing a structured roadmap toward Level 5. During this transformation, he built large-scale automation capabilities delivering thousands of modular scenarios and more than 3,000 daily executions, significantly expanding validation coverage and increasing operational confidence.

Across healthcare, supply chain, and enterprise software environments, Paul has led initiatives where the consequences of quality failure extend far beyond defects to include financial risk, regulatory exposure, system instability, and organizational credibility. His work is grounded in real-world transformation leadership, where quality is not treated as an abstract discipline, but as a business-critical capability tied directly to trust, resilience, and operational performance.

Paul holds a Master's degree in Technology Management from Georgetown University and is certified by the International Software Testing Qualifications Board (ISTQB) at both the Foundation Level (CTFL) and Advanced Test Manager Level (CTAL-TM). He is the author of the Q

Intelligence™ Body of Knowledge and the architect of the QACE methodology, which redefines quality as a governed, end-to-end system rather than an isolated function or phase.

Paul's philosophy is grounded in a disciplined and practical principle: technology management supported by servant leadership. Elevate people. Clarify processes. Apply governance intentionally. Select tools that amplify—not replace—engineering discipline. When these elements are aligned, quality becomes not only a control mechanism, but a strategic differentiator.

He is not a theorist writing about transformation—he is a practitioner who has led the transformations he describes, with credibility measured in results.

About the Founder

Paul G. Kanaris is the founder of the QACE Institute, a standards-focused organization established to advance quality engineering from a fragmented delivery function into a governed enterprise capability. QACE was created in response to a persistent reality across modern organizations: quality failures continue not because effort is absent, but because quality itself remains structurally underdefined, operationally fragmented, and weakly governed.

Through the QACE Institute, Paul developed the Q Intelligence™ Framework and the QACE operating model to address the systemic conditions that prevent quality from functioning coherently at scale. This work is grounded in the belief that quality must be treated not as an inspection activity, testing phase, or tooling concern, but as an enterprise system requiring architecture, governance, diagnostics, validation, and institutional continuity.

The QACE Institute is designed as a body of practice and standards development, not as a conventional consulting model. Its purpose is to define and advance the structures, vocabulary, learning systems, and operational models required to make quality intelligible, governable, and sustainable across complex enterprises. Through its frameworks, assessment systems, training materials, and publishing work, QACE aims to establish a durable foundation for the next evolution of quality engineering.

Under Paul's leadership, QACE serves as both an intellectual and operational platform—one that connects real-world transformation experience with formal system design. The institute exists to help organizations, practitioners, and future leaders move beyond reactive quality activity toward a disciplined, coherent, and institutionally grounded model of enterprise quality.

About QACE Institute

QACE Institute is a standards-focused organization dedicated to advancing quality engineering as a core enterprise capability. The institute's work centers on the belief that quality must be designed, governed, and continuously interpreted as a system—not treated as an isolated role, downstream activity, or collection of tools.

QACE develops the conceptual frameworks, operating models, governance structures, learning systems, and assessment methods required to make enterprise quality coherent at scale. Its purpose is to support organizations in building quality capabilities that are structurally aligned, diagnostically visible, operationally governable, and sustainable across changing conditions.

Through publications, practitioner guidance, assessments, and educational pathways, QACE Institute seeks to establish a durable body of knowledge for the future of enterprise quality architecture. Its role is not merely to improve existing practices, but to redefine how quality is understood, structured, and led in modern organizations.

About the Q Intelligence™ Series

The Q Intelligence™ Series is not a prescribed reading sequence. It is a structured body of knowledge designed to support real-world quality transformation within complex organizations.

This volume, The Umbrella Playbook, serves as the entry point. It establishes the foundational framework, operating model, and diagnostic approach required to understand how quality functions as an enterprise system.

Transformation does not begin with selecting the next book. It begins with assessing the organization.

Leaders responsible for improving quality must first establish an accurate understanding of the current state, including:

Where breakdowns exist across the lifecycle

Where quality remains reactive rather than engineered

Where decisions lack evidence, structure, or governance

Where the greatest opportunity for meaningful change resides

Only after this assessment can a transformation path be defined.

In many organizations, improvement begins at the source—product definition and requirements—where unclear intent and inconsistent inputs create downstream inefficiencies. In parallel, development practices and validation approaches must be aligned to ensure that quality is engineered into the system rather than inspected after the fact.

From this point, additional domains may be engaged based on need, including automation architecture, non-functional quality, observability, governance, and AI-enabled quality engineering.

The Q Intelligence™ Series provides dedicated volumes for each of these domains. These volumes are not intended to be consumed in a fixed order; they are applied selectively based on the organization's maturity, constraints, and transformation priorities.

In this way, the series functions as an extensible system of knowledge—one that is engaged deliberately rather than followed sequentially.

As organizations evolve, additional volumes will be introduced to address emerging challenges and expand the depth of the framework across new domains.

www.ingramcontent.com/pod-product-compliance
Lightning Source LLC
LaVergne TN
LVHW021740071126
851857LV00039B/574
* 9 7 9 8 9 9 6 6 7 0 7 0 3 *